BACK TO MANDALAY

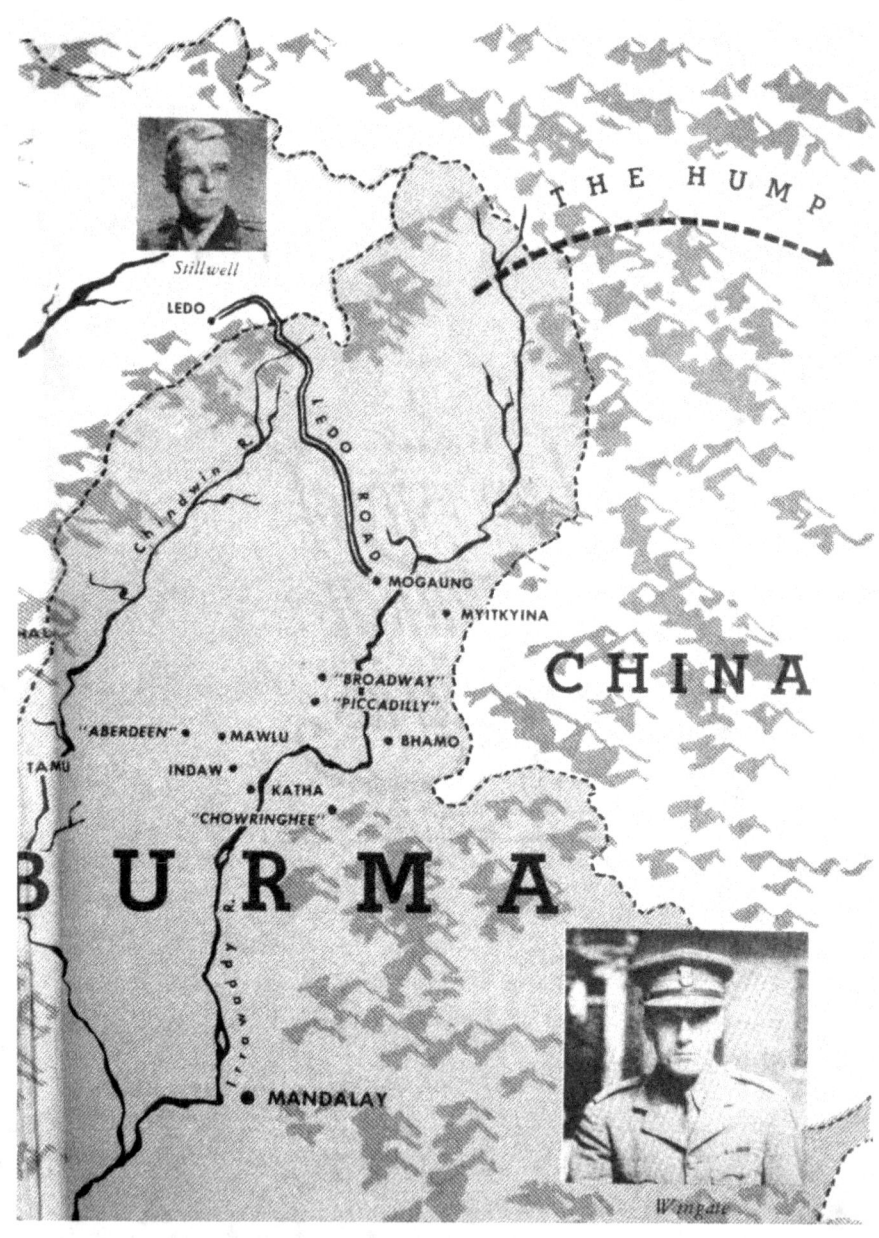

GENERAL WINGATE WITH COCHRAN AND ALISON: Cochran stands at the right, Alison at the left. Wingate wears his campaign beard and helmet.

Back to Mandalay

By LOWELL THOMAS

Author of *With Lawrence in Arabia, The Sea Devil, Raiders of the Deep, Beyond the Khyber Pass, Pageant of Adventure,* etc., etc.

NEW YORK
THE GREYSTONE PRESS

COPYRIGHT 1951 BY LOWELL THOMAS
PUBLISHED BY
THE GREYSTONE PRESS
100 SIXTH AVENUE
NEW YORK 13, N. Y.

ACKNOWLEDGMENTS

The Publishers extend their thanks to Lowell Thomas, the United States Department of Defense, and the British Information Service for making photographs available for use in this book. William Taylor aided in the planning of the end-paper map, which was drawn by Jesse Jacobs. Cartoons from "Terry and the Pirates" were released by News Syndicate Corp., Inc., and are used through courtesy of the Chicago Tribune-New York News Syndicate and Philip Cochran. Thanks are also due to the editors of Colliers, where a brief and different version of this work has appeared; the chapter titles from Kipling's poems appear in this book with permission of Doubleday and Company, New York.

UNCOMMON VALOR SERIES EDITION
ISBN: 978-1951682767
May 2023

Printed in the United States of America

CONTENTS

I.	"Two Strong Men Stand Face to Face"	11
II.	"The Captains and the Kings"	20
III.	"Give Us the Men Who Do the Work"	31
IV.	"Ordered to Burma"	52
V.	"Come You Back, You British Soldier"	57
VI.	"Make Allowance for Their Doubting"	71
VII.	"He Used the Earth, the Seas, the Air"	85
VIII.	"Youth That Trafficked Long with Death"	97
IX.	"And Men Esteemed Me Bold"	108
X.	"You Long-Eared Old Darlin's!"	123
XI.	"We've Fought with Many Men Across the Seas"	143
XII.	"Gentlemen Unafraid"	166
XIII.	"Their Lives Are on My Head"	176
XIV.	"Good Hunting, All That Keep the Jungle Law"	189
XV.	"In Jeopardy We Steer"	198
XVI.	"The Rush Throughout the Mist"	211
XVII.	"The Wildest Tales Are True"	232
XVIII.	"How Long Will the Lull Endure?"	247
XIX.	"They Come from the Ends of the Earth"	261
XX.	"The Blindfold Game of War"	266
XXI.	"Jungle-Favor Go with Thee!"	273
XXII.	"There Was a Man"	289
XXIII.	"For Their Work Continueth"	298
XXIV.	"Victory at Last"	305
XXV.	"Lest We Forget"	313

… BACK TO MANDALAY

1. "Two Strong Men Stand Face to Face"

MILLIONS OF AMERICANS would have found it hard to believe, but for once the daredevil American pilot was really worried. He wasn't, as the funnies so often pictured him, caught in the toils of a beautiful but wicked woman spy. He wasn't being chased through the clouds by Nazi planes—he could always outguess those. He wasn't in the hands of the Japs; he was looking forward to meeting them. Right now he was all alone, grounded in the gray streets of wartorn London.

London wasn't what it had been, since the blitz two years before. But the adventurous Yank wasn't looking for old English landmarks, and he didn't mind the sandbags that hid many of the buildings an ordinary tourist would have wanted to see. Instead, he cast a professional eye over the damage—the gaping holes in the pavement, the piles of rubble yet unremoved, the spaces as if whole buildings had been extracted like teeth. Air war could do plenty when it hit a big town.

"TWO STRONG MEN STAND FACE TO FACE"

He ought to know, this young man wearing the uniform of a lieutenant colonel in the American Air Forces, with a row of fruit salad to show he'd already seen rather more than his share. It was a snappy turnout and he'd taken some trouble with it, from badges to boots. You could sleep in your clothes if you had to—he'd worn the same leather jacket and the same pants through the campaign in Tunisia, not taking them off night or day—but on occasion you had to show off. This was the occasion. No time to be called down for wearing black-and-white sports shoes with a uniform, as he had once back in the R.O.T.C. at Ohio State.

Now he was conscious of looking trim enough to represent the United States. He had thick dark hair, wavy and streaked with premature gray, like a movie actor's, although he'd seen enough to make it gray all over. His nose was small but it had a touch of beak about it, and his jaw was heavy and hard, a fighter's jaw. His dark eyes looked a challenge. He had things on his mind. He was Lieutenant Colonel Philip Cochran, in London on a mission arranged for by the top brass on both sides. The British, in fact, had asked for him—well, not specifically for him, Phil Cochran of Erie, Pa., but for air aid of the kind he was authorized to supply. Winston Churchill had told the President help was needed to recapture Burma, and it couldn't be done except with American planes. The planes would require men to fly them and a top-ranking officer to handle the pilots. They'd combed the Air Force and given him the job.

It wasn't a job he wanted. He had trained to be a fighter pilot and he wasn't really happy except at the controls of a fighter plane. He had told them that, although he didn't have to tell them. Most people knew. If they didn't know Phil Cochran, they knew Flip Corkin, the daredevil pilot of the "Terry and the Pirates" comic strip that was running

COCHRAN wearing his celebrated Flip Corkin smile.

in the newspapers at home, and read by men on all the battle fronts. Phil Cochran was Flip Corkin. They'd drawn him for the strip, fighting chin and all.

Flip in the strips hadn't had to do anything as cockeyed as the job he was on now, Cochran thought. This was an assignment full of mystery and politics, entirely out of his line. So he figured, but what could he do? They'd sold it to him. General Hap Arnold had actually made a sales talk about the terrific potentialities of the projected Burma campaign. Imagine a top general selling you a job, when all he had to do was order you and you couldn't talk back! But they wanted you to be enthusiastic about it.

All right, he was enthusiastic—about part of it. The equipment they were giving him was out of this world, and there'd be a chance to fight. Arnold had almost promised that, without saying anything you could pin down. After what he'd been through he was lucky to get the job, lucky to be promised all sorts of planes and guns and even rockets for the asking—after Tunisia, where he'd had to beg, borrow or steal the stuff. The way they were promising things bore out the story that the whole hush-hush project had been dreamed up by the top men at the Quebec Conference, and it really was important.

Certainly the British were taking the thing seriously, although they'd started off on the wrong foot as usual. That morning at Lord Louis Mountbatten's headquarters, where he'd reported as ordered, he'd run into a conference of British admirals. You never saw so much gold braid in your life. They introduced him around just as if they'd been waiting for him, and the admirals talked and talked of things he knew nothing about. But that didn't worry him; he could sit tight and say nothing with the best of them. You couldn't understand half they said anyhow, gargling their words the way the English did. Back in Erie you could get a laugh just by imitating them, only nobody would believe you. Every once in a while they looked at him and he'd look back, and everybody would smile and nod. The conference was over before he suspected, and Mountbatten realized, that he was in the wrong meeting. This one was working on ships and staff for Mountbatten's whole Southeast Asia Command.

Just to straighten everything out, Mountbatten took him home for lunch—a real break, with the British meals the way they were at the time. Mountbatten himself was a regular fellow and easy to talk to, even if he was own cousin to the English king. He was better-looking than the newspaper pictures showed him to be, and a friendly, affable, hospitable chap. Cochran felt at home with him and enjoyed lunch at the Mountbatten house with Lady Mountbatten and other guests who included, he discovered, government bigwigs—the Secretary for India, Mr. Amery, and the Soviet Ambassador, Mr. Maisky, and their wives. Cochran sat next to the Ambassador's wife and got on with her very well. But of course everything was pretty British, the talk and the servants, and even the food. Once or twice he said to himself, "What are you doing here?"

The whole morning had marked his first contact with the English in large numbers. He'd known some Britishers before, of course, like the limey with the group in North Africa, a young officer whose job was to lay booby traps. They hadn't understood each other's kidding and it had bothered Cochran. He could tell when an American was crazy but not, it seemed, an Englishman, and he kept thinking a crazy man with booby traps would be something. In Tunisia, though, the young limey had been in the minority and everybody kidded him. Here Cochran was the minority.

And the afternoon was taking him into something else

completely unknown. Mountbatten had lost no time in sending him to the War Office to see General Wingate, who had thought up the Burma campaign. Maybe it was just as well he'd been careful about the polish of his boots.

Later he felt it wouldn't have mattered. The place wasn't much, when he got there. It looked like an old post office and smelled like one, too. It didn't awe Cochran and it didn't inspire enthusiasm. The private office they showed him into, finally, was just a grim little cubbyhole, hardly where you'd expect to find a general that Mountbatten had described as a great hero, another potential Lawrence of Arabia. Prime Minister Churchill, he said, had the utmost confidence in this Wingate, although there seemed to be something about him that they didn't make clear, either because it was a secret or was just naturally lost in the British way of speaking around a mouthful of hot potato.

Anyhow, Cochran naturally expected to see something impressive in a general, maybe looking a little like Pershing, or MacArthur. Instead, here was a small, oldish-looking man, yes, he looked old and tired, although he was only seven years older than Cochran himself. He spoke in a raspy sort of voice, with a nervous stutter. He had blue eyes like any Englishman's, but set deep in his head, and they seemed to look right through you. His shoulders stooped a little and his whole appearance was somehow sloppy and uncombed, as if he didn't care. Yet he sat stiffly in his chair as if he were posing for one of those old-fashioned photographers who put a clamp on your head.

Cochran plunged into the report that had been so well received by Mountbatten. He had word from General Arnold about promised planes, and when Wingate asked what kind of planes, he was able to say any kind, every kind that might be needed to do the job. "We've got 'em all—"

WINGATE on his way to the War Office in London.

General Wingate looked at him, not just turning his head but his shoulders and his whole body, and said only, "You have?"

That was the British for you, always belittlin'. By their doubting manner they seemed to keep saying that Americans talk big. Well, they didn't have to believe him, Cochran felt, and Wingate didn't have to like him either, though as they would have to work together it would be better if they could get along. Cochran didn't think too much of Mr. Churchill's pet general. Explaining it afterwards, he said:

"He saw in me less than he expected, and he didn't try to conceal it. He never went out of his way to put on anything. So my attitude towards him was antagonistic—who the hell is this guy? I gave him back the attitude that he had toward me."

Implicit in Cochran's reaction was of course his own sense of achievement, and his feeling of the importance of his own country. But he had knocked around enough to know the advisability of giving the other man a break, and he'd heard Wingate praised. Why not let him show his stuff? So Cochran asked, what was this new Wingate method of jungle war that they talked about? What was the big idea?

The response he got, as Cochran describes it, was like a public address.

"I found out then and there that Wingate had a habit of making speeches. You might ask him a specific question requiring a one-word answer, and he would go off on a long harangue about a lot of things. You might ask a military question, like the average rainfall in Burma in March, and he would go off on a lecture about the effect of rainfall on Burmese monasteries and the Buddhist religion. In our first talk I said, 'What do you intend to do?' And he went into one of his orations.

"He told me the war in Burma was stupid, the way the

British were conducting it. He said the brass hats in India didn't understand modern war or jungle war. He referred to his idea. He called it 'long-range penetration.' The gold braid in India couldn't comprehend its importance, but Churchill did and so did Mountbatten. He kept talking about 'long-range penetration,' which meant nothing to me.

"He mixed everything up with scholarship and the history of war. I didn't know what he was talking about. A lot was about things that were over my head and that I didn't care about. I had trouble with British accents in general, and his was exaggerated and all the more obfuscating because of his gurgling defect of speech. He had a habit of mouthing and dropping the last phrases, and I'd have to ask him to repeat something if I wanted to get it. I soon got tired of asking, and sat there wondering what it was all about. We finally ended it by saying that I'd come back next day, I hoping for a better break."

Cochran left the shabby cubbyhole in the War Office little wiser than he had entered it. Wingate's secret was "long-range penetration," which presumably meant thrusting far into the jungle, but how that was to be accomplished Cochran couldn't guess. He thought Wingate arrogant and opinionated, egotistical, self-centered.

Wingate, no doubt, thought the same of Cochran.

2. "The Captains and the Kings"

BEFORE THE MEETING of Cochran and Wingate in London there had been a bigger public meeting, at which England and America had reached an impressive accord on the larger questions of the war. Wingate had been present on that occasion. Cochran wasn't there, but the issues discussed affected his life.

At the Quebec Conference of 1943, which had as its setting the picturesque and historic Citadel in the capital of Old French Canada, the central figures were the American President, crippled of body but proudly erect in his bearing, and the rotund British Prime Minister, who, as Admiral of the Cinque Ports, loved to appear in a nautical cap and a glorified pea jacket. These central figures in the international pageant were attended by lesser statesmen, generals, and admirals, who were in their turn accompanied by experts to hold discussions over maps and concentrate on the ponderous calculations of logistics. To the job of conducting a global war, all available authority, rank and gold braid and attendant military genius were summoned by the mighty Republic and the globe-girdling Empire.

On that Empire the sun, surprisingly, seemed to be setting in the East. Singapore and Rangoon, all Burma, had fallen to the Japanese. Would the British soldier go back to Mandalay? Admitting what he called in Commons "a painful series of misfortunes," Winston Churchill had to say, "I cannot encourage the House to expect good news from the Burma theater." This astonished and impressed many high-placed observers, including some Americans, who forgot how many battles England could lose before she won a war. Harsh things were said about British ineptitude in the colonies, in the Treaty Ports, in all the East.

Churchill of course had no intention of writing off Burma as a permanent loss, and hoped for American help to retake it. Ever sensitive to American opinion, he came to Quebec prepared to answer the criticism that said Burma could not be retaken, even with American help, by a British army. He had said of the war, "Give us the tools and we will finish the job." Now he had to make good on this promise of capable leadership and man power. Specifically, in the case of Burma, he had to prove that Britain possessed commanders who understood jungle fighting and tough guerrilla combat of the sort necessary to oust the Japanese.

One of Churchill's trump cards at the conference was Lord Louis Mountbatten. The spotlight was focused to shine full on this smiling, handsome cousin of King George VI. Mountbatten's appearance was preceded by the prewar reputation which pictured him as a royal playboy, a social lion of the fast international set, a decorative figure of what had been Europe's gay world. More recently, in the war, Mountbatten had made a hero's mark as a naval officer, daredevil skipper of destroyers in action, and leader of Britain's Commandos in desperate raids. Now Mountbatten was being given the Southeast Asia Command, which would include the area where a new offensive, it was hoped, would reconquer northern Burma.

In the Burmese campaign the important figure would be Churchill's second and perhaps more important trump, General Wingate. Still wearing Burma battle dress, Wingate presented a maximum contrast to the more decorative figures at the conference. Here, it was explained, was a man who really understood jungle fighting. In this Quebec region, where memories of Wolfe's death and, alas, of Braddock's defeat held glory but no great promise of triumph for British arms, Wingate could be talked of with pride as a jungle tactician who knew as much about hiding behind trees and sniping at savages as any American of the French and Indian wars. In fact, although the conference was too busy to go into genealogy, an American branch of the Wingate family had been well-represented in those wars.

In two other important campaigns, but more recently in Burma, raiders trained and commanded by General Wingate had demonstrated a novel technique of battle in the tropical wilderness. Penetrating the Burmese jungle in bold advances, they had struck at the Jap with slashing blows, ripping his communications, destroying his supplies, and wrecking his transport. These exploits were becoming known, Wingate was becoming famous. Churchill's proposal at Quebec was to expand the previous Wingate raids in Burma into a full-fledged campaign.

He had brought Wingate to Canada after whispers reached England that out in Burma could be found "another Lawrence." In his early forties, Wingate was, like Lawrence, a man of small stature but commanding presence. You noted his face, weatherworn and marked with lines of mental travail. His eyes were attentive and studious, used to reading people and events. His expression was wry and dour rather than smiling, and he made no attempt to please strangers. But the stories told of the end of his first Burma campaign marked him as the man to make the second.

He had come out of the jungle, they said, crossing Burma's Chindwin River, after an ordeal in which men had gone hungry or eaten boiled mule meat or even python. Wingate himself had lived on rice, and his hollow cheeks, with the beard he grew on the campaign, gave him the look of a prophet. But he was a prophet with conviction. He had walked up and down, wearing shorts and playing with an orchid, while he dictated a report about the possibilities and requirements of jungle fighting. Commando training, plus enthusiasm, plus special equipment—the first two of these he had been able to provide. The equipment for long-range penetration of the jungle, specifically air equipment that could drop enough supplies for fast-moving columns without supply lines, was still insufficient.

His report written, Wingate went to a party and drank a toast in brandy: "Here's to the next time we cross the Chindwin." Perhaps this story reached Churchill's ears, to delight him with Wingate's stubborn tenacity. But of course Churchill had watched Wingate since his campaign in Palestine, and quoted his reports in Commons. And Churchill badly needed a British officer who knew his way around a jungle.

Although they approved the jungle battle dress for its effect, they took time to make Wingate a major general before they flew him to Quebec. There Churchill, with his unfailing sense of showmanship, presented the fighting Scot as a successor to Clive of India, "Chinese" Gordon, and Lawrence of Arabia, and strongly recommended the Wingate method of jungle fighting as the way to win back Burma.

"THE CAPTAINS AND THE KINGS"

On the desirability of retaking Burma, Roosevelt and Churchill were agreed. Both men saw the difficulties, and Roosevelt, as the record shows, did not feel that reconquering the country was a major objective; but control of Burma was, for America, a matter of military importance.

To the American people Burma might appear a faraway country remote from any strategic need. But American policy, at the time, was all-out support of Chiang Kai-shek in China. Although Burma was originally a province of India, it is close to China, as Kipling showed in the poem *Mandalay*—"the dawn comes up like thunder outer China." To supply Chiang's armies, in desperate and perpetual need of munitions, Americans were flying the Hump, over the Himalayas from India. If northern Burma could be won, an overland supply route would be open.

That Americans would participate in the campaign, as well as furnish supplies, Roosevelt promised Churchill. Next, Lord Louis Mountbatten, in his new post as commander-in-chief for Southeast Asia, consulted with United States Army Chief of Staff General Marshall. To Marshall it was clear that Americans should have as large a part as possible in the proposed Wingate campaign. He suggested that one-fourth of Wingate's troops be Americans. It was decided to form a special outfit of jungle-trained American rangers as one of Wingate's columns for the Burma push. This column was formed, but, known eventually as Merrill's Marauders, it worked instead under General Stilwell in China.

Wingate had his own idea for American participation, and one thing he asked for above all. He remembered only too well that on the campaign in Burma the year before it had been necessary to abandon the wounded. His method of long-range penetration of the jungle, sending columns ahead without supply lines and keeping small parties constantly

HE WAS LUCKY: Wounded in Wingate's first Burma campaign but rescued by the R.A.F. plane which was able to carry the worst casualties.

THEY WERE NOT: These men wave a cheerful goodbye to the plane which took out a few, left the others behind.

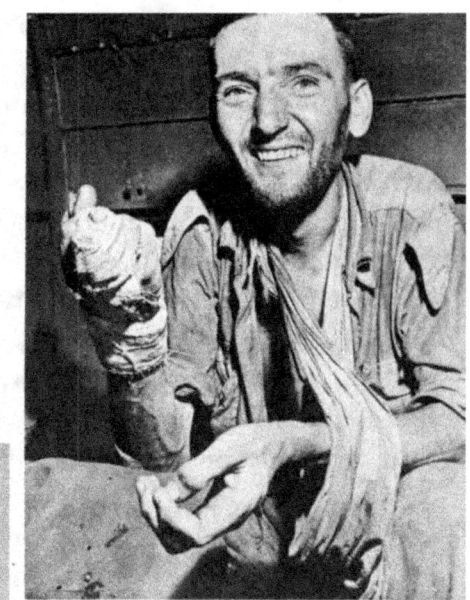

on the move, provided no means of transport to the rear for men unable to keep up. One of Wingate's closest friends had been left behind; sitting under a tree, to die, after he had given Wingate a farewell message for his wife. This abandonment of the wounded had been bad for morale, with soldiers downhearted and embittered by having to leave their comrades to the mercy of the jungle or the Japs, and fearful of the same fate for themselves.

One thrilling rescue of the wounded was made by an R.A.F. plane, and more could have been made had the planes been available. Wingate, a ground officer, understood little about air. But he had with him in Burma men who had flown with the R.A.F. One, an American called "Carolina" Gibson, had joined the R.A.F. in Canada, and had been with the Wingate column commanded by Wheeler. Another, "Tommy" Thompson, had been with Wingate and had made a constant outcry for planes when they had to leave the wounded behind. Light planes, he told Wingate over and over, would be able to land in jungle clearings. The wounded could be carried to nearby clearings, and evacuated by air. If they only had planes, just a few planes!

To Quebec, Wingate had brought Tommy Thompson, who was later to make a speaking tour of military centers in the United States, telling the story of the first Wingate jungle campaign. He was at Wingate's side to prompt him. Would the Americans provide light planes? With these he could evacuate his wounded, and moreover light planes could fly supplies to parties of jungle troops. They could do a two-purpose air job, providing a line of mercy and a supply line.

This threw Wingate in with the commander of the United States Army Air Forces, General H. H. Arnold, smiling Hap Arnold, whose buoyant cheeriness was a byword in the world of air power. He was impressed by Wingate. He saw in the grim English zealot a stubborn originality, a ruthless dedication to a new idea in the war. Hap Arnold, too, was a seeker of the new, trying forever to find broader fields for the employment of air power. If Wingate was chronically at odds with the limitations of standard practice, Arnold was forever discontent with the restrictions imposed by routine on wings in war.

What Wingate asked was nothing new. The evacuation of wounded and transport of supplies by light planes in jungle campaigning had been done before, in the Solomons and New Guinea. But the Wingate style of war in Burma was unorthodox, and that caught Arnold's imagination. He had a quick intuition that air collaboration with Wingate might develop surprises. Light-plane operations of evacuation and supply could go beyond the obvious, and far beyond what Wingate had in mind. Why not add American planes and American air-mindedness to the stubborn originality of Britain's zealot of the jungles, and see what would happen? Toss in young American flying talent with Wingate—the combination might flash with something new in the world of air power.

In military conference, the American Air Force commander was asked how many light planes we could let them have.

"How about two hundred?" laughed Hap Arnold. "Or no, let's make it three hundred."

That many?

Mountbatten beamed his surprise. Always something of a boy was this debonair commander, with his matinee-idol good looks. Wingate, turning head and shoulders, smiled his astonishment with more reserve. His austere and often saturnine face was little given to smiling.

Mountbatten and Wingate were of one mind in taking

the promise with a grain of salt. The British in the war were used to little and seldom expected to get as much as needed or promised. These Americans spoke so cheerfully in large figures, which no doubt was the American way. But Mountbatten and Wingate were British, and knew how hard it was to get planes by the dozen, let alone by the hundred. However, they might as well encourage this American enthusiasm, expecting, meanwhile, only a few.

After the Quebec Conference had ended in a blaze of headlines, Mountbatten went down to Washington to continue military conversations. There he reminded the American Air Force commander of the promise of light planes for Wingate. The response he got was another surprise for the British mind, with its resignation to insufficient means in war. Arnold's idea about planes for Wingate had developed. He now promised what he called an aerial task force.

Arnold sought more mobility for air power, was in revolt against air power tied down. The squadrons on high might seem to represent mobility at its far-ranging widest, and it might seem a paradox to speak of planes as being tied down. But the air forces in war were restricted by organization, by the vast routine of bases, elaborate installations, intricate systems of supply. Air units integrated in the larger whole were as if held on a leash of organization.

Arnold looked forward to a more mobile kind of air unit, one that would operate outside of the systems. Such units had been used for single jobs, one-time strokes of war like the Doolittle bombing of Tokyo. Why not extend the idea to regular operations through a campaign? To adopt Navy parlance, why not set up an aerial task force? The Wingate campaign provided an opportunity: an aerial task force would be an apt vehicle for light-plane cooperation with Wingate and might develop into something more, something new in the war of the air. Arnold saw a chance to test not only the soundness of the Wingate plans but the possibilities of air and ground warfare over the jungle. His idea was to find a young American of outstanding ability, one you could match with Wingate in ingenuity and daring, and give him a chance to top Wingate's jungle-fighting tactics with flying skill.

Arnold sent out an inquiry for candidates to be nominated for the post. The requirements were rigorous. The flyer must be young. He must have a flair for novel ideas, enough imagination to want to use air power in ways hitherto untried. He must be an innovator with the courage of his convictions. He must be tough. The Wingate way of jungle war was a fantasy of peril for ground fighters in the equatorial forest, and was likely to have unforeseeable novelties of difficulty and danger for men charged with air cooperation.

Deputy Air Force Chief of Staff General Craig made suggestions, and out of the mazes of the Air Force organization two officers appeared, both fighter pilots with great war records. One of these was Phil Cochran.

Cochran would have competition. He was told that another candidate had been sent, a fighter pilot from the 4th Fighter Command. He said at once, "That would be John Alison." He said it naturally and spontaneously, though he had no ground for the surmise other than his knowledge that Alison was attached to the 4th Fighter Command. Alison had served with General Craig under Chennault in China.

When the two candidates met in Washington, they exclaimed:

"Hello, Phil!"

"Hello, John!"

They were friends whose intimate association in times past had made them Air Force blood brothers, but whose trails had since taken them to opposite ends of the world. Now, after being long separated, coincidence had brought them together again as rivals for the command of the aerial task force to aid Wingate.

It was up to General Arnold to select the man for the job. He began by scheduling separate interviews with the two recommended candidates. He wanted to look them over, question them, sound them out. Hap Arnold was a shrewd judge of men.

3. "Give Us the Men Who Do the Work"

ARNOLD TALKED FIRST with Cochran. Describing their interview later, he said, "In walked the toughest little Irishman I have ever seen." When he asked Cochran about his war experience, Cochran mentioned his air fights in North Africa.

"Did you win any of them?"

"I lost them all."

"What do you mean, lost them all?"

Cochran explained that against first-class opposition the P-40s they had in Africa were good only for defending. You couldn't really win with them and could only hope not to lose too badly.

"He asked me," relates Cochran, "if I wanted a top job. I said, 'What is it?' He said he couldn't tell me, but spoke of the jungle and the roughness of it. He asked me if I thought I was up to a rugged physical job. I answered that I thought I could take a tough job in the jungle."

31

"GIVE US THE MEN WHO DO THE WORK"

Arnold told Cochran to come back the next day. Phil had survived the first round.

Cochran's fame in the Air Force began even before he went to war. One of his friends at Ohio State, a classmate of his brother's, had been Milton Caniff—the cartoonist who drew the "Terry and the Pirates" comic strip. As the war threat loomed in America, Caniff decided to add the thrills of military aviation to the pen-and-ink adventures of Terry and his pals. He felt the need of more knowledge of real planes and pilots. He went to Phil Cochran to learn about an airman's life of flights and frolics, and Phil, spending his leaves in New York while he trained P-40 pilots in Connecticut, knew much about both.

At the Army base at Groton, Caniff received a bigger welcome than any ordinary newspaper artist could have expected. Commanding officers at the flying field reasoned that the introduction of Army aviation into a popular comic strip would be a valuable boost for Air Force recruiting. Flying demonstrations were put on for the visiting comic-strip artist. Planes swooped in the dizzy maneuvers of air battle. He went to parties with the pilots, and hobnobbed with the ground crews.

Putting air adventure into his comic strip, Caniff would, in the nature of things, likewise introduce an airman here. It was part of his professional belief that comic-strip characters were best when modeled on real people. His choice was obvious—Phil Cochran. That swaggering young officer, with his mop of wavy hair, piercing eyes, and muscular jaw, was the physical type. He had likewise the mannerisms, the animated smile, the swift tenseness in action, the rollicking, chatty gaiety, the abruptly incisive word—richly dramatic qualities in the fighter pilot.

"GIVE US THE MEN WHO DO THE WORK"

Presently the new issues of "Terry and the Pirates" were sky-high with air adventure and aviation dialogue. The new air hero appeared, a shrewdly cartooned replica of Phil Cochran. It took only a minor twist of sounds to get a name—Flip Corkin. The new transformation of "Terry and the Pirates" was a success, and the singular detail of an Army flyer living the fictitious life of comic-strip fable became a detail of the American scene.

Contemporary history probably presents no counterpart of the twofold career of Phil Cochran and Flip Corkin. His promotion to "Terry and the Pirates" pleased Cochran—what young American wouldn't be tickled by such fame? "At first it was fun," he says, "and then it was odd to live your life with everybody regarding you as that fellow in the funny paper."

Cochran won the Soldier's Medal for a daring exploit of rescue. The plane of a comrade pilot, crash-landing on the flying field, burst into flames. Cochran dashed in, and, in imminent danger of being incinerated, dragged the imperiled pilot out of the explosive blaze. But that was a passing trifle compared to funny-paper marvels. Here Phil Cochran was eclipsed by Flip Corkin.

Comic-strip fame was hardly sufficient to make Phil Cochran a candidate for the Project Nine job, but that was only the beginning of his career. He did in fact do his best, consciously or subconsciously, to achieve a war record worthy of his cartoon counterpart.

Given a squadron of P-40s to train, he worked like mad to prove the possibilities of the planes and improve the capabilities of the pilots. He planned, of course, to lead the outfit overseas.

They called it the Fighting Cock Squadron. For a mascot it had a game rooster, for insignia, a picture of a fighting cock with a chip on his shoulder. This was drawn by Milton Caniff of "Terry and the Pirates"—another tie between Phil Cochran and Flip Corkin.

The Fighting Cock Squadron was in a group ordered to Egypt, where Wingate had gone as an officer a decade before. In that ancient land headlines and history were being made. German Field Marshal Rommel and his formidable Afrika Korps stood at the gateway to the Nile. The British, under Montgomery, were soon to launch the offensive before which Rommel would make one of the most spectacular retreats in the annals of war. American aid was being rushed to Montgomery, and Cochran's Fighting Cock Squadron was one of the aviation units dispatched. Pilots and planes sailed for Egypt to fly and fight in the battle of the desert.

But Phil Cochran remained behind—in a hospital bed. He had overworked, worn himself out into illness. It was part of the intensity of his character to overdo things, and he had overdone things so badly that he had developed a kind of combat fatigue. You might say that Cochran had combat fatigue before he ever saw combat. He had driven himself so hard, training the squadron he expected to lead into action, that now he was out of action—apparently for good. Cases of exhaustion were not likely to be sent into combat. Flip Corkin might be a hero in the funny paper, but Phil Cochran was a wartime stay-at-home.

There was a small turn of mercy. A general sympathized. The American invasion of North Africa was being launched, and General John K. Cannon, whom they called "Uncle Joe," was organizing air forces for it. A group of replacements was to be sent, thirty-five P-40s and pilots. A commander was needed to take them over and deliver them to squadrons to which they would be assigned. General Cannon, out of sympathy and regard, gave the task to Cochran. It

"GIVE US THE MEN WHO DO THE WORK"

would enable him to go overseas, if only in charge of some replacements to hand over to others. Cochran, just out of a hospital, knew it was all he could expect.

They crossed the Atlantic on a British carrier, from which, at Casablanca, they were launched by catapult. They say that Cochran virtually talked his pilots off. Landing, all they saw was confusion—the invasion of North Africa was in its early days. Cochran and his replacements found no place to go and nobody to tell them where..

They decided to stick together and prepare for a little action on their own. Cochran headed for the general direction of the war, but when interrogated always said they were headed for Casablanca—just as another famous young Irish-American pilot, "Wrong-Way Corrigan," had claimed he crossed the Atlantic by mistake. Wrong-Way Cochran took his gang off to a spot on the desert where they teamed up with an infantry outfit, only too happy to have an air umbrella. There he trained his men—carrying on with his old job under new conditions. The replacement pilots were green youngsters, fresh from flying school. Cochran taught them just as he had taught squadrons before, just as he had schooled his own Fighting Cock Squadron. Green though his men were, he transformed them speedily into a competent unit, some becoming crack pilots. They called themselves the Joker Squadron because they had no number, having been formed outside Air Force routine. When their existence was discovered, the Air Force Command was pleased to find well-trained flyers instead of raw recruits. Cochran was ordered to take seven of his best pupils as replacements to the fighting front in Tunisia.

They flew by hops across the North African desert and along the coast, but in Tunisia found nothing to join. In the still-prevailing confusion, they couldn't locate the outfit to which they were assigned. Cochran was on his own again. He saw a chance for action, independent action. He took his lost outfit down to a place where he could stay unattached. This was possible in the hurly-burly of a new campaign, when a unit might find itself left to its own devices.

Southern Tunisia was the spot. Not much attention was being paid to it by the Allied Command at the time. Rommel was in hasty retreat from Egypt, his North Afrika Korps in full flight along an immense length of coastline. If he planned to join forces with German units in northern Tunisia, it would be by way of the southern Tunisian corridor. But that was thought unlikely. For the time being, the corridor was a neglected area, where skeleton enemy forces were keeping land connections open. An ideal place for aerial guerrilla warfare, and there Cochran led a minor independent campaign.

This was his chance, his first and last, he believed. The recent fatigue patient who had gone overseas from a hospital bed could not have expected this much, and certainly could not dream of more. It was a great chance for the thing that Cochran was best at, the independent fight. He led his planes in dog-fights against whatever enemy planes he could find. They shot up trucks and parties of troops. They strapped bombs to their P-40 fighters and went on bombing missions.

More Germans and Italians appeared, men and equipment. Things in southern Tunisia were becoming busier, much busier. Activity increased daily. Rommel was coming through, and enemy forces were moving in to hold the south Tunisian corridor open for him. The Allies were pushing to close the corridor. It was evident that a violent battle would develop. Cochran, for his minor aerial guerrilla campaign, had picked a sector that was rapidly becoming a key point of the global war.

"GIVE US THE MEN WHO DO THE WORK"

His improvised air war was discovered and reinforced. Incorporated into the Air Force organization, his unit was given more planes, more fighters, some bombers, level and dive. He could now experiment with the combined tactics of different kinds of aircraft, strafing and bombing against artillery positions, troop concentrations, tank squadrons. He hunted German light tanks all over southern Tunisia.

The commander of the American Air Force in North Africa came to see him, General James H. Doolittle. Phil Cochran's tensely observant eyes studied the small, baldish, smiling air commander. Jimmy Doolittle, the great old-time stunt flyer who had made daredevil history in the early days of aviation, who in the spring of the previous year had flashed into war fame with the Doolittle bombing of Tokyo, and who was now moving into greater fields of the war of the air. The gods of adventure must have smiled at the two of them, Jimmy Doolittle and Flip Corkin, the one the hero of exploits as dizzy as the comic-strip fables of the other.

Doolittle said to Cochran, "I hear you are doing a great job of ground support down here."

Cochran answered, "Well, we happened to find ourselves set down in this place, and we were looking for a war."

"What do you need?"

"More airplanes."

Cochran got more airplanes, Doolittle saw to that. Thereafter he made weekly visits, keeping an eye on the Cochran development of ground support.

The Germans had been the first to devise air-power tactics in modern war. Their Stuka dive bombers, used as flying artillery, had terrorized the world in the first phase of the global conflict. That was followed by a swift development of more formidable equipment, the United States leading the way in turning out advanced machinery for air power. The improved aerial weapons had to be coordinated with operations on the ground, and the hard school of experience in battle was in Tunisia, as Rommel came through the southern corridor.

Cochran saw the confusion, the blunders and defeats of the dark days when the Americans were learning how to fight a war. He saw American forces battered and hurled back by Rommel's panzers, in the bad days of Kasserine Pass. He saw the lack of understanding of air and ground cooperation, the mistaken ideas about the use of air.

"At first," he recalls, "the ground forces would get into a pickle and call to the planes, 'Come and get us out of here.' They thought the Air Force was a cure-all for their mistakes. When we couldn't pull them out they blamed it on the airplanes. We said, 'You ground people don't understand air, and you think we're here to straighten out all your damn mistakes.'"

He virtually insulted General Giraud, who was then head of the French Government in Africa. His outfit was supporting French troops and these were badly cut up. Giraud stormed at Cochran. "There should be more planes," he shouted, "hundreds, thousands."

Cochran shouted back, "You've got to fight on the ground and quit thinking that airplanes are the magic wand. You've got to stop thinking you can hide behind a rock and have the planes do the job."

He was not too clear about who Giraud was, and later blinked a bit when he realized he had bawled out the head of the French North African Government. Superior officers were bothered. Then Giraud sent an apology, telling the American major that, after thinking it over, he realized Cochran was right.

Out of the turmoil and trouble in North Africa grew the

American idea of a tactical air force for immediate ground support. In the development of this, Cochran was a pioneer. North Africa, too, produced the strategic air force for long-range aerial blows.

Cochran, the air tactician, was still the infatuate fighter pilot. He led his planes into wild action every time he could, and that was nearly always. Believing that in North Africa he was having his first and last chance in war, he saw to it that he had enough nerve-chilling adventure to last one man for the duration of any war.

Near the Tunisian city of Kairouan, a German divisional commander had his headquarters. Cochran had the building spotted. At night he woke up laughing, thinking how funny what he was going to do would be. With a bomb attached to his fighter plane, he flew at dawn to the German commander's headquarters. All was quiet, the Nazi general and his staff fast asleep. Cochran made his bombing run so low that he had to pull up to get over the building. He let go the bomb, and looking over his shoulder saw enemy headquarters go up into the air, a shower of debris. "Just like a movie," he described it.

Suddenly Cochran found a Focke-Wulf 190 shooting at him with a cannon, shooting accurately. Away went his right aileron and most of his tail. He would have to make a crash landing. He started down. The Focke-Wulf kept after him to finish him off. Cochran, looking like a sure goner, tried a desperate measure. He swung around and went straight at the German, giving him a machine-gun burst, again "just like a movie." The enemy pilot apparently thought it all a trick maneuver, suspected a ruse. He turned away, and Cochran resumed his trip earthward for the inevitable crash landing.

He drove himself to the utter limit. He drove his men the

same way. Air power was desperately short in the climax of the Tunisian campaign. Every pilot had to be in the air for every possible hour, and every pilot had to fly as much as he could, and more. "We flew thirty or forty missions a month."

Night landings were difficult because of inadequate lighting. Finally, as they approached the field, Cochran had bursts of ack-ack fired to guide the incoming pilots, probably the first time ground firing was used to help rather than harass planes. "The ack-ack seldom hit anything anyway," Cochran explains.

Living conditions were an ordeal. The only food they had was British field rations, savorless to the American taste. Agreeable and varied food means much to men under prolonged strain and pressure, and this was an unending monotony. There was no semblance of town or barracks anywhere near this corner of the desert. At first they slept in foxholes. Then they took over a great ravine and dug caves in the sides, which they expanded into spacious caverns. Two thousand men, who incessantly fought in planes and worked on planes, existed like cave dwellers. Facilities for civilized grooming were nil. Officers and enlisted men looked like tramps.

One day General Cannon arrived and saw some of Cochran's pilots in disreputable sweat shirts.

"Are you United States officers?" he demanded.

"Yes, sir."

"Do you mean to say that Cochran lets you go around like that?" he exploded.

"Oh hell, General," they replied, "you ought to see him. He's dirtier than we are."

Cochran admits that for one stretch of six weeks he didn't take his clothes off.

With the outfit inhumanly overworked and living in subhuman conditions, the inevitable came about—they began to crack. The men were being worn out, urged on to exhaustion and illness, driven to collapse from sheer strain and fatigue. This Cochran realized clearly. He himself had been a fatigue case. "I knew it was going to happen. I asked a full month ahead of time, 'Take this squadron out. Give these men a rest.' But they couldn't be taken out. The Command was too short of air power. The planes and the pilots were needed too badly. They couldn't be spared, and the squadron was just run into the ground. Some of the kids went crazy. One killed himself. They all got sick." When they were finally relieved and sent home, most of the pilots were too badly spent ever to be sent into combat again.

At Mitchel Field, Cochran was doing a training chore when the order came to report to the Commander of the Air Forces in Washington. His reaction was typical, "What have I done now?" He had an uneasy misgiving that he had committed some error and was being summoned to answer in Washington.

About Alison, Arnold had heard from presidential advisor Harry Hopkins. He had also noted work Alison had done in Russia with shipments of lend-lease planes. Responding to Arnold's questions, Alison offered a brief account of his fighter-pilot service under Chennault in China.

The Air Force commander gave an attentive eye to the smiling reserve of this mild and shy little sky fighter from Florida. Alison was in striking contrast to what Arnold called "the toughest little Irishman I ever saw." But then Hap Arnold, who had grown up with the Army Air Forces, knew well enough that the formidable warrior of the sky may have almost any outward characteristics, from swashbuckling bravado to a suggestion of Sunday school.

"GIVE US THE MEN WHO DO THE WORK"

He told Alison to come back the next day. This candidate had also survived the first round.

John Alison was a young Southerner from Gainesville, Florida. He was Cochran's opposite in coloring, of fair complexion, with blue eyes, wide open and alert, and light brown hair moving back to give him the high forehead of early baldness. His bearing was one of bland and smiling modesty and simplicity, combined with keen intelligence. He spoke softly, yet with little trace of Southern accent. What he said was expressive, aptly worded and often vivid, sometimes dramatic with exhortation, yet always he retained a touch of good-mannered self-depreciation. Somehow you were not surprised to hear that his brother was a Methodist minister down in Florida.

Alison's war experience had been different from Cochran's. Sent to England with the first squadron of P-45s for the Royal Air Force, he went on to an assignment flattering or disappointing depending on the viewpoint—a diplomatic post. He was ordered to the Soviet Union, to become assistant air attache at the American embassy in Moscow.

This was an ornamental job. Then, as later, the Russians were keeping their military affairs darkly secret. Allied observers were permitted no significant observation of the Red Army in action. Alison, like Cochran a fighter pilot keyed up for combat, found himself shunted off to exile in a meaningless desk job. Yet he found ways of distinguishing himself.

He flew to Moscow in the same plane with Harry Hopkins, emissary of the President on a mission to the Soviet Government. Alison and Hopkins struck up an acquaintance, which Cochran, Alison's old friend, loved to describe:

"Hopkins, just as you and I, became intrigued with this little fellow. He would say, 'Alison, have a drink.' And John

"FATHER ALISON" his friends called him. The Japanese thought differently.

would reply, 'I'm sorry, sir, but I don't drink." Hopkins would exclaim, 'Oh,' and have a drink. So would everybody else in the plane except John.

"A little while later, Hopkins, forgetting, would say, 'Alison, what will you drink?' Again John would say, 'Nothing,' and all would have a drink except John. This happened several times and finally Hopkins said, 'Alison, I don't mind your not drinking, but don't be so damn superior about it.'"

In Moscow Hopkins and Alison attended the customary great Soviet banquet with the usual round of Russian toasts, which brought a crisis for Alison. "If the Russians propose a drink," Cochran, who often spoke for the more quiet Alison, has related, "you have just got to drink, for the Russians don't understand a teetotaler. John sensed this. He drank the toasts, slugging down the vodka. When Harry Hopkins saw this, he grinned and said, 'Alison, that shows a definite lack of character.'

"He was wrong about that. John's drinking was really an exhibition of strength of character. He was doing it because it was part of his job. He drank all the toasts, guzzled vodka like mad. Yes, and he was the last one to drink with the Russians. A lot of people got sick, and had to leave, or passed out. But not John. There he sat, putting away the vodka with the best of the Ruskies."

During his months in Russia, Alison worked with lend-lease shipments. At Archangel, in the Arctic, he did a job on a hundred P-40 fighter planes. For this he had the help of one of the surprising personalities of the Air Force, Colonel "Hub" Zemke, whose parents were born in Germany, who had cousins in the German Army, and whose wife was an Italian, daughter of a former Italian consul at Miami. Her two brothers were in the Italian Army, one a medical officer, the other a pilot in the Fascist Air Force. Having such close ties with both ends of the Axis, Zemke, as an American air officer, was a rather remarkable sort of chap. He later became a top-ranking ace, with a string of German planes to his credit. He himself was shot down over Germany, then walked out, looking like a German and talking the language perfectly. In the bitter cold of the Arctic he aided Alison in the task of assembling the hundred P-40s, trying them out in test flights, and sending them to the Soviet war front.

Then Alison repeated this performance, at the opposite pole of lend-lease for Russia. "He went down to Persia," says Cochran, "where a lot of lend-lease planes were coming in for the Russians and where a very bad job was being done. John walked in and, as a mere captain, said, 'That's not right.' Without being told and without an order from Washington, he took over the lend-lease business down there in Persia and straightened things out. For five months he supervised the assembly of planes, B-25s. He put them together in the right way, and flew every one. There must have been seventy-five or a hundred. He did a test pilot's job on each, and then turned them over to the Russians in proper shape."

His journeyings took him to China, where again teetotaler Alison did his duty as he saw it, braving Demon Rum, or, in this case, the Chinese dragon called rice wine. "If a Chinese," Cochran explains, "invites you to his house and gets out the rice wine, he says *Gombay*. That means drink the whole thing down. You must do it, and John did. The Chinese like to see a white man drink so much that he gets befuddled. They love it if he passes out. It pleases them to see that a white man can't take it. The white man loses face. John sensed that and, every time the Chinese said *Gombay*, he downed the rice wine. They didn't reckon with this little fellow. John has a terrific competitive spirit. Everything he does is competition. He was holding up the American end, and said no Chinese would drink us under. It was a competition, and he won."

After much wirepulling, Alison was transferred to the American Air Forces in China and served under Chennault, the commander who had made fantastic air history with the Flying Tigers earlier in the war. The secret of the fabulous Flying Tiger exploits had been the bold use of new tactics. Chennault was the arch progressive of the air, a master of the unorthodox, and serving in his China outfit meant scope and latitude for originality and experiment.

This was possible because of Chinese distances. American air bases were scattered widely and were only loosely integrated. Individual squadrons were more or less on their own. A gift for independent action was at a premium in what was largely an aerial guerrilla war. In China, Alison had as much chance to initiate and improvise as Cochran in North Africa. He availed himself of the opportunity to the full, became one of the best fighter pilots of Chennault's China Air Force, ran up a string of enemy planes shot down, and earned impressive decorations. Then he was sent home.

Both Cochran and Alison were brought back for training jobs, set to teach green squadrons the lessons they had learned in action. This was what they were doing when Arnold's summons reached them.

Their association had begun in flying school, where Cochran, escaping from business administration, arrived just ahead of Alison, up from the University of Florida. As Cochran tells it, "We lived on the same floor, and I knew him as that little fellow in a lower class who wanted to learn things I had already been taught. I was eager to tell him. I have a peculiarity that makes me want to tell the other fellow what I have learned. I can't stand to see somebody who wants to know something that I know, and not give it to him. In flying school, when a new batch of kids came in, it was natural for me to think, 'Cochran, tell those fellows what you know.'"

Alison was shy, Southern and grateful. "John claims that nobody in the school paid any attention to him except me."

After flying school they were in the same squadron together, Cochran four months ahead of Alison, with four months more of things learned. Again the one was eager to learn, the other eager to teach. "John adhered to me because I was the Old Man."

Their backgrounds were as different as possible, yet both represented a large section of the greatly diverse American people. Up in Erie, Pennsylvania, Phil Cochran's family was prominent in local politics. His father was a lawyer, and real estate adviser to the city. Because so many of his friends called him Barney, Phil's mother tried to give her boys good sober saints' names that couldn't be twisted into nicknames. She could hardly foresee that her son Philip would be known to a generation of young Americans as Flip.

Although he seldom rose at dawn now, unless it was to fly, Philip had been altar boy at early Mass and had sung in the boys' choir. He had played football at Central High School, although he admitted he wasn't remarkable, because at the time he weighed only 114 pounds. He didn't go to college—Ohio State—until he got his weight up to 128, but then he did more singing than football, to pay expenses. He sang in night clubs and roadhouses, sometimes making as much as eight dollars a night, sometimes just singing for his supper. He also worked at a desk job for a paper company and, what with these various jobs, he managed to delay graduation until he was twenty-five. Although his degree was in business administration he had by this time an abiding distaste for business and administration of any kind, and especially for what is called "paper work." Also it was in the mid-thirties, when business jobs were few and far between, but the country was beginning to think uneasily of war. Cochran was just under the age limit, twenty-six, for the Army Air Force. To get his fare to Detroit, where the examination was held, he sold his grandfather's gold watch and played a game of professional football. He passed.

Down in Florida they also had night clubs and roadhouses, but Alison was a native brought up to have no traffic with the Yankees who disported themselves in such hot spots. His family was religious, his home background of the God-fearing Bible Belt type, which made it natural for his elder brother to be a Methodist preacher. He was a teetotaler by upbringing and as such an eternal source of surprise and amusement to Cochran, whose college crooning had given him a fondness for night life, show girls and what he called "hat-check chicks."

"John was always the Boy Scout," Cochran sums it up. "He likes to help people and he is always rescuing bad boys. Though a teetotaler, he has a great following of drunks, whom he is forever getting out of trouble. Time and again, I'd say, 'John, you're going to be sorry.' To which he replied, 'Yes, I know, but there's nobody else to help them.' We called him Father Alison."

The tie between them was fighter aviation, for which they had similar gifts—animated intelligence, restless appetite for adventures physical and mental, driving competitive energies, fierce individualism. Cochran's approach was hotly aggressive; Alison's, that of a crusader, was to have more in common with Wingate's.

The art of air battle can be as intricate in theory as a game of chess, as skillful in practice as billiards. There's enthrallment in the moves and countermoves of air combat, guess and

"GIVE US THE MEN WHO DO THE WORK"

outguess, the finesse of hand and eye. It's a superb game at high speed in the great spaces, and the stakes are life and death. It's a game in which the teamwork is a cooperation of individualists. The fighter pilot, alone in his single-seater, is the individualist in the war of the air. His victories are personal glories, his reward is an individualistic title, ace. Fighter pilots deem themselves the elite, and are the prima donnas of the air forces.

Cochran and Alison talked fighter aviation, thought fighter aviation, lived fighter aviation. "It got so that John and I thought exactly alike. People regarded us as synonymous. They'd say, 'We're going to have a party. Are John and Phil coming?' We lived together. We rented a house, and bought our own furniture. People gave a shower for us, as for newlyweds, donating pots and pans."

Their house was named John-Phil-John. Another John lived with them, John Aiken. Alison was Little John; Aiken was Crazy John. They were stationed first at Langley Field, Hampton, Virginia, then at Mitchel Field, New York, and all was fighter aviation.

"Little John, Crazy John and I," Cochran remembers, "ran competitions, each trying to make his squadron the best. We'd have air fights, squadron against squadron, and would fight our heads off all morning. Then, sitting at lunch, we'd fight the battles all over again. Our cook used to say, 'Will you boys talk about something else?' She'd have something special for us, and would expect us to say, 'Wasn't it lovely?' but we'd pound the table and argue about who had won, and didn't eat. That made the cook angry no end. She was a big fat colored woman."

Crazy John was killed. This is the story in Cochran's words: "He was trying to help a kid they were going to wash out of fighter aviation. Crazy John said: 'Don't wash him

49

out. Let me take him for a week.' They turned the kid over to him, and day after day Crazy John in one plane went through fighter maneuvers with the kid in another. The kid ran into Crazy John, and killed him."

Then Art Salsbury lived with Phil and the remaining John. He was Cochran's protege. "I had confidence in Art. They wanted to wash him out. They said, 'He's a fine fellow and has a strong mind, but he just can't make the grade as a fighter pilot.' I said, 'Anybody with as strong a desire as Art Salsbury—let me have him.' They let me take Art in hand, and he became a magnificent fighter pilot."

Cochran and Alison each had the temperament for experiment. The Phil-John team tested new tactics of air battle, devised new ways of combat on high, new squadron maneuvers, new acrobatics in dogfights. They practiced original methods of giving tactical fighter support to ground forces, of strafing the enemy, of using fighter planes to bomb.

Curt Moffett, Cochran remembers, was the commander. "Twenty years before he had done extraordinary flying. For nine years he was test pilot at McCook Field. When the war came he was forty-three years old, but did some great combat flying. He was shot down in Tunisia, his hands badly burned, but today he's okay. As our squadron commander he gave John and me anything we wanted. We would say, 'Major, we've an idea.' And he'd reply, 'Let's try it.'

"John and I used to do a lot of formation acrobatics which were absolutely off the books in the Air Forces. With older and slower planes stunts in formation were all right, but with modern high-speed jobs it was too dangerous. When John and I with our squadrons flew acrobatics, Curt Moffett and our group commander, Will Kepner, looked the other way. Finally, however, they asked us to stop it. We were a bad example to the other kids. So we thought up something else, twisters of another kind to try."

The Phil-John team was kept together, Cochran and Alison always in the same outfit. Air Force routine was arranged so as not to separate them. Their partnership in experiments, their mutual seeking of the new and trying the untried, was recognized as valuable.

When war drew near to America, there was a swift expansion of the Air Forces, with urgent need for skilled pilots to train recruits. After their separate war adventures in Tunisia and in England and Moscow, both, as experienced war flyers, were reassigned to training jobs, so that once more their careers synchronized in a curious way. Their homeward paths crossed for a brief meeting in New York, a quick chat before destiny took them in opposite directions. Cochran was detailed to the 1st Fighter Command at Mitchel Field, Long Island. He hoped for an assignment to the sky war in Europe. Alison went to the 4th Fighter Command on the Pacific Coast, to train a squadron for the Pacific for air battle against the Japs. Now destiny—and Hap Arnold—were bringing the two together again.

4. "Ordered to Burma"

ON THE DAY following the first interview, Arnold had Cochran and Alison in together, and told them what the job was. He referred back to the Roosevelt-Churchill conference at Quebec, the appointment of Lord Louis Mountbatten to a newly formed Southeast Asia Command for a major offensive against Japan. He spoke of Wingate. Neither Cochran nor Alison had ever heard of Wingate. Arnold reflected the vivid impression that the singular British genius of war had made on him. He told them briefly about Wingate's raiding operations against the Japs in Burma the previous year, and stated that a new and greatly expanded Wingate campaign for the reconquest of northern Burma was planned. In this, American air aid would be given, and Chief of Staff General George C. Marshall wanted as much American participation as possible.

Arnold outlined Wingate's jungle war problem, the evacuation of the wounded and the bringing in of supplies, and repeated Wingate's request for a unit of light planes for evacuation and supply. For this a task force of light planes,

Cubs, one hundred or perhaps two hundred, would be formed, the command of which would be offered to one of them, Cochran or Alison.

The response of the two crack fighter pilots to the offer of a light-plane command was, in a word, hostile. Arnold said later that Cochran "just about snapped my head off, saying it was a sissy job." Which required temerity. A lieutenant colonel seldom takes an attitude toward the commander of the Army Air Forces at all suggestive of snapping his head off.

As Cochran tells the story: "I have a habit of talking for Alison. This may seem peculiar, because John is entirely capable of saying things for himself. But he has a habit of not explaining what is in his head. When General Arnold said to us, 'Do you fellows want this job?' John hesitated, and I remember him saying to the general that he didn't know quite how to explain. Then he looked him straight in the eye and said, 'General, I want to fight.'

"I knew General Arnold didn't know what he meant. So I spoke for Alison. I said, 'John means he is a fighter pilot, and you are asking him to give up, just as you are asking me to give up, a career that we've spent seven years in developing. We are fighter pilots, and we don't want to change.'

"John looked at me and said, 'Yes, that's what I mean.' My angle," Cochran goes on, "was that I was just back from a lot of air battle, fighting and studying fighter-pilot tactics. I had some ideas that I wanted to develop. So I didn't like this light-plane project for evacuation and supply one bit. In fact, I told General Arnold that, in place of the best job in the world he was offering me a sissy job. John had been over in China, where he had done a lot of fighting with very little equipment, the little that Chennault had. He had been sent home to build up a new group, and he had built one, a good organization. There he was, all set to go, and now he was being offered the job of running a light-plane supply-and-evacuation business of some sort."

Alison added his own voice: "General Arnold said, 'I'm going to give you two hundred Cubs. I might even give you another hundred.' What I told him was, 'Sir, if that's all you're going to give us, you don't need Cochran, and you don't need me, because anybody can run those Cubs. We are fighter pilots, and want to stay in the fight. There are no guns on those Cubs.'"

In the Cochran-Alison competition for the Wingate post all was anticlimax. Instead of vying with each other for it, they were fighting to get out of it. It was rivalry in reverse, a contest in ducking the job.

The Air Force commander understood their fighter-pilot point of view, and undertook to convince them. Alison says, "The general gave us a sales talk." It was seldom that a four-star general had to use salesmanship on lieutenant colonels, but it was a good sales talk.

Since his last conference with Lord Louis Mountbatten, Arnold had been mulling over the Wingate idea, and had developed the picture of air support still further. What he had in mind was something not to be stated too plainly. There were international implications that called for tact, subtlety, discretion. Cochran and Alison were not to be told flatly. The idea was to be transmitted by hint and inference.

"General Arnold told us," Cochran recalls, "that the idea was to give the Wingate jungle campaign air support in every possible way. Wingate had been promised light planes to evacuate the wounded and bring in supplies. That was what Wingate had asked for; he hadn't thought of anything more. But air support could mean a lot more. He said that Chief of Staff General Marshall wanted the fullest American participation in the Wingate show. And fullest meant just that, everything that a bright airman could think of. General Arnold himself could see far beyond the original idea of mere light planes, Cubs. What he wanted was somebody to pick up the vision of an unorthodox air campaign in the jungle war and work it out with a ruthless originality of mind. I, personally, read into General Arnold's words a thing that actually he never said—'Go over and steal that show.' "

Alison's version: "General Arnold seemed to say: 'Who can tell? It might turn into an air show. I want somebody to get on the job and see if it can't be turned into an air show.' He didn't put it into so many words. That one little idea was only eye to eye. I mean, when General Arnold looked at you, you saw a certain twinkle in his eyes, and you knew pretty much what he meant. I looked at him and felt I could tell what he meant, the way he smiled. His eyes and his mind told me that what he wanted was the transformation of the Wingate campaign into a new experiment in the use of air power."

The sales talk concluded with a challenge and a promise. "The general," says Alison, "told us, 'I am going to leave the door open, and if you have sense enough to put your foot in it, you can have anything you want.' " Meaning they could have for the Wingate task force not only light planes, but all other types of aircraft and equipment that they could fit into the picture of a jungle-war air show.

Cochran adds, "I don't think he had us sold on the idea, but when the Commanding General of the Air Forces says, 'Do you want this job?' you don't say, 'No, sir.' You say, 'When do we start?' "

It remained for Arnold to make a selection between the two, and pick one for the command. But he never did make the selection. The Cochran-Alison competition came to an odd conclusion.

"I think," explains Cochran, "that General Arnold sensed that John and I were very close to each other and thought for each other. Every once in a while, in talking, John would look at me as if saying, 'You finish the statement,' and I would pick up where he had left off. I was talking for John, and John was talking for me. We still thought he would pick one of us, and then he asked something like this, 'Which of you two monkeys ranks?' We said we didn't know. I was the older in the Air Forces by four months, but John got his Regular Army commission as a pilot before I got mine. The general said, 'Well, Cochran, you rank.' The meaning was that one of us two, by ranking the other, would have to take the final responsibility. He was, by implication, appointing us both to the command. Seeing how close John and I were, he thought, 'What the hell! Send them both.' It was very unusual."

Decidedly unusual, a partnership command. Instead of tossing one young American in with Wingate, Arnold would try two. At first thought it might seem a little like the joke about Hollywood lavishness, "If one is good, two would be better." But Arnold, of course, had seen Cochran and Alison as complementary types, their abilities dovetailing. Together, they worked as well as he hoped the team would work with Wingate.

Arnold's last remark to the two of them, and his first order, was, "See Wingate in London." They were to fly to England and report to Mountbatten, who would arrange the meeting with Wingate.

Talking it over hastily, it was decided that Phil Cochran, as senior officer, should go. This balanced Alison's previous experience in London. In view of Wingate's character, of his and Cochran's first reactions to each other, it might have been easier had Alison made the trip. But Phil went.

5. "Come You Back, You British Soldier"

THE MAN PHIL COCHRAN MET at the War Office, that afternoon in London, had a wide experience in war, but so far it had not included working closely with Americans.

Orde Wingate was no great writer of English prose, but in other respects he may even have outpaced another British soldier to whom he has often been compared, Lawrence of Arabia. In various stages of his career Wingate was known as the Lawrence of Judea, of Ethiopia, and of Burma. This comparison is said to have irked him, not because he felt himself to be in any way unworthy of the comparison, but because he was not "another" anybody. He was himself. He had in fact made his career in three fields to Lawrence's one.

Like Lawrence, Wingate started as a brilliant student of Arabic. Like Lawrence too, he was a brilliant professional soldier without having what is called a military mind. He said himself that he would never have become a soldier except for a conclusion which he reached, reluctantly, when he was seventeen. At an age when young Phil Cochran was worrying over his football weight. Wingate heard a lecture in 1920 by Professor Gilbert Murray, the Oxford savant, on the future of the League of Nations. Wingate was so impressed by the importance of the League and, at the same time, by its weakness, lacking a police force, that he decided "soldiers will be needed again in my generation." This may well have been rationalization of a youthful decision to follow a profession for which he had a natural bent, and one in which there was a family tradition of success. But he did find it necessary to justify the decision, which he confirmed when a bicycle trip showed him a Germany unconvinced of fair defeat in World War I, and determined to try again.

After schooling at Charterhouse, army training at Woolwich (his branch was the artillery), and studies in the School of Oriental Languages in London, Wingate went to Egypt, where his uncle, Sir Reginald Wingate, had succeeded Kitchener as governor-general of the Sudan and sirdar of the Egyptian army. Uncle Reginald (a character in Lawrence's *Seven Pillars of Wisdom*) had been chief intelligence officer for Egypt and it was simple enough for young Orde Wingate to be given a small intelligence job. There, however, family influence of a material sort stopped.

Family influence of a less tangible kind was to continue through Wingate's life. His grandfather was a Glasgow merchant who learned Hebrew and turned missionary for the Plymouth Brethren, a nineteenth-century British sect whose fervor was more nearly matched, in the United States, by the early Puritans than by any group of the later era. The Plymouth Brethren were serious folk who denied themselves small comforts and amusements for salvation's sake, but clung stubbornly to their own opinions, which they held by direct inspiration, free from any intervention or interpretation by the organized clergy. Like the Quakers, they listened to an inner voice; then they went out to preach their own gospel, Salvation Army-wise, to the poor. In the Wingate family this religious discipline, combining with the discipline of the Army, was to produce the kind of zeal which distinguished General "Chinese" Gordon and has marked occasional British soldiers since Cromwell, or perhaps since the Crusades.

Orde Wingate's father was Colonel Charles Wingate of the British Army in India. He was reported to pray five times daily and do his best to avoid battle on Sunday; unquestionably he did devote his spare time to a mission for the Pathans at the Khyber Pass. Born at Naimi Tal, a hill resort six thousand feet up in the Himalayas, Orde was the eldest son among seven children "brought up on porridge, bread and dripping, and the sincere milk of the Word." At home in Woking the text *Fear ye the Lord* greeted visitors, who were later to say that this was the only fear Colonel Wingate taught his son.

The colonel never rose quite as far in the service as his brother Reginald, perhaps because he nagged at his superiors with reports on the financial condition of the Budanee administration and the advisability of dam-building on the Krishoo River. His son Orde was to move up faster, due to remarkable ability and a series of opportunities to make good as a trouble shooter, but he never ceased to criticize the Empire he fought to save. In Palestine, in Egypt, in Burma, he carried with him his father's and his grandfather's zeal for trying to improve the world.

In the Sudan young Wingate could, it was said, "think like a Sudanese." But he spent an uneventful apprenticeship under orders from Cairo, its high point an expedition on leave to find "the lost tribes of Zerzera," among the shifting sands of the Libyan desert. This independent enterprise took him to a "lost oasis" called Zina, celebrated in an Arab ballad. To afford the trip, he economized by giving up cigarettes for a year, and never smoked again.

Then he went home to England and met on shipboard the girl he was to marry, dark-haired Lorna Patterson, daughter of a tea planter in Ceylon. Her intention was to go to Oxford, but when she married young Wingate she went with him instead, in the early years of world depression, to a dismal assignment at Sheffield. There he persisted, as a few years later a young king was to do, in poking his nose into industrial slums, visiting the hovels of unemployed miners in the "distressed areas," and muttering that something would have to be done.

Something was done with so unorthodox an officer. They found Wingate a berth even worse than Sheffield, from the Army point of view. They sent him to Palestine.

He was delighted, and so was Lorna. He began at once to learn Hebrew by the method of comparing Bible texts. For him Palestine was, first of all, the Bible country, and Lytton Strachey's famous description of General Gordon—"a solitary English gentleman . . . wandering, with a thick book under his arm, in the neighborhood of Jerusalem"—would have applied equally well to Captain Wingate some fifty years later.

Times, however, had changed. British piety, as exemplified in Gordon and, later, in the high religious aims of Allenby and the Balfour Declaration, had somehow vanished. A British mandate to protect the Jewish homeland had gradually deteriorated, until the model farms under British supervision were raising pigs, for neither Arab nor Jew but for the British Army. As between the two Semitic

"COME YOU BACK, YOU BRITISH SOLDIER"

peoples claiming the country, the Arabs were rather favored by the Army because they could, at least, talk to the men on horseback about horses. Also, in the cold wars of the early thirties, Axis funds flowed freely, and subsidized sheiks were pleasant hosts to British officialdom.

Among Zionist Jews it would have been hard to find a time when British prestige was lower or British friendship less prized. The British might govern by day, although even then they dared not walk alone. By night the Arab bands ruled the country, and that year Arabs seized and held, for days, the Old City with its Jewish and Christian shrines.

When Wingate declared his support of the Jewish position and wanted to join in the battle for a free Palestine, Jewish leaders, at first, were understandably cautious. He looked like an intelligent man, with his deep-set eyes and his long, stubborn Scottish chin. But he was, after all, not only a gunnery expert but an intelligence officer of the British Army.

Time was to prove his sincerity. He and Lorna, then only eighteen, turned their little house on the Bethlehem road into a replica of other Palestine homes. They furnished it with low couches and tables and bookcases, most of the books being in Oriental languages. They filled it with the flowers and fruits of the country and, in time, with Jewish friends. Wingate, those friends were to recall, liked sitting on a rug to play Bach and Beethoven on the phonograph, his fair hair falling in his eyes, one lanky arm out to crank the machine when it faltered. He said he never grew tired of Christian religious music and Jewish religious literature. The Wingates served local food, and Captain Wingate made himself unpopular by suggesting to Haifa headquarters that the health of the occupying army would be improved if Jewish bread were served at mess.

All that he did and was made him unpopular, naturally, with his fellow officers. This disrespect was mutual. Wingate was frank and bitter in his denunciation of the old school tie and Whitehall policies in general. They tried to run Palestine at arm's length, he complained, with no real knowledge of the country.

The Wingates were determined to live in Palestine as citizens of the country rather than as members of an occupying force. They spent as much time as possible with young friends in the cooperative farms. "We never traveled in armored cars," Lorna Wingate recalled afterwards in explaining how they were able to know the real Palestine. "How could we, when, going along the road, we would meet young Jewish girls in their shorts, without any weapons, singing happily, fearlessly and defiantly?"

There was some danger in such travel because 1936 was a time of trouble in Palestine, with the highways and the farms, the outlying villages and even the Jewish suburb of Jerusalem never safe from Arab attack. But Wingate argued that the much-discussed enmity between Jew and Arab was less important than the dislike felt by both Jews and Arabs for the British.

To prove this, given leave by General Dill, he set forth on an adventure directly in the Lawrence tradition. He went to Tirat Zvi, a village on the trans-Jordan border, and there, with the help of a Jewish friend, Gerson Ritov, he disguised himself as "Brother Jacob," an orthodox Jew of Tel Aviv. The two then traveled for six weeks through Arab villages, after which Wingate was able to report that he was better treated as a Jew than he would have been as a British officer.

This basic possibility of agreement between Arab and Jew, given a hands-off policy on the part of the British, was important to Wingate, because he believed in the ultimate peaceful development of the country under Jewish guidance. With Lawrence, who had advised Emir Feisal to concur in the Balfour Declaration, Wingate saw the Jews as "the leaven of the Middle East," their progressive civilization giving a necessary impetus to their neighbors. "Only the Jew can save the Arab," he was fond of saying. More practically, he reported, from a military standpoint, that "the Jewish settlement in Palestine is the only bit of real strength in the whole of the Middle East."

Meanwhile Arab insurrection (fed by Axis funds), which killed children and cattle, burned houses, ruined crops and chopped down trees by night, mocked British control. Wingate wrote: "I was appalled to find that Jews had to hide their women and children behind bullet-proof walls, while the menfolk patrolled their farms with antiquated rifles to protect their crops and livestock. The whole trouble could be settled overnight if the Jews were allowed to raise their own army."

Later, Wingate wrote directly to Winston Churchill: "These Jews in Palestine are hard-working, intelligent people, leading good lives, cultivating soil that has not been tilled for thousands of years, raising orchards where there have been deserts. They are entitled to our protection not only for what they have done to the soil but also for the culture they have brought with them. Give the Jews the right to defend themselves, let them have access to arms, and the Axis-inspired Arab revolt would fade out like snow upon the desert's dusty face."

Actually England, sending successive commissions to Palestine to whittle down the "homeland" area and placate the Arabs, might have preferred laying down the Mandate, could that have been easily and safely accomplished, to arming the Jews. But then the Grand Mufti's men went too far; they made too many punctures of the oil pipeline from Haifa to Mosul.

A certain number of punctures were expected, and every day in the Haifa office they marked them down on a map. The official police could do nothing because the Arabs did their work at night, when all Palestine police were ordered to be in barracks. The situation grew worse when Arab hatchet men were given sanctuary in an Italian monastery conveniently situated for work on the line. If the flow of oil were seriously threatened, it must be an Empire concern. Fuel for British ships meant control of Suez and the East. So young Captain Wingate, with his odd proposals for Palestine defense, could go ahead with that private army he wanted, just six hundred strong. As two hundred of his men would be British soldiers, this meant arming four hundred Jews and forming what would be called "Special Night Squads" to cope with the Arab marauders.

In six months Wingate's squads, given a certain amount of commando training and a little equipment, accomplished what the twenty thousand men and officers of the British Army had found impossible. The Arab revolt was broken, their raids reduced to a point where Jewish settlers could go about their farming in relative safety. This should have earned Wingate a promotion, and did win him the D.S.O., but he was, understandably, not popular with the British high command. When General Dill was succeeded by General Auchinleck, Wingate was ordered to disband the Special Night Squads and relieved of duty on five days' notice.

This was not personal failure, and Wingate's work did not end with the order, for the men he had trained went home to their villages to train others, and the future of Jewish resistance was assured. As for his own career, he had used Palestine to test his theories of guerrilla warfare and the test had been successful.

Wingate's method of guerrilla fighting was in fact based on the Bible, and he had tried hard to live up to the exploits of Gideon—the commander sent to save Israel, with the promise of the Lord to help him, and orders to do by night what must be done. When he was given a tiny group with which to accomplish the impossible, Wingate may well have read in his mother's Bible, which he carried, how Gideon rejected a sizable force, indeed, sent home for cowardice some twenty-two thousand men, an army even larger than the British had in Palestine, and by careful testing chose, instead, only three hundred. *And the Midianites and the Amalekites and all the children of the east lay along in the valley like grasshoppers for multitude; and their camels were without number, as the sand by the sea side for multitude.* But Gideon blew a trumpet and said, *The sword of the Lord, and of Gideon,* and Gideon prevailed.

Wingate too had picked his men carefully. The project was hush-hush, no fanfare. But from Haifa to the Dead Sea, young men gladly gave up good jobs to serve in the Night Squads for a monthly wage of six pounds. They liked and respected Wingate even when they did not understand him. His application of Bible tactics to Bible terrain might be his own. When he set up headquarters at Ein Harod in the valley of Jezreel, he noted that the strategy of King Saul there was shortsighted; Saul should have put his headquarters at the top of the hill, not by the well. But fighters in a modern Jezreel noticed that Wingate always said "We," not "You," and shared with them the dangers and hardships of guerrilla warfare. More than they knew, he took their part, as a good commander must, against those over him. And he was consistently regardless of his own life, either in foolhardiness—and he was never a reckless man—or in sincere belief that his life would be protected until his job was done. "I believe that no enemy's bullet will harm me," he was quoted as saying. *And the Lord looked upon him (Gideon) and said . . . "Have I not sent thee? . . . Fear not: thou shalt not die."*

When he was relieved of the Palestine command, Wingate flew to London to protest the British White Paper forbidding further immigration into the country. Of course it did no good. It might be true enough that he was the "ideal and the idol" of the young Jewish fighters, the David of the Jordan valley farmers; that Palestine "viewed this pious, eccentric, ingenious British officer as its very own," making his exploits a legend "in Kinnereth and in Tel Aviv, in Sharon and in Tel-Hai, in Givat Brenner and in Jerusalem." But to his own compatriots he was, by now, "a crank, a maniac, a soldier too much interested in politics, a prophet in uniform, a genius perhaps, but more noticeably for the moment a tiresome, arrogant fellow with a strange obsession about the Jews." The wind was blowing from another quarter and Jewish arms were again forbidden. Within a year, some of Wingate's old squadmen were to be arrested for drilling. Wingate sent them messages of cheer; they replied from prison.

Wingate's personal concern for Palestine was only part of the general concern felt at this time, 1939, by observers of the world struggle. Everywhere, that year after Munich, there seemed to be only appeasement and defeat. Wingate's sister had worked and fought with the Republican armies in Spain, and he declared himself prouder of her record than of his own. But the Spanish war was lost. In Abyssinia, Mussolini had been given his way, while civilized men felt the reproach of Haile Selassie's last vain appeal to the League

TO RESTORE AN ANCIENT THRONE: Emperor Haile Selassie, left, with General (then Major) Orde Wingate at the Ethiopian border, Jan. 20, 1941.

of Nations. The truth of Gilbert Murray's warning that had so impressed seventeen-year-old Orde Wingate, that the League of Nations, lacking a police force, must need professional soldiers, was more than ever plain. When his wife wept over the fate of Abyssinia, he said, "Don't cry. You'll see. I'll bring back the Emperor."

This might seem a large order for one British officer, but again, when things got out of hand, the proconsuls gave Wingate a chance. They had made him a major now. And in Abyssinia he was to repeat his Palestine success with a significant similarity in the pattern.

This time he could not count on the quick intelligence of local groups already organizing for guerrilla war, but he did have able help. Daniel Sandford, another British subject long familiar with Ethiopia from residence there and active trade in the country, joined with Wingate to restore the ancient throne. In January, 1941, Wingate crossed the Ethiopian frontier. Again he commanded a "Gideon's army," this time of some two thousand men—a Sudanese battalion, a small force of Ethiopian patriots, and a few non-commissioned officers from Palestine who were never to be mentioned in dispatches. Again he used Gideon's tactics of dividing his small force into three main columns, and dividing again into small units for night raids and quick thrusts. In constant harassment and action over a wide terrain, Wingate's little army engaged Italian forces ten times its size. In six months, just as in Palestine, the enemy was destroyed, more than half taken prisoner, the rest killed or dispersed. Wingate advanced and the Italians retreated so fast that communications fell into his hands. On one occasion the *Christian Science Monitor* correspondent, Edmund Stevens, told of seeing Wingate in a tent where the Italians' field telephone was still working. The enemy commander was on the other end of the line. Stevens spoke good Italian and Wingate persuaded him to assure the Italian commander, in frightened tones, that a force of ten thousand British was on the way. There were, of course, only the men of a small detachment sent out to dynamite bridges, but the lie enabled Wingate to take the Blue Nile crossing with only a few hundred men.

When the Italians demanded an honor guard for their surrender, Wingate was unable to comply because he lacked the man power. The only frills of the campaign were reserved for the return of the ever-dignified Haile Selassie. In a newsreel, Lorna Wingate was to see her husband, just as he had promised, greet the Emperor when he stepped from a transport plane onto Abyssinian soil. Later, riding a white charger, Wingate escorted the restored Emperor through the streets of Addis Ababa. It was the fifth of May. As in Palestine, victory had come less than six months from the time he had undertaken the job.

Wingate liked and respected the Abyssinians, civilized, as he was fond of pointing out, since the days of Solomon. He praised his Ethiopian "patriots," saying that their value in the campaign was greater than was ever publicly admitted. But because he did like the country, he felt sick at heart even in the moment of triumph. He saw too much of what went on behind the scenes. The disillusionment which dogged Lawrence after his Arabian adventure descended on Wingate more quickly, in every moment of victory. He realized that restoration of the Emperor, to him an act of historic justice comparable to the restoration of Palestine, was to the British a matter of political strategy. It was openly so considered, and there was no assurance of support beyond wartime experience. Nor did the top brass wish to press on and take Libya, to Wingate obviously the next objective.

"COME YOU BACK, YOU BRITISH SOLDIER"

The Cairo staff, notoriously languid and indifferent to the war, was unimpressed by the whole Abyssinian campaign.

General Wavell, however, had watched Wingate's work in Palestine and saw the significance of his guerrilla tactics. Now, little as the war in Ethiopia meant to Cairo, Wavell recognized it as another triumph for a competent trouble shooter. And there was plenty of trouble in other quarters. Wavell himself was to leave Africa for another tough assignment. Burma, by now, was an area like Palestine or Abyssinia, in which British arms were reduced to the point where guerrilla tactics could be useful. From Rangoon to Mandalay the sahibs had given ground and the little yellow men were swarming. Wavell was going to Burma and he wanted Wingate as brigadier.

Wingate meanwhile was miserably unhappy. To him, as to Lawrence, personal triumphs meant little. He hoped instead to see some permanent result of his work. Frustrated, disillusioned, his plans brushed aside and the whole force of his activity pent up at a time when he felt his talents to be most needed, Wingate had what was called a "nervous breakdown" and, in a Cairo hospital, slashed his throat in desperate protest against the trend of events. He recovered, but his voice now had a rasp, and a mannerism remained to plague him and puzzle others—rigid neck muscles required that when he turned his head, he must turn his shoulders too.

Had Phil Cochran known the whole story when he met Wingate in London, his first reaction might have been different. For here was a man in whom there was less patience with tradition, less respect for British authority as such, than in Cochran himself. Wingate, of course, wasn't even an Englishman. He was a Scot.

6. "Make Allowance for Their Doubting"

Cochran, facing the wiry English general for the first time, had sensed a surge of antagonism in the air. Was it really there? In far-off Burma, victory or defeat, life or death, might hinge on the way Englishman and American hit it off together.

Wingate wanted the American equipment, of course. To call him only a Scripture-reading crusader and a tough jungle fighter is to neglect a third side of his genius, which was for grasping and using new mechanical techniques. This mechanical aptitude, perhaps even more than his other qualities, distinguished Wingate from other British commanders.

Readiness to see good in gadgets was characteristic of the Wingate family, if one is to believe the story told about an early American Wingate, a New England clergyman, who possessed an umbrella, a rarity in Colonial times. He insisted upon using this outlandish contraption, even after sober people made it plain they considered it unseemly in a minister of the Lord to do so. Wingate's own methods of killing flies afforded a later example. That he did kill flies energetically, in the various tropical countries where his duty lay, in itself marked his dissent from the Army sahibs at Cairo, who notoriously preferred a gentleman's defense, the horsehair fly whisk of the Orient, which shoos without destroying. Wingate meant business. Clad in shorts, he received more than one interviewer, while he leaped erratically about swatting flies with a towel. Brother officers were known to complain that he did not hesitate to swat flies on them. Wire swatters he welcomed as an improvement over towels or folded newspaper, but his delight was unbounded when he first saw a Flit gun.

So here was Cochran to promise the equivalent of a fleet of Flit guns for killing Japs, and Wingate had to be grateful. He wanted to like the purveyor of such rich gifts.

On the other hand, he knew that the American flying officer assigned to work with him would be the opposite end of a liaison requiring tactful, ticklish collaboration. A great deal would depend on the kind of American they sent.

And here, with planes beyond any reasonable hope, was what seemed to be a cocky child. If Wingate seemed old to Cochran, Cochran seemed young to Wingate. It wasn't a matter of years, of course, but of temperament, training and background. Cochran's hair was gray but his face, still unlined by deep trouble or really harassing thought, was youthful. Of course youth controlled the air and the R.A.F. was full of boyish officers. But an English leftenant colonel would surely have had some of the cockiness knocked out of him while he was still a subaltern. Instead, obviously, they had bolstered this Cochran's ego in the States until he was, in his own mind, cock o' the walk.

In Palestine and in Abyssinia, championing the underdog, part of Wingate's problem had been to imbue his men with

"MAKE ALLOWANCE FOR THEIR DOUBTING"

confidence. This was a job he obviously wouldn't have to do for the Yanks. Rather, this young man looked as if he had early acquired the military assurance which Wingate had fought in Whitehall and Cairo and Delhi. He appeared to feel that all was for the best in the best of all possible worlds. These were not qualities that Wingate esteemed. How could he put up with them in a junior officer, no matter how important his status?

Cochran must of course have outstanding ability of its kind, or they wouldn't have sent him over. He would doubtless be an innovator in techniques, as all Yanks were supposed to be. But talk to him a bit and you found him quite uncritical about the larger issues. Wingate, a dissenter all along the line, felt it might well be difficult to work with so orthodox a mind. His triple requirement for winning—training, conviction, equipment—would be only two-thirds realized if, with all his modern skills and American speed, this young fellow failed to share a sense of what the war was being fought for and why it must be won.

In Wingate's mind the problem was all of a piece, the struggle for a free Palestine, for a free Europe, for a free world. But his first few words with Cochran made him feel that here was a young man unworried about the world, untouched by the world's problems. Asked about the basic cause of the war, he might even have defined it as Japan's sneak attack on Pearl Harbor.

Wingate, wearied by a lifelong consciousness of struggle, could go on in comfort only when he had satisfied his own conscience about all the moral implications of the war. Willing as he was to fight Japs, his heart had been in the European struggle even before it started. Years ago, when one of the Englishmen in Palestine had asked, "Why should the world save the Jews?" Wingate had answered, "Because

"MAKE ALLOWANCE FOR THEIR DOUBTING"

the Jews can save the world." Something told him, now, that discussions of this nature, even amicable differences in the realm of abstract ideas, would have no part in his relations with Cochran. And they were the breath of life to him. There were plenty of bright, forward-looking young Jews in the American Army. Why in God's name couldn't they have sent him a Jew?

These thoughts, or something like them, may well have gone through Wingate's head, giving occasion for Cochran's sense of his disappointment. But Wingate's habits of discipline began with himself. He would have reproached himself, on second thought, not only for uncharitableness but for narrowness of mind. Why should he expect or hope for an immediate meeting of minds?

A young American would, presumably, have great skill in the use of machinery. To the Yanks, fast-moving cars and planes were as ordinary as elephants and camels to the African. You had only to look at those comic pictures of which Americans were so fond. Wingate liked American cartoons but his taste ran to Disney's expressive animals, rather than to the strips in which men were shot from guns or propelled great distances at incredible speeds, and otherwise involved in mechanical miracles. These things were so strange to Britons that only an unorthodox British mind, like his own, could contemplate them. But familiarity with American products must come naturally to Americans, and so it argued no real originality of mind, no special insight. With these young men one must have patience, explaining carefully the things not previously a part of their experience, beginning with the things understood, talking simply, and leading gradually into new fields.

So on the following day Wingate delivered himself of what Cochran considered to be another harangue. But by now Cochran was a little more accustomed to the general's peculiarities of speech, and this time Wingate varied excursions into philosophy, scholarly lore, and long-range penetration with a discourse on a topic that Cochran could appreciate.

He talked communications, radio. Cochran, the fighter pilot and veteran of the air war in North Africa, had a zealous understanding of radio communications. Wingate told how he had learned, while operating against Arab anti-Zionist guerrillas in Palestine, the feasibility of sending parties far ahead and directing them by radio.

In Ethiopia, in a larger kind of war, he had operated against the Italians with a more complicated coordination of raiding groups by radio over wider spaces of wilderness. In a series of brilliant successes he had found that guerrilla parties, when controlled by radio according to plan, could thrust far and seize districts from regular troops. This tactic he had adapted to the tropical jungles in his Burma campaign of the previous spring.

He had split his forces into groups—columns, he called them—which had made their way through jungles, operating as a many-headed unit by radio direction. Each column threading its way through the equatorial forest had carried a small, highly efficient radio set, and had maintained constant communication with the central headquarters. From his control base, Wingate had moved the jungle parties in coordinated action, manipulating them like pieces on a chessboard. The campaign of raiding columns scattered through an immense jungle area had been integrated into a single operation, directed at predetermined objectives.

This was "long-range penetration," Wingate's invention in the war. It was, he indicated, his contribution to history, and he never concealed his belief that he would have a place in history.

To Cochran came luminous understanding. "I suddenly realized that, with his radio direction, Wingate used his guerrilla columns in the same way that fighter-control headquarters directs planes out on a mission." This was realization with a flash for a fighter pilot.

"I saw it as an adaptation of air to jungle, an application of radio-controlled air-war tactics to a walking war in the trees and the weeds. Wingate had hit upon the idea independently; he knew little about air. In his own tough element he was thinking along the same radio lines that an airman would about tactics among the clouds."

Wingate was dogmatic in saying that the forthcoming campaign would result in the reconquest of northern Burma. His long-range penetration columns, operating against communications and supplies, would so disrupt the Japs that northern Burma could then be occupied easily by regular invasion. His forces in his previous Burma campaigns were to be greatly increased.

He would have four brigades, some twenty thousand troops, especially trained for jungle war, and in addition the unit of American rangers promised by General Marshall (the ranger unit that was to become famous as Merrill's Marauders). The total was not a great host in the terms of the European war and its millions, but a formidable power when used in a pattern of radio-controlled raids in jungle country, where military forces were necessarily sparse.

Then Wingate got around to a theme about which Cochran was to hear much, to his unending amusement, the matter of mules. "I never could get over Wingate's belief in mules. To him transport meant mules. He had used them in Palestine, in Ethiopia, in Burma, mostly American mules. He was always saying that the only way you could get stuff through the jungle was on muleback. He delivered discourses on mules. Long-range penetration went clumping along with long ears and a heehaw. It seemed cockeyed to me, the combination of mule transport and the ultramodern radio elaboration of Wingate's scientific guerrilla war."

It was, of course, in this ability to grasp and use diverse elements that Wingate's genius lay. Radio and planes added extra dimensions to jungle war, but it remained, after all, a problem of covering ground without roads. There no invention as yet surpassed the mule. In Ethiopia they had used camels, but the camels died. In Burma they had used mules and bullocks; the mules were faster.

Wingate would yield on only one point. He said, with his own dry brand of humor, that mules weren't very good eating. Otherwise, the fact that they were going to a place where he had been, where he knew the terrain and the conditions it imposed, gave him the final say-so without pulling rank. There would be mules. After all, they were American beasts and Americans couldn't object if Wingate insisted on them with truly mulish stubbornness.

He did admit to Cochran that, as transport, mules had limitations. You couldn't take the wounded out on muleback. That had been the tragedy of his previous Burma campaign—abandoning the wounded. He told Cochran what he had told them at Quebec about having to leave the wounded behind. But Cochran's light planes would solve the problem, said Wingate hopefully. They could land in jungle clearings and on flat sandy river banks, which abound in northern Burma, and could take out the men unable to move.

Mule transport placed, likewise, a limit on equipment. Mules could carry only light equipment, machine guns and small mortars, but then the Japs in the jungle were similarly limited. They had only light equipment. There was no possibility of transporting heavy armament, like cannon, large mortars, armored cars, tanks—not on mules.

In the previous Wingate campaign they had supplemented mule transport by dropping supplies by parachute, but parachutes could accommodate only light weights. Cochran's light planes would be limited similarly as transport, but they would help as an auxiliary to mules. Sometimes Cochran thought that in Wingate's mind all air power was an auxiliary to mules.

They were getting along much better now, Flip Corkin and the crusading Scot. So Cochran spoke of fighter planes, told Wingate about the fighter squadron he'd have. He promised that, as the long-range penetration columns pushed deep into jungled enemy territory, American fighters would rip Jap communications and supplies, make strafing and bombing attacks against enemy units, and assail whatever targets the ground forces might direct, the kind of aerial guerrilla war that Cochran had led in North Africa.

What about bombers? They could use some, Wingate nodded, but said the Royal Air Force would provide them. The R.A.F. had promised to cooperate with a force of medium bombers. There would be no need of bombing planes in Cochran's aerial task force.

The campaign would begin, said Wingate, when the rainy season ended in Burma, early in February, less than five months hence. Operations would last through the dry season, about three months. Cochran said okay, he'd be there with an aerial task force of light planes and fighters.

Cochran parted from Wingate with a new appreciation. "I realized there was something very deep about him. He spoke with a conviction that he couldn't have had unless

SUPPLIES DROPPED FROM AIR, first Burma campaign.

he was a thinker and a philosopher. He knew he was on the right track. He was the kind to convince his men by saying, 'We're going to do this or that, and we're going to win,' in such a manner that there was no argument. He made you feel that here was a man who could look into the future and tell what was going to happen tomorrow. One of the things awfully upsetting in war is not to know what is going to happen, but Wingate could tell his men what was going to happen. When I left him, I was beginning to assimilate some of the flame of this guy Wingate."

On Wingate's side, doubt still lingered. Always, Cochran felt, the dour and introspective Englishman was studying him, trying to figure him, still uncertain about the cocky Irishman, so very American, whom the commander of the United States Army Air Forces had sent with promises so large. Cochran knew that when they met again in India, Wingate would still be doubtful of mind, still trying to figure him.

Relations were simpler with Lord Louis Mountbatten. The young Irishman from Erie, Pennsylvania, was more at ease with the debonair cousin of the King. They hit it off famously. On his last day in London, Cochran took Mountbatten to a hospital for treatment of an infected hand, driving him to his residence to pick up clothing and shaving material, and then to the hospital. He was happy about Lord Louis, and looked forward to seeing him again in India.

Flying home, Cochran reflected. He had learned about Wingate's new idea, about radio-controlled long-range penetration in jungle war. But he had contributed no new idea of his own. General Arnold had said let's transform the Wingate show into an air show. But Cochran had hit upon nothing novel for that. Lounging in the great transport plane as it sped high above North Atlantic waters, his thoughts drifted to the obvious weak spot in the Wingate long-range penetration theory, the factor symbolized by Wingate's mules. Transport, with light planes to be used as auxiliaries to mules. Warfare limited to light equipment, machine guns, small mortars.

Cochran knew from his experience in North Africa the meaning of heavy equipment in battle, the might and devastation of major armament, cannon, large mortars, armored cars, tanks. That was what Wingate needed, heavy equipment against the light equipment to which the Japs were limited. What would happen, thought Cochran, if the Wingate radio-controlled long-range penetration parties should suddenly show up with heavy stuff? Cochran could laugh to think of the surprise and confusion of the Jap and the crushing of the lightly armed enemy at every point where heavy equipment was brought to bear. But neither mules, parachutes nor light planes would do the trick. Nor would large transports. They could carry heavy equipment, but needed regular air-base flying strips to land on.

Cochran thought suddenly—*gliders!* It hit him in a flash. He knew that large gliders, capable of carrying artillery, large mortars, armored cars and light tanks, had recently been developed to high efficiency. These could land, crash-landing if necessary, any place where a light plane could and places where a light plane couldn't. If the aerial task force had a unit of gliders, it could supply the long-range penetration columns with heavy armament at key points in the middle of the jungle. Cochran could laugh, not only at the surprise of the Japs when it hit them, but also of Wingate and his British when they heard about it. Gliders were the idea for turning the Wingate jungle campaign into an air show.

Because of weather the plane made a stop in Iceland, Cochran was delayed for a day. "On my way back, I got stuck in Iceland because of bad weather. At the officers' mess I noticed a great to-do, people running hither and thither. I asked, 'What goes on here?' They told me that General Arnold had made a quick emergency trip to London for a couple of days and was on his way back. He had been in London while I was there, though I didn't know it. Now our trails were meeting in Iceland, and he had given me the Wingate job in Washington just five days before. Things moved fast in this war, I thought.

"Then pretty soon, as I was hanging around the officers' club, the general came in. He had with him Bernt Balchen, the great old-time Arctic and Antarctic pilot, who was now doing superb war flying up there in the north. General Arnold sat down to have a meal, and I was over in a corner reading a magazine. I saw no reason why I should walk over to him and say, 'Remember me, I am that fellow.' So I sat there reading the magazine. I could see the general glancing over at me, and realized that he wasn't quite sure who I was. He had had a good look at me in Washington, of course, but my being in Iceland didn't make sense. He couldn't figure that I had moved so fast, that I had already been to London to see Wingate and was on my way back. He was puzzled, and finally made motions in my direction. 'You, come over here.'

"I walked over and said, 'General, I'm Cochran.'

"He asked, 'What in hell are you doing here?'

"I replied, 'I've been in London, sir, seeing Wingate and Lord Louis Mountbatten.'

" 'What do you mean?' he exclaimed, 'I've been in London, and didn't get a chance to see Mountbatten. He's in the hospital.'

" 'Yes, I took him to the hospital.'

CHINDITS crossing river with rubber boats in General Wingate's first Burma campaign.

" 'You did?' he grinned. Then asked, 'How are you getting on?'

" 'General,' I burst out, 'we're going to surprise even you.'

" 'Atta boy,' he laughed, and gave me a clap on the back.

"I felt like shouting 'gliders,' but thought I wouldn't bother the general any more at his meal. He'd find out about the gliders when, at his office in the Pentagon Building, Alison and I walked in and gave him a list of what we needed for the task force to support Wingate. He might blink when he saw all that would be on that list. He might throw us out."

Back in Washington, Cochran hurried to Alison, burning to tell the news, the great idea, the secret of air support for Wingate. The moment they were together, Cochran blurted: "You know what Wingate really needs?"

"Yes," Alison responded quietly, "he needs gliders."

Alison, the quiet introvert, had been reading Wingate's voluminous reports on his Burma jungle campaign of the previous spring. He had come independently to the conclusion reached by Cochran as he flew home.

7. "He Used the Earth, the Seas, the Air"

"Draw up a list of what you want," General Arnold had said to Cochran and Alison. At first hearing, this sounded like an invitation to two bright boys to write a letter to Santa Claus. But of course there was a catch in it; the list would have to go to the general for his okay. Its composition, they saw, would tell him what he still wanted to know about their ability to handle the job. In terms of equipment it would present their plans, the ideas they had for an aerial task force not only to support Wingate's jungle campaign but to justify the general's hope that the campaign could be a testing ground for new uses of air power. And until they had that famous H. H. Arnold signature on the list the whole project would lack actuality.

So, although they might detest paper work, it was now to be the key to success in their assignment. They'd stand or fall on the document they had to prepare. The list had to be good.

Fortunately, while Cochran was in London, Alison had established an office in the Pentagon Building and had begun to assemble an administrative staff. With their grudge against files and records, both Cochran and Alison would have been happier without desk men; as some were necessary, they resolved to keep the staff small but efficient.

For an administrative officer, Cochran, before going to London, had suggested a candidate. "I knew him from the time when I was just out of hospital. The doctors told me I should do something every day. I said, 'Well, squash.' Were there any squash courts at Mitchel Field? A captain in the Operations Office said yes, there were courts, and he played squash. He was the only one around who did and he'd be glad to help. So at four o'clock every afternoon we had a session at squash. His name was Charles Engelhardt, but everybody called him Willie. He had been an insurance broker in civilian life, and his wife was connected with the theater. She was Irma Cells, an artist who drew theatrical caricatures. I was always beguiled by the the theater, and got to be pretty close to Willie and his theatrical artist wife. He was tremendously competent, and Willie Engelhardt was known for his loyalty."

Engelhardt was recruited in unceremonious fashion, as he relates: "At Mitchel Field I had a call from Washington, from Colonel Alison, whom I didn't know. He asked me how I liked the idea of my new job. I said, 'What job?' Oh, hadn't Colonel Cochran told me? No. Well, Phil had told Colonel Alison he'd phone me about the job, but had been too busy or something, and had gone to London, and there I was, administrative officer of the aerial task force without knowing it. I could have taken it or left it, but it never occurred to them that I might not volunteer, or to me, for that matter."

For a sergeant at the typewriter they recruited Berky—

"HE USED THE EARTH, THE SEAS, THE AIR"

Irving Berkowitz. Cochran calls him the best master sergeant in the Army. "He was a Jewish boy from the New York West Side, where his father ran a delicatessen and restaurant. Berky had worked as a clerk in the New York Police Department, where he hadn't distinguished himself particularly, and hadn't been happy. The Army brought out his talents as a paper man under pressure. He was quiet, shy, unassuming, and had more loyalty in him and more sense of responsibility than 90 per cent of the people in the world, more than most officers. Willie and I had known him at Mitchel Field, and realized that he had to be our top paper man."

Berky had a family situation that made duty in the vicinity of New York a welcome thing. He had sufficient reason for not volunteering for service overseas. He solved the dilemma rather obliquely, saying to Engelhardt: "Of course, Captain, if you should order me—" The captain had no authority to order him, but Berky solved his inner conflict by asking to be ordered.

Sergeant Berkowitz was the answer to the Phil-John grudge against paper work. "Everything funneled through Berky. None of us thought of him as merely a sergeant. We regarded him as a capable officer. We called him 'The Brain.'"

For an executive officer they had Major Arvid Olson, whom everybody called Oley Olson. He was a tall, blondish Scandinavian from the Northwest, good-looking, thin and energetic, whose qualifications Cochran describes: "Oley was a top-notch pilot with lots of administrative ability. He paid more attention to detail than either John or I. He was at the time an air inspector in the Fourth Air Force on the West Coast. Oley knew Burma, had served out there with a squadron of American planes early in the war. He had been kicked out of Burma by the Japs. With his squadron, starting at Rangoon, he had been forced back until he had found himself in India. We said we would get that guy because he knew the district, knew the jungle, knew Burma from Rangoon to Mandalay."

With Cochran and Alison staking their own fitness for the assignment on the list, and administrative cooperation that combined personal liking and loyalty—Engelhardt, with special intelligence, Berkowitz, experience, and Olson, eager to go back to Mandalay and blast the Japs out of there—Project Nine could begin to take form on paper. Cochran and Alison began writing down specific items.

Light planes, of course, were first on the list, evacuation and supply being the beginning of it all.

They would, moreover, have fighters, that was implicit in the silent agreement with Arnold. It was part of the indignant fighter-pilot reaction to light planes to take it for granted that an aerial task force they commanded would include a fighter squadron.

What else? Cochran had flown and fought in the North African desert, Alison in the valleys and mountains of China, but neither knew the jungle. Only after Cochran talked to Wingate, and Alison read his reports, had they hit on the glider idea. But now they marked down one hundred and fifty gliders, the large cargo-carrying kind the Army had recently developed. These could accommodate artillery and light tanks.

Gliders needed transport planes to tow them. So next they listed thirteen large cargo planes, which, in addition to towing gliders, could carry freight. Materials and men would have to be hauled around in haste, particularly in India. They didn't want to have to depend on an Indian railroad and highway traffic, overburdened in war and not too good at best. A squadron of transport planes would give them added mobility.

They listed a squadron of thirty fighters for a small but effective striking force with the latest aerial weapons. But no bombers. In London, Wingate had told Cochran that in India the R.A.F. would provide them with a squadron of bombers.

They marked down a swarm of light planes, one hundred for evacuating wounded from jungle clearings and shuttling supplies. What else? What else could they think of? Helicopters. These contraptions were new and a hitherto unheard-of wonder, something special. They could rise from and descend upon the smallest of spaces, and might be used to take out wounded from exceptionally difficult places. Mark down light helicopters.

Mark down the tops in guns, miscellaneous equipment, clothing, medical supplies, everything needed for the best-provided air outfit that ever operated in jungle territory. In drawing up the list, they were greedy. They listed as much as they thought they could get, and more.

To an air tactician the list was valid and graphic in meaning, signifying an air-ground unit for all purposes. Cochran and Alison were planning a small but complete tactical air force, the first air-ground task force on record.

They took the document to the office of the Commander of the Air Forces with some trepidation. "We half expected General Arnold to look at the list and say, 'I told you guys I would give you a liaison air force for evacuation and supply. Gliders. What do you mean gliders? Now forget this nonsense and get to work.' Well, he didn't even read it."

The list was something you wouldn't have to go over carefully. You either saw its value at a glance or else you missed it completely. General Arnold saw what they were up to. He confirmed his quick judgment by asking members of his staff, who had scanned the list, whether it made sense to them. "They said yes and he signed it," Cochran summarizes. "We were disappointed that he didn't show some surprise at what we were asking for, and were disappointed that we hadn't asked for more."

Handing back the list, now signed and a formal order, the general told them, "Think up a name for this unit." He suggested, tentatively, "Something like Air Commandos. Think of something better."

Nothing better, nothing else, was ever suggested. The British had made their sea and land commando tactics famous. Adapt the British amphibious unit to the air, and you logically had the task force of the sky. The name of Air Commandos was all the more appropriate because Mountbatten, in whose Southeast Asia Command the Burma area was included, had won renown as the leader of Britain's commando forces. So they were the First Air Commando Unit, but not publicly, not until much later.

The assembling of their aerial task force must be shrouded in mystery, not publicized. The plan to reconquer Burma was an international secret, and the Wingate re-entry was darkly hush-hush. The Japs were to be taken by surprise. They might expect a repetition of the Wingate jungle raids of the previous spring, but must not be permitted to guess that the raiding would be expanded into a full-fledged back-to-Burma campaign, with American air aid.

So the aerial task force was officially on the books under the pseudonym of Project Nine. In Air Force parlance, a project was a special outfit for a special job, a group formed and acting independently of the general organization. Project One had been the Doolittle raid on Tokyo, with Jimmy Doolittle creating and leading his unit of Tokyo bombers as a small, close-knit group, separate and apart from the large interlocking system of the Army Air Forces. There had been other projects, there would be more. Now there was Project Nine.

Even the fact that the aerial task force was to go to India was kept secret. Burma was never mentioned. The name Wingate was never mentioned. They called him "The Man." "The Man thinks this." "The Man may not like that."

The secrecy requirements made equipment-getting both easier and harder. They couldn't explain why they wanted what they wanted, say how and where they expected to use the material. But the magic high priority of Project Nine gave them opportunities which they never neglected to improve.

Of course the equipment problem was not solved when Arnold signed the list, for they had still to obtain the authorized material. Also, as science was drafted for the Army, new inventions were heard of and they found new things to ask for.

Thus, for their fighter squadron, thirty P-51 Mustangs, they procured the latest armament of assault—rockets. These were becoming the new sensation of the war.

"We were the first air outfit to do a rocket-firing job. We had heard about the air bazooka, and knew that rocket equipment was being built for planes, but when we asked for the gadgets we found that none had been put into production to fit our P-51s. We had to make the rocket equipment, ourselves, have it constructed in a private machine shop."

For this they had to get authority and have money alloted to them. They had to get drawings, blueprints that technicians were reluctant to give up. "We had to do an awful lot more than just asking. In the Army you can't just go out and buy something. We tried to get the North American plant at Dayton to make the air bazooka equipment, mounts for rockets, but the factory was building P-51s. The people there had been told: 'If you stop building P-51s, we'll kill you. Don't dare do anything else but build P-51s.' They told us, 'It takes draftsmen, it takes tools, it takes machinists, it takes man hours, and to hell with you.' They wouldn't do it."

They had to go to a small businessman who had a machine shop. He could make the rocket mounts, but in his plant it had to be done by hand. "We had to get $27,000 of the Government's good money for that." The construction job was supervised by gun specialist Ajax Baumler. He had been a pilot in the Spanish Civil War, on the Republican side, and had served with Chennault in China, where he had known John Alison. Ajax had a flair for armament, and presently Project Nine had its air bazookas, thirty planes equipped with them. The Man, they figured, would be dazzled by the rockets.

They had 150 light planes, L-1s and L-5s, those and something special. On his way home from his talks with Wingate in London, Cochran had stopped off in Canada, and there seen a new type of plane, a medium weight-lifting plane. "I asked the people around there what it was, and they said a Norseman. It would carry two thousand pounds on a single engine. In Washington I spoke about the Norseman, and was told, 'The Army has just bought fourteen of them from Canada.' I said, 'We want them.' We got twelve. We took them from somebody else. The Norseman, as a medium-sized weight lifter, bridged the gap between our light planes and the big transports."

The hardest battle was for the helicopters. "We weren't sure of getting those egg beaters at all until just before we left. It took a terrific argument. Those were the only helicopters in the country, and the Navy said, 'We need them.' The British Navy said, 'We need them.' Wright Field said, 'We need them.' The thing went right up to the Joint Chiefs of Staff, and got into the hands of presidential adviser Harry Hopkins. We got the helicopters, eight egg beaters. They followed us to India. Helicopter training was done there. Twenty-five boys volunteered to fly the eight. One little kid said, 'I'll go to war in a free balloon.' He later turned into a fighter pilot, he had the spirit." The Man, with his profound concern for the evacuation of the wounded, would appreciate the helicopters.

They got the first of the collapsible carbines, a light gun that could be strapped on a man if he had to jump from a plane by parachute. They didn't know it existed. They went to a man who knew his guns, Colonel Freeman of the Ordnance Department, and said, "We are going to be in very close touch with the enemy. We will probably land in places where a man has to use a gun awfully quick. We are not infantry fighters, and we don't know anything about infantry guns or infantry tactics. But we are going to be in a spot where we will have to do something awfully quick. We want a gun that we may have to carry in the jungle for months. We may be lost in the jungles."

Colonel Freeman replied, "You sound as if you need the collapsible carbine just coming out. Nobody else has any."

The men of Project Nine were the first air unit to be trained in jungle ground tactics. The idea was that anyone might, in the course of operations, find himself a jungle fighter. They were all armed for this. "When we asked for the weapons, we were told, 'Well, the only men in the Air Forces who carry pistols are officers.' We demanded pistols for all our enlisted men. They said, 'All other Air Force people have only one tommy gun for fifty men.' We replied that, between tommy guns and carbines, we should have one weapon for every man.

"We knew the normal Air Force uniform was not going to be adequate for people who would be flying over and living in jungles. We attempted to design a sensible good uniform for our use, and ended up with paratroop pants and jacket and Marine Corps jungle boots. We wanted the paratroop jacket and pants because of the number of convenient pockets they have. In case of a crack-up in the jungle or a parachute jump, a man should have enough things with him to keep him alive until we could get him out. We had to have the best knives we could get, and decided on paratroop knives and a big jungle knife. We needed pockets to carry first aid, a hand grenade, additional ammunition, food. We planned even to carry opium. That drug will buy things out in the Orient in places where money is useless. We found out later there were three commodities that could get you more in the Burma jungle than anything else—opium one, salt two, kerosene three.

"It was odd and against all rules in the Army that air people should have paratroop clothing. That was made for paratroopers. It is a very, very nice piece of clothing. Everybody wants it. Everybody would want a paratroop jacket. We had quite a bit of argument to show that we needed it. Not being allowed to tell people what we were going to do made this difficult. It took a lot of special orders and a lot of wrangling to persuade them to say, 'Yes, you need that.'

"The Marine shoes were hard to get. It was difficult to persuade people in the Army that just the plain G.I. shoes that other soldiers were wearing weren't just the thing. It took a lot of conniving to make Army Air Force officers see that we must go to the Navy for shoes — to the Marine Corps. We had to fight for them, but got them." It pleased them to think how The Man would note that their men were better equipped for the jungle than his own jungle soldiers.

They took too much. Not knowing what they would really need, they overdid it. "Somebody would suggest we should take along ten of some article or other." Cochran would reply, "Take twenty," or maybe thirty. "We had no arguments about stuff for fighting.

"We did have a big argument about typewriters. I said we'll have a minimum of paper work, or none at all, and told them to give me a list of organizational equipment, and keep it down to the barest essentials. Lo and behold, when I saw the list, one item was twenty-four typewriters. I had been charged to hold down shipping space to a minimum, and I wasn't going to take typewriters. I was going to take bullets and bombs and bazookas, things to shoot and drop. I could picture no use for typewriters. So, going through the list and drawing lines through silly things they had on it, I knocked out all the typewriters except three. 'What are you going to do with twenty-four typewriters?' I found they had simply copied the normal equipment list for Air Force squadrons, and were taking clerical equipment for five squadrons, because we had five. They finally sneaked eighteen typewriters on the list when I wasn't looking. That was the only equipment they ever got by me.

"Alison said, 'Man must be paid and man must be buried.' I said they have to be buried but they don't have to be paid. The paymaster's job in the Army is a cumbersome necessity. No man is paid like another man, because of his insurance, his allotment, his savings, his war bonds, his wife, his sister. I said, 'I'm not going to take a bunch of people to be paid every month.' Our men would be taken care of medically better than soldiers ever were taken care of before, but no pay.

I also said no cooks. I was wrong, but that was my first impression. We got cooks when we arrived over there.

"They even ordered bicycles. These could be useful, I knew, but I figured when we got over to India we would chisel them or steal them. But I let them have the bicycles, and they did turn out to be useful."

8. "Youth That Trafficked Long with Death"

THE RESTRICTIONS ABOUT SECRECY made a real problem of recruiting for Project Nine, when the need was for special talent. Arnold's directive to the team had specified not more than five hundred men. Of this small group, many must be experts and all, Cochran and Alison hoped, would be men of outstanding ability.

In some fields—gliders, for instance—they had to be people who could be trusted to carry on more or less on their own. Neither Cochran nor Alison had glider experience; neither of them had even seen one. All they knew about them was what they had read in the newspapers, that the Germans had used gliders with melodramatic effect in the invasion of Crete, that the United States Army had an ambitious glider program, and that large cargo-carrying gliders had been developed. They were acquainted with no glider people from whom they might recruit a leader for this group. All they could do was go to the Glider Division in the Pentagon, and inquire for one.

"We were referred to Captain Bill Taylor, a glider enthusiast from Mississippi, who had worked on glider-loading tests in Florida and experimented with glider and liaison planes in Panama. His experience in the Canal Zone had been with glider landings in jungle country. We said, 'He's our man.' All we had to do was to ask Bill Taylor if he wanted a tough and exciting job in a war area something like Panama. He jumped at the chance. Not only Bill, but also his assistant, Lieutenant Vincent Rose, and we had our glider leaders number one and two."

To each group they gave a double command, just as General Arnold had named a twofold Cochran-Alison command for Project Nine. This fitted in with their antipathy for paper work. With records kept to a minimum, number one and number two men would have necessary data in their own heads, each knowing what the other knew. If something should turn up while one was absent, the other would have the facts.

They procured the asked-for gliders and glider equipment. There were difficulties. They were an independently formed project demanding material wanted by regular units of the Air Force organization. But General Arnold told his staff to give Project Nine high priority, second only to the production of big bombers on which the Air Forces were concentrating.

They recruited glider pilots, seventy-five of them. They had to be exceptional. Glider pilots were told, "We're going out on a deal. It's a tricky one, and it's dangerous, and it's got to be voluntary. If you have a terrific desire to go out and do a hell of a job, and a real nasty one, and a dangerous one, we've got a spot for you."

"YOUTH THAT TRAFFICKED LONG WITH DEATH"

Glider pilots, thus approached, were eager to go. "We told Bill Taylor to pick fellows who had other skills. Since we were limited to five hundred men, we wanted to get men who could double up on jobs. Pick boys who had been carpenters. We could use them for hammering things together. Pick farm boys who knew how to run tractors. They would come in handy for running a bulldozer to fix up a flying field. We said, 'Find a glider pilot who has been a sign painter and can slap a brush around for us.' He got one fellow who had been a dentist's assistant, making false teeth. Another, on being asked what he could do besides flying a glider, said he could play a piano. We grabbed him. We also got a guitar player and an accordion player. They would help morale by whipping up entertainment."

Among their recruits was Jackie Coogan, former boy star of the movies, who could play all sorts of music and could sing, solo or in a quartet. They procured musical instruments for Project Nine, shipped a guitar to India and sent an accordion in a box labeled "Official Documents."

Most fully trained glider pilots had been sent to the Mediterranean for the invasion of Sicily. Some had gone to England for the D-Day invasion of France. Project Nine had to complete the schooling of the glider pilots it enlisted. Bill Taylor took them to Goldsboro, North Carolina, and there put them through a rigorous training grind, gliders working with tow planes, transports.

Pilots for the transports were recruited in unorthodox fashion. A cargo-plane leader whom they had recruited flew to air bases of the Troop Carrier Command. "His main trouble was to beat off people. As soon as he would land, and they would hear that he had this intriguing job, he was swamped with people. He selected some of the finest pilots in the world, most of them instructors. The Troop Carrier

Command was reluctant to give up these high-class training people, and three different commands in one day called Washington, wondering what was happening. Here their best people were being enlisted to go on a never-before-heard-of campaign. What was going on?

"It was our own fault, because we didn't go through the proper individuals. We just said to the kids, 'Do you want to go to war?' And the kids wanted to go to war. On one occasion thirty key enlisted men put their names on a list and signed a petition asking to go with Project Nine. That could make the job of the commander running a training field in the United States very difficult. We were in a hurry, and didn't approach the job properly. It wasn't right for us, with an arrogant attitude, to walk on somebody else's field and start recruiting. That upsets a whole command. It had happened in other cases, commanding officers were tired of it, and we were the last straw. We were censured for it, and properly so. It got to General Arnold, but he just laughed it off. He knew what we were doing. He had told us to do it, although he didn't quite like the way we did it."

Cochran went to the glider-transport training field at Goldsboro. "I watched them at work and said, 'People that fly airplanes are fool enough, but anyone that gets into one of those gliders is a damn fool.' John felt the same way about it, but we knew we had better find out about the contraptions. Both he and I went glider riding. We actually flew those things. You can't lead anybody unless you know the thing yourself."

The glider training specialized in night work. Glider operations in Burma were likely to be by night. In the Burma dry season nights were bright, with a brilliant moon. The difficulty, they found, was accuracy in night landings. Says Cochran, "It is hard to land things at night. Darkness triples your inaccuracy. You have difficulty because your eyes are not

"YOUTH THAT TRAFFICKED LONG WITH DEATH"

picking up the things you see in daytime. In daytime you see ground go past and you get a horizon and an angle of descent. But at night you have no references, and just aim at a bunch of lights. Here were these pilots without any engine power. They had to develop a great sense of glider angle, distance and speed in darkness. It was hard enough with lights on a field, and they had to learn to land without ground lights, with nothing but perhaps some moonbeams, sixth sense and second sight.

"Bill Taylor drilled them incessantly to have everything down pat. We knew they were going to be frightened to death when they first did their stuff in action, and we trained them so they would go through the routine of glider landing even if they were stone drunk and almost paralyzed with fright. We pounded it into their muscles, rather than into their heads, so that when they'd come in to land for the first time at night in Burma, and gliders started to crack up, they would just automatically do what they had been trained to do, because they couldn't do anything else."

They had accidents. Gliders hit barns, and landed in places other than flying fields. But on the whole the development of their glider force progressed rapidly and effectively. They were pleased. The Man, they thought, would be mightily impressed by the gliders for the transport of heavy armament in the jungle.

Cochran told Alison: "There is an air line, a peculiar outfit, that operates near my home down in Erie. They snatch mail off the ground by flying over it, and the plane has a mechanism to pick it up. They're a crazy bunch of barnstorming fools, and I know pilots who got jobs with them. It's in the hill country, where there are few places to land planes, and a fellow just goes out and picks up a load of mail by the snatch method."

Gliders, too, could be snatched off the ground by a speeding plane, and here was an idea for the jungle campaign—pick gliders up from clearings and riverbanks, retrieve gliders, empty or with cargoes. The Man would be surprised by that.

They found that the Army had been experimenting with glider pickup mechanism, and had built a snatch reel, only one, the only one in existence, an experimental reel. "We said, 'We'll have some of those, even though we have them built especially for ourselves.' That was a tough one, because some of the parts that finally went into the reels were needed for B-24 bombers, and bomber production would have to be delayed. Air Force attention was focused on bombing at the time, and they wanted to kill us when we told them that we needed some bomber material for our snatch reels. We finally had to appeal to General Arnold, and asked him to let us have those reels built, even though it hampered bomber production. The general didn't like the idea, but he saw our point. He wanted Project Nine to have everything possible to make it effective, and so he signed an order."

They procured the experimental reel, and made tests to see if their glider pilots could use it successfully. A bulky transport plane flying at 120 miles an hour had to hit a small piece of rope close to the ground. It was difficult in daytime, and seemed almost impossible at night.

"We got off to a bad start. On the test ground at Wilmington, our first attempt was a tragedy. We sent one of our best boys in as a sort of test case to see how the thing was going to work. He was killed. When the transport hooked onto him, he overcontrolled. The glider got into the air, but then plunged right down and smashed on the ground. We never will know why he did it, or why the other man in the glider with him wasn't killed. It was a miracle that he came out alive."

GLIDER SNATCH: At left, "snatch poles" in position and ready for a glider pick-up.

Below, a Douglas C-47 tow plane snatches a glider off the ground.

They were discouraged, but kept at it, and learned they could do the glider-snatching trick. Says Cochran, "I took a ride in a picked-up glider, so as to be one of the boys. John Alison, watching, said, 'Look at that old fool being snatched off.'"

The snatch reels made to order were not complete by the time Project Nine left for India. The reels would have to follow, and the training of the glider force in the use of the snatch mechanism would have to be completed over there.

But as experimenters on the ground, Cochran and Alison were a maverick outfit in the mazes of the Pentagon Building. "There were agencies in the Pentagon Building that could do almost anything, if you knew where the agency was and what people to see. We had the misconception that we could have to do it all ourselves. The first thing we did was to get lost in the halls. I still don't know how to get around in the Pentagon Building. We didn't understand the way the wheels worked in the large offices. Therefore in many instances we butted our heads against walls and went down many a blind alley. When we started we made twenty calls in order to see the right person. We got a reputation in the Pentagon Building—'Here come those fellows who run down aisles.' Sometimes it would take us two weeks to get a thing done, and on the last day we would find a fellow we should have gone to on the first day. The people were willing to cooperate, but we were always asking the wrong people. Toward the end we got so that we could get things done fast because we knew where to go and push the right button."

Disliking paper work, they did everything they could by telephone or personal interview. In their office, telephones were going all the time, calls all over the country, wrangling for equipment, receiving reports about this, giving orders about that, talking with flying fields where training jobs were being done or with factories from which equipment was being procured. They had three Wilmingtons—a training job at Wilmington, Delaware; factory work at Wilmington, Ohio; and at Wilmington, California, material was assembled for shipment to India. Call from Wilmington, and a yell, "Which Wilmington?" People barged in and out. Half a dozen talks might be going on at once. The place was pandemonium. If they had a really important interview, it was likely to be transferred to the hall outside to avoid the noise. Some of their most important business was transacted in the hall.

At night, they took the job to their hotel, the Hay-Adams House, a place frequented by theatrical people. There Willie Engelhardt's artist wife had procured quarters for them after they had been ousted from hotels in overcrowded Washington. From the Hay-Adams House they might transfer for an evening to a night club, where planning air support for The Man would go on amid the gaudy revelry.

Project Nine was building up a tense and vibrant morale. It was essential for the project. "Limited to five hundred men, we were certain to be desperately overworked. Each man would have to double and redouble his normal effort. To drive men as we would have to drive them, there would have to be morale plus." Fighter pilots themselves, Cochran and Alison tried to instill the fighter-pilot spirit. They wanted glider, transport and light-plane flyers to have the pugnacious, unrelenting drive of the air-battle individualists. They picked leaders who had that quality, so that it would seep down to the men under them, who were selected because they were the type to be infected with the fighter-pilot mentality.

They sought to develop a fierce team loyalty. "It's habitual for American boys to want to say, 'My team is better than yours, my high school team can beat any team.' We did everything we could to build up that spirit by cultivating in our fellows the idea that ours was an exceptional outfit and they were exceptional guys. When they were recruited they were told they were volunteering for something top secret, and tops. They knew they were picked because they were better than average. They could see from the way the thing was run that it was an exceptional outfit. They could see that if we had any trouble getting something, we'd grab a phone and call Washington, top level, and would get what we wanted. They thought, 'Hell, we must be some gang!'

"They saw all that special equipment, which nobody else could get, the snatch-glider mechanism, the rocket equipment, the helicopters, the new special carbines. They knew they were the only ones in the Air Forces to get jungle training. They had more guns than anybody else. They were getting paratroop jackets and pants, which everybody wanted, with special knives and jungle gear. They had those Marine Corps shoes, and knew they had got them in no ordinary way. Usually the corporal asks, 'Does that shoe fit?' And the G.I. says, 'Well, I don't know, maybe it doesn't feel too bad.' To which the corporal answers, 'It's all right. It says so here on the list, that's your size.' We had an officer go along, and he would say, 'Wait a minute, we're going to get the right shoe for this fellow. Walk up and down. Does it hurt a little at the heel? Try another.' Our fellows might be walking out of jungles, and shoes might mean life or death."

Morale soared so high that sometimes it was a problem. Discipline could suffer from too much morale. When the glider pilots left Goldsboro, North Carolina, they shot up the railroad station. The train was late, and they riddled the station. Flight Surgeon Cortez Enloe says, "They had the greatest morale of any outfit I ever saw, but not such strict discipline."

The final touch in the building of morale came with the

move to India. Equipment and supplies went by ship from the West Coast across the Pacific. The personnel went the other way, by air. Normally G.I.s, and officers too, crossed oceans in boats, grubby transports. But all five hundred of Project Nine were flown to India. They went with highest priority. An airplane mechanic would look at his orders and see "A.P.R.-1," and he'd say, "My God!" Enlisted men saw themselves put on airplanes, when colonels were taken off. They thought, "We sure must be something." That spirit affected the whole outfit.

In India one glider pilot told a Red Cross nurse that Project Nine was going to invade Tokyo, slam right into Japan from Siberia. The nurse, startled by the loose talk about so great a military secret, reported it to Army Intelligence. G-2 discovered that the military secret was nothing more than Project Nine morale.

They all got to India except one sergeant, an expert radio man who had had experience as a mine planter and had been a pharmacist's mate in the Navy, a useful man. He got wrong shipping orders, and was routed to Australia. There he tried to find Project Nine, while tracers were being sent through.

"Where is Sergeant Finlay?" They located him, but routine got the sergeant in its toils again. He was sent from Australia, not to India, but back to America, then from America finally to India. When at length he found Project Nine, the campaign was almost over.

9. "And Men Esteemed Me Bold"

COCHRAN WAS FIRST OFF TO INDIA, while Alison stayed behind to look after men and materials.

On the way to Delhi, where he was to meet Wingate, a song kept running through Cochran's head. *Come you back to Mandalay,* the chorus began. The old Kipling song, old back in the days when he'd been singing in college. Mandalay was in Burma, of course. He wasn't going back there, because he'd never been there, though The Man had.

But he was going there—to give The Man an eyeful of what the United States could do. He grinned to himself at the prospect of placing Project Nine, in all its beauty, before The Man. Skeptical about what Cochran had promised in London, Wingate would be astonished at getting so much more. Cochran could imagine the deep and burning gratification of the British zealot in the possession of so novel and modern an air arm, especially the gliders to provide heavy armament in the jungle. In London, The Man had not been impressed by the Irish-American fighter pilot from Erie, Pennsylvania. Now he would see, Cochran gloated. Flip Corkin was prepared to dazzle the British.

But in Delhi Wingate was ill, recovering from a dangerous attack of typhus, and could be seen only for a few minutes at a time. When Cochran got in to him, The Man lay prostrate with sickness of soul as well as of body.

"It's all off," said Wingate.

"What do you mean, off?"

"The campaign has been canceled."

"What?"

Wingate said that the Supreme Command in India had decided to call off the offensive to reconquer northern Burma, had ordered the Wingate operation to be stricken from the plans.

The Wingate campaign and Project Nine had been caught in a trap of high policy. At the Quebec Conference the North Burma Campaign had been a Roosevelt-Churchill decision. Wingate had the support of the British Prime Minister. It had been scheduled as the major feature of operations in Lord Louis Mountbatten's Southeast Asia Command, and Mountbatten was a Wingate enthusiast. But meanwhile, the Cairo Conference had been held, with new Roosevelt-Churchill promises of aid to China. Chiang Kai-shek was to get more armament, more supplies. There was not enough for everything that had been planned. Something had to go. The India-Burma theater was short of resources, and the Wingate plan required things that now could not be provided. It made demands now impossible to fulfill. So, out with it, which did not displease some of the hierarchs in India.

To Wingate the disappointment was intolerable because it came as the latest in a series of such setbacks. In Delhi, the year before, weary weeks had passed while headquarters sat on his plans, shoved them aside, forgot him. Compared to the red tape of the Indian army command, he discovered that Palestine and Abyssinia had been simple and easy little adventures. In Delhi, he had ample facilities for planning, a technical library, a room tapestried with maps, a chance to use the Royal Air Force in his calculations. He had Wavell, who was responsible for his being assigned there, to back him up. But to the Joint Planning Staff, the official group concerned with more orthodox measures for the recapture of Burma, Wingate's proposals had been something to be filed and forgotten.

Of course he had gone on planning, and had argued with those who would listen. As one who knew him in those days quoted him, "If I think I can do a thing better than anyone else, why should I keep silent about it?" But inactivity and frustration wore him down; he was seen as morose, moody, absent-minded, and careless in his dress or neglectful of haircuts, while his shoulders were acquiring an "almost simian" stoop.

He had come through to make the first campaign in Burma, and, as was said of him later, "He was retained in leadership when events had justified his heretical judgments, and nothing can be more irritating to superiors." But here was another frustration, and he was tired.

Oddly enough, Wingate's disappointment was matched, over the border in China, by a man supposed to benefit from it. General Stilwell, whose need for air transport was one of the reasons why it was denied to Wingate, was also unhappy over the mess being made of plans for retaking Burma. As Stilwell saw it, the root of the trouble was British fear that Burma would be taken by the Chinese, with of course its corollary, Chinese fear of the British. The British "viewed with distaste" Stilwell's Chinese force, felt we "can't have the dirty Chinks," while, when he dealt with the Chinese, Stilwell noted, "How they hate the limeys." To Stilwell himself, changes in the Burma plans were by no means for the better. He preferred the original "X-Y" plan, which had given him seven divisions, to the new "Saucy" plan, which cut him down to three. He argued endlessly with Chiang Kai-shek, not only over dishonesty and incompetence but over strategy, considering, for instance, that to retake Burma it was quite unnecessary to capture Mandalay, although Chiang thought so. Stilwell's definite and picturesquely expressed convictions were, on many points, opposed to those of Wingate. Stilwell had no use for Wavell, who backed Wingate, and preferred Wavell's rival, Auchinleck, "The Auk." In *The Stilwell Papers*, the American general's candid opinion of Wavell is, "Well, to hell with the old fool." His long-term battle with British red tape, as related in his correspondence, is so similar to Wingate's, his characterizations of timid authority are so in line with Wingate's own, that it seems a pity these two fireaters never got together. Certainly there were times when Wingate must have echoed feelingly Stilwell's "The limeys squawk that 'it can't be done' and look on me as a crazy man, as well as a goddam meddler stirring up trouble."

These intricate conflicts were hard, at the time, for Cochran to grasp, but without understanding Wingate or the reasons for his differences with those in authority, Cochran nevertheless could sense the savage disappointment of The Man. Proud and inflexible, Wingate was witnessing the death of his idea. His great opportunity was vanishing. Britain's present-day Clive of India, "Chinese" Gordon, Lawrence of Arabia, was not now destined to become Wingate of Burma. The jungle troops that he had laboriously trained in tactics of long-distance penetration were to be distributed among regular units of the Indian army. Once again General Orde Wingate was being cut down by the higher-ups and by the perversity of destiny.

Cochran's own disappointment at Project Nine coming to so ignominious an end was equally savage. "It was a bitter pill. It was a bitter thing to have to admit. There we had excited all our people, bringing them across the world in an arrogant state of mind, and suddenly we would have to tell them it was all over nothing. We had built them up so high, built them up to a ridiculous letdown. It was a laugh. I'd have to tell John Alison, when he arrived, that we were leaders of a task force without a task.

"People who had sneered at us and said we would never get anywhere were right. We had been so positive, and now we were shown to have been so utterly wrong. All our wonderful equipment and expertly trained people would be absorbed by the hungry India-Burma theater, starved of first-class equipment and competent men to run it. Project Nine, equipment and men, would be distributed among regular air units in India."

The second time Cochran went to the Wingate sickroom, the patient, stricken with fever and chagrin, gave in detail the reason why the jungle campaign had been called off. Now Cochran learned just what military moves Wingate had planned, the larger strategy. Hitherto he had known only in general about the tactics of long-distance penetration, the method of using jungle columns in a radio-controlled pattern.

With Cochran that day was Executive Officer Olson, joke-loving Oley Olson, now as glum as Cochran and Wingate themselves. Wingate got out of his sickbed, and unrolled a great map on the floor. He took off his own sickroom slippers, and had Cochran and Olson remove their army shoes so as not to damage the floor-covering map while crawling over it.

WINGATE THE PLANNER, with pointer in hand, map on floor, at the Delhi headquarters.

They crouched together, while The Man pointed to places on the map, places in India, Burma and China.

His plan, he said, had been to push into Burma from three directions. One of his brigades was to have advanced from India, from the west. Another brigade was to have come down from the north, in advance of General Stilwell's American-trained Chinese. The third brigade was to have thrust from the far side of Burma, from the east, from China. The three columns were to have converged upon a critical area in the middle of northern Burma.

The brigade thrusting from China was to have played the dominant part, taking the Japs by surprise. They would never expect a Wingate raid from that direction, the China side. The Japs would be looking toward India. That brigade would have to be flown to its China base. Wingate had planned a fleet of transports to carry three thousand men with supplies and mules to the Chinese city of Powashan, over the Hump, along the stupendous trans-Himalayan airway.

That was what had turned the High Command against the Wingate campaign. Moving the brigade to China would require a great amount of air transport over the most difficult and critical sky route in the world. Among the shortages in the India-Burma theater, the shortage of air transport was the most critical of all. Wherefore the High Command had decided that the air lift Wingate needed could not be provided. It was required elsewhere, in accordance with the new Roosevelt-Churchill decision at the Cairo Conference, the promise of more supplies for China. General Stilwell's Chinese army demanded air transport, as did the British army operating in south Burma, General Chennault's American air forces in China, and Chiang Kai-shek's own armies. There was not enough to go around. So Wingate was out.

"AND MEN ESTEEMED ME BOLD"

As the three crouched on the map, Wingate pointed to the north Burma area to which he had planned to march through the jungle after flying one brigade to China.

"How long would it take your soldiers to walk that trip?" Cochran asked.

"One month," replied Wingate.

"But I can fly it in an hour and a quarter," Cochran expostulated.

"Yes, I suppose so."

"But it's not sensible to walk it," Cochran argued, "it's medieval. I can fly soldiers in there."

"My God, can you?" Wingate exclaimed.

"Yes, with gliders."

Certainly, Cochran thought, if he could land heavy armament by glider in jungle clearings, he could land troops also.

He told Wingate about gliders. He had 150, with which he had planned to provide the Wingate columns with cannon and tanks. The gliders could, just as well, bring in soldiers, fly soldiers from India to the area to be invaded.

He explained the small space of not-too-level ground in which gliders could land. Wingate nodded. Yes, there were places like that in the area to which he had planned to march his men. He had studied the country, and knew of a number of jungle clearings where, according to requirements laid down by Cochran, gliders could land.

Wingate's mind was in a ferment. New ideas, new plans came flocking. Cochran, too, was thrown into a process of new thinking. He sensed possibilities of which he had never before dreamed for air-ground action. Both saw the dawn of a new chance—The Man to save his north Burma jungle campaign, Cochran to rescue Project Nine. They talked eagerly, with Olson chiming in. Their ideas developed and clarified—how to throw Wingate forces into the middle of northern Burma by air. Land soldiers in a jungle clearing to hold it long enough against the Japs to build an airstrip. Then, by regular transport planes, bring in a Wingate brigade and turn the clearing into a stronghold from which columns could operate in the tactics of long-range penetration.

These ideas were hastily sketched, half-expressed and half-implied in the quick talk of the three men in the sickroom. The Arnold idea of tossing young American flying mentality in with Britain's genius of jungle war was boiling. The air invasion plan, with no need for transporting a brigade to China by airlift over the Hump, eliminated the objection that had canceled the Wingate campaign.

Wingate said they would have to act instantly. At Delhi that very afternoon would be held a decisive meeting of the highest ranking leaders in the Southeastern Asia theater of war. At this top level conference the final plans for the India-Burma area would be affirmed, plans that included abolition of the Wingate jungle campaign. If that went through, there could be no appeal. Their new air-invasion scheme would have to be presented that afternoon if there was to be any chance of getting it approved.

Wingate couldn't go. Doctor's orders prevented him from leaving the sickroom. Cochran would have to go. They decided that Cochran should present to the Command Conference a letter from Wingate propounding the air invasion. Cochran was then to answer questions, meet objections and fight it out.

The Man was rapidly getting better. His ailments always improved when things went well for his plans. He called in a military stenographer, and dictated. He had a ready flow of incisive speech, a gift for logical exposition and the lucid presentation of military ideas. It was afternoon now, the meeting of the High Command already in session. Cochran took the letter and, accompanied by Olson, hastened to a government building near the palace in New Delhi.

Around a big conference table sat Lord Louis Mountbatten, British General Auchinleck, other heavily gold-braided British admirals and generals. With them were General Stilwell, American Commander in China, General Chennault, American Air Commander in China, General Stratemeyer, Commander of the American forces in India. Enter Cochran, accompanied by Olson.

"Here I was charging into this very formal meeting, not having quite digested the fact that I was pushing into the highest-ranking conference I'd ever seen, or probably ever would see. I handed the letter to Lord Louis."

Mountbatten greeted Cochran like an old friend. He and Cochran always hit it off. Others gazed at the intrusion of a mere colonel.

"Nobody realized what kind of force we had and what we were doing in India. They didn't know we had 150 gliders, a dozen transport planes, fighters, light planes and even helicopters. We had not even got into their minds, let alone their plans. And here I was presenting a paper that said Wingate and I had a plan.

"They had already ruled Wingate out. China had to have so much air transport over the Hump. Chennault had his requirements. So did Stilwell. This amount of air tonnage was needed for southern Burma, and that amount of tonnage for something else. None could be spared for that Wingate show. They had gathered to put a final okay on their plans, and in those plans it was definite that the Wingate thing was out. So what was this new blast from Wingate, with this American air fellow barging in?"

Lord Louis Mountbatten read Wingate's letter to the gathering. Cochran listened tensely, as the very English voice

"AND MEN ESTEEMED ME BOLD"

of Mountbatten recited, from the pages of the letter, the proposal to reinstate the north Burma campaign on the basis of a cancellation of the air transport that Wingate's plans had previously required.

There was quick interest around the table. How could Wingate, who had demanded so much air lift, dispense with it now, requiring none at all? How could he get around the need of transporting a brigade with armament and supplies "over the Hump"?

The Wingate letter, as Mountbatten read it, sketched in the swift strokes of an accomplished writer of military topics the plan for an air invasion by Wingate forces and the American aerial task force, the seizing of a jungle clearing by glider, the establishment of a Wingate base behind the Japanese lines in northern Burma. The letter enumerated the resources of the Cochran-Alison aerial task force, and argued that these would be sufficient for the first all-air invasion in history. Characteristically, The Man advanced the ideas as mostly his own.

"They all listened, and were all surprised. They asked me to tell them why I thought I could do this thing. They fired questions at me, and I remember that sometimes I gave very fast answers that I wasn't quite sure of myself. I knew this was no place to let anybody buffalo me. I knew also that I was the only one there who knew the answer when they asked what a glider was and how much it could hold. It was new to them, and I was the only one who had the information."

Cochran, flying in war, had had to fight his way out of many a tight corner. This was the crucial battle of his career, battling to save the Wingate campaign and Project Nine from annihilation. He talked. He answered questions. He fought. He was in his element.

"AND MEN ESTEEMED ME BOLD"

He was aided by the negative fact that the whole tone of the meeting of the High Command had been glum. There had been a scaling down of plans, a reduction of ambitions. Resources in India did not fit ambitious ideas for offensive operations against the Japs. The Mountbatten Southeast Asia Command, so brilliantly announced at the Quebec Conference, was being curtailed to disillusioning proportions.

Cochran was aided by the positive fact that in the Allied invasion of Sicily gliders had been used dramatically. In military circles in India, they knew little about the technique of gliders, but were aware that a successful glider job had been done in Sicily.

Moreover, there was the cold fact that the new Wingate plan made no demand for air transport. It required nothing of anybody.

The verdict was "Go ahead." To Cochran, Lord Louis Mountbatten said, "My boy, you are the only ray of sunshine we have had in this theater this year."

Cochran had a talk with Chennault, commander of the Flying Tigers, who knew more about the air-war methods of the Japs than anybody else. "I asked his opinion about Jap fighter interference. He said we would get interference during the day. I replied that we would do it all at night. His assurance was, 'Then you will have no interference.'"

General Stratemeyer, American Air Commander in India, was strong support. General Arnold had recommended Project Nine to him, and he was alert to new uses of air power.

General Stilwell was the ground soldier, the proponent of infantry. "Vinegar Joe" was in heroic fashion the walking soldier. The Japs had driven him from Burma and he had refused to be flown out. With his soldiers he had walked out. He was determined to go back the same way, walking.

American Commander in China, he was to invade Burma with his American-trained Chinese, a walking invasion. His joy was to lead his infantry slogging through the jungle.

In India a story was told about Vinegar Joe. On one of his walking campaigns in the jungle, the yarn related, he was trudging through a heavy rain in his old campaign hat, style of the Spanish-American War. Down the line was an American mule skinner, wet and disgusted. He saw the Stilwell party coming along the rain-swept jungle trail, and growled, "Christ, duck hunters!"

Vinegar Joe, the inveterate foot soldier, was vastly amused by that. He was also amused when Cochran talked gliders. "I found him exceedingly pleasant, very affable. I think he was intrigued with the glider idea. I remember he laughed about things I said we could do. I told him about our ability to snatch a glider off the ground, a plane flying over and snatching it up. He thought it was funny."

In terms of strategy, Stilwell was of course delighted to have the Wingate penetration scheme go ahead, provided it did not require the expenditure of planes in an air lift. And he was not anxious to interfere in any way with the Southeast Asia Command. He had troubles of his own with Chiang. He had Merrill's Marauders, the rangers trained under Wingate, and hoped to be allowed to keep them. And he had no use for Mountbatten, whom he called "the Glamour Boy."

When Cochran and Olson emerged from the conference and walked to their jeeps, Oley Olson said, "How are you going to do it?" Cochran replied, "I don't know."

They flew to Calcutta. There Bill Taylor and his glider men had established themselves to receive and assemble the gliders as they came in by ship. They were having some trouble with sickness. They lived in old barracks with thatched roofing, and slept at night with dust falling on them from the thatch. But that day they had made test flights with newly assembled gliders, the first glider flights ever made in Asia.

Cochran greeted Taylor with the brisk remark, "Well, Bill, I sold you down the river."

"Down what river?"

Cochran replied that he had committed the glider force to more than it could do. He told of the new plans for air invasion, and concluded in a hard-boiled manner, "Now, can you do it? I said you can."

Taylor replied that probably he could, that probably he could overload the gliders sufficiently for troop landings. But they had better get some more gliders, fifty more. Cochran sent a cable to the United States asking for fifty more gliders.

Wingate ordered maneuvers. The Man was great for that sort of thing, realistic war games, pitting one brigade against another. For any operation he trained his long-distance penetration troops to the last detail. Now they would experiment with something new, a routine of seizing jungle bases by air, sham battles woven around air invasion. Project Nine was to display its tricks, glider tricks. Be ready, said Wingate, for glider troop landings. Be ready to give the first demonstration of the possibility of the seizure by glider of positions behind enemy lines in an all-air invasion. Prove that it can be done.

Wingate was not competely convinced. The Man had grasped at the air-invasion idea as the only thing that could save his campaign. He threw into it the rich reserves of his imagination. He supported it argumentatively. But deep down in the jungle foot soldier there was lurking doubt about whether this madcap air adventure would work. Nor had Lord Louis Mountbatten any unshakable belief. Venturesome and optimistic, he was delighted with the daring brilliance of the air-commando scheme of jungle invasion. But would it work?

Most of the high brass in India was unbelieving. Royal Air Force officers ridiculed the air invasion, and in written opinions stated that it could not be done. The plan was to tow two gliders behind each transport plane. Air officials in India stated that a two-glider tow was impossible.

Alison had arrived in India, and he and Cochran went into a Phil-John huddle. They faced realities. By the air invasion plan, Project Nine had been saved from obliteration, but all was tentative. They still existed, but only on sufferance. Everything depended on the showing of their gliders in the Wingate maneuvers. That would be the proof. Until then, Project Nine was still liable to be washed out at any time.

10. "You Long-Eared Old Darlin's!"

EQUIPMENT FROM THE UNITED STATES was arriving, most of it according to schedule. A shipment might appear at Karachi that should have gone to Calcutta, or at Bombay when it should have gone to Ceylon. A few things arrived in India months later, after the show was over. Gliders were being unloaded when, on December 5, the Japs made their last bombing raid on Calcutta. Flights of enemy planes assailed the waterfront with a rain of high explosives, and bombs narrowly missed Liberty ships full of gliders.

Most equipment came in good shape, but some was damaged in transit. "We started out badly," Cochran admits. "With our first P-51's coming in, a shipment of eight, the boys were thrilled. Then we heard that one of the Mustangs had its wing twisted and another had its tail off. We went charging down to the docks and found that water had seeped into the planes, had got inside the wings, and the wings were corroding. It looked as if the eight Mustangs were ruined. But the boys went to work and fixed them up.

"The next consignment of P-51s, twelve, came in a boat that had been hit by a typhoon and had almost sunk in the tremendous storm. The pitching of the ship had twisted the structure of the planes. One was so badly damaged that we could never use it. To save the others we had to send back to the States to get spare parts for repair jobs.

"We got what we could at Calcutta. Our engineering officer, Joe Jeanette, did a lot of chiseling, and actually swiped tools and parts of other planes. We stole one entire plane. There it was, sitting on a field. It had been damaged and couldn't fly. Soon there was no airplane. It disappeared part by part, assimilated into our planes."

Supplies came late to the glider section. They had to use army field telephones and telephone wire for communications between gliders and tow planes in flight. Equipment for snatch pickups came late. They had to go into the jungles and cut bamboo poles to use, instead of what they called the "pretty poles" made in the United States.

"Our stuff was like a dream, and it came into a theater that was starved for equipment and wanted to take it up like a sponge. The people out there saw this beautiful material, and decided that things like that belonged to their own outfits. We had a constant fight to keep our own property." The weapon they had for defense was a letter signed by Generals Marshall and Arnold stating that Project Nine was an independent outfit and was to operate as such.

The glider section was getting ready for the Wingate maneuvers, the air-invasion test on which the fate of Project Nine would depend. At Pangarah, north of Calcutta, they used a base by courtesy of an American bomber squadron, which housed and fed them. They labored short of equipment and men, everyone pitching into sweaty work, practicing glider troop-landings by day and by night. They experimented with overloaded gliders to carry a maximum of soldiers and equipment, calculating and planning.

The British were more of a hindrance than a help, so Cochran and Alison thought. Cochran was now better able to understand what had seemed to be ill-tempered complaints about mismanagement made by Wingate at that first meeting in London. "We figured there were a hundred planning staffs in India and none knew what the others were doing. They estimated everything down to pounds, and gallons of gasoline to miles of distance. We would say to Oley Olson, 'Let's see, that's 175 miles, so much extra gas, sure we can do that!' Then a planning staff somewhere would get out the ruler and say, 'If the wind is blowing that way, it will mean such and such.' Half the time they would tell us it couldn't be done when we knew it could.

"We had to keep selling them gliders. The planning staff would say, 'How much will a glider hold? How many pounds?' Then they would keep asking more questions with a lot of *ifs* and *buts*. We finally had to go to Lord Mountbatten and say, 'For God's sake, call off the planners!'"

The Man retained his predilection for mules as transport. In London Cochran had marveled at the place accorded to long ears and heehaw in Wingate's modernistic long-distance penetration tactics, patterned by radio control. Now the campaign had been transformed into air invasion, still more modern, but The Man had to have his mules as part of the force to be landed by glider. This would have to be demonstrated in the maneuvers. Cochran and Alison said they could fly mules in gliders, though so far as they were aware this had never been done before.

"We consulted the British mule people, and they reacted in

typical army fashion. They said we'd have to have stalls in the gliders for mules, and they got carpenters and tools. In a couple of days, they had fancy stalls built. We didn't like this, the stalls weighed too much.

"We asked a veterinarian whether we could dope a mule for two hours to keep him from kicking a glider to pieces. The veterinarian said sure. So we figured that instead of knocking a mule unconscious with a smack on his head we'd give him a shot of dope. Then we figured how would we get him out of a glider? Maybe we'd have to carry out the doped mules, and that would be awkward in the heat of action. Anyway, when would the mules wake up?

"We finally ended by discarding all these bright ideas. We just put the mule in a glider and let him stand there, tied in such fashion that he wouldn't bounce up and down. It worked. All you had to do with the mule was be nice to him, and he'd ride in a glider without trouble.

"The British, however, had to get in one fancy idea. They trained each mule to get used to the sound of an airplane engine, the roar of the motor of the transport ahead that a mule in a glider would hear. They would tie up some mules, and then nearby they'd race airplane engines like mad. We finally proved to them that it wasn't necessary, that the mule didn't care whether he was in a glider or where he was."

The aerial task force was having insignia made. Milton Caniff was drawing it back in the United States, the same Caniff who had put Phil Cochran into the comics as Flip Corkin. Cochran wanted each unit of the task force to have its own insignia as well, especially the gliders, now that these had become the spearhead of the Wingate operation. The glider men decided on a design of yellow and blue, the Air Force colors, a G standing for glider, and a winged mule's head with a knife in its mouth. This last detail sig-

SOME MULES did not like the idea of leaving Mother Earth.

nified the Gurkhas of the Wingate force, Gurkhas traditionally attacking with knives in their mouths. Cochran was delighted with the insignia and Wingate liked it so well that he later wanted to adopt it for all his forces.

Glider leader Bill Taylor fell ill with malaria, an old story for him. Back in Mississippi, and on service in the tropics, he had had malaria twenty-four times. Chief Flight Surgeon Page ordered him to bed. Cochran established himself at the training base, substituting for Taylor, as glider practice went on for the Wingate maneuvers. The Christmas holidays were observed with scant celebration and much work, tension mounting. The maneuvers were to be held in a few days. They had their final test on New Year's Eve. Everything went wrong. Bad landings were made. Gliders were damaged. They forgot to remove the control locks of a C-47 transport plane and it crashed. Nobody was hurt, but they were minus one good transport plane.

Taylor, still sick, was confined to headquarters. "I was hanging around when they all came in with long faces, glum and downcast, after losing a transport plane and everything going wrong. I knew it was because of strain. They had been under terrific tension. I told them to bring out the accordion, and get some liquor. Claude Waller, one of the glider pilots, played the accordion. Cochran sang *Uncle Bud,* his favorite song, about the gamecock mascot of his old fighter squadron.

"They had a hilarious New Year's celebration. That was what I wanted, to get them roistering and singing in that godforsaken country. The next morning they weren't so pretty, but the tension was broken."

The maneuver was held in the Indian state of Gwalior, south of Delhi. There jungle conditions were approximated. Taylor was better, and Cochran went off to Delhi saying that he would wire Bill when to have his gliders at Gwalior.

"YOU LONG-EARED OLD DARLIN'S!"

The telegram was delayed. Taylor got it one day before the time named, the shortest possible notice. Rush orders brought tow planes from scattered fields. Frantic work assembled twenty-four gliders for take-offs. They flew to Gwalior in two hops because of the distance. The twenty-four-glider fleet made it within minutes of the time assigned.

"As soon as I landed," as Taylor tells it, "Phil rushed up to me on the field. A slow drizzling rain was falling, and airplanes were all over everything. Cochran shouted, 'Get ready immediately. You've got to pull the first maneuver right now.'

"I balked. I told him it was impossible to expect us to do it on such short notice. Everything was against us. I proved to him it was impractical. It wasn't a fair test, it wasn't giving us a break, the more so because of clouds and rain. Phil went back to Wingate and told him to put the show off until the next morning.

"Wingate said, 'No, do it now.'

"The general commanded it, and we had to do it, regardless of what might happen. I gave the orders, and the boys started lining up the gliders on the rainy field."

Maybe Wingate's insistence was ill-advised. But it must be remembered that he had been compelled to stress haste in all his campaigns, usually in countries where swiftness of attack was unusual or unknown. The Special Night Squads, in Palestine, were taught to move more swiftly than the Arabs, to strike and vanish. When they had to travel by day, their vehicles ran at high speed to hide their numbers in a covering cloud of dust. In Ethiopia, commanding mixed troops and striving to impress them with the passage of time, Wingate formed the habit of walking about with an alarm clock in his hand.

Now he was dealing with Americans and although reason

and observation taught him that they could move fast, he no doubt felt that he had to make sure that they would do so, in the required synchronization. The bad weather would be hard on equipment, but there might be bad weather in Burma before they got out.

Wingate drove off by car to the jungle clearing in which the glider landings were to be made. He wanted to be there to witness the arrival of the air invasion. According to Cochran, he still didn't quite believe it could be done.

There was no time for glider pilots to fly over the jungle clearing and see what it looked like. Tow-plane pilots did, and had a glimpse of the landing area through the clouds. Taylor could brief the glider pilots only by drawing on a board a rough sketch of the clearing that he derived from a map. As commanding officer, he would fly the first glider. Cochran said, "Bill, I'll ride with you as co-pilot. I've seen the place, and can tell you when you have reached the landing area."

The tactics they had devised for air invasion were brand new. With a token force of twenty-four gliders, there were two pathfinders. In the first, with Taylor and Cochran, rode a party of Wingate assault troops. They were to seize the ground and beat off sham battle attack. They were Scots of the Black Watch, who had never even seen a glider before, but were eager for the adventure. The second pathfinder was a communications glider. Its crew would lay down field markings for the landing of the main force, and its radio would guide the glider trains to the area. These were to start after an interval of half an hour.

The two pathfinders took off, in double tow behind a transport plane. They flew for miles. Bill Taylor looked down through the rain on unfamiliar country of Indian jungle.

"YOU LONG-EARED OLD DARLIN'S!"

Then Cochran sang out, "There it is, Bill, the space near that tree up ahead."

Taylor cut loose from the tow plane, and immediately realized he had too much altitude for a slow, safe glide. He had to swing around, and nose down for a fast wet landing. It wasn't the safe way, but he made it. The field was soft and rain-soaked, the mud similar to his own native Mississippi gumbo.

They all piled out, the soldiers of the Black Watch marching off to take defense positions at the edge of the field, seizing the ground. The communications glider with radio and field markings came in for a good landing. Its crew hopped out, and began laying landing strips for the main wave.

Cochran saw someone coming across a newly plowed field. "It was muddy, and I saw him running and falling down in the furrows. Then I recognized him. It was The Man. He stumbled up in a wild hurry and gasped, 'Phil, you've done it!'

" 'I've done what, sir?'

" 'You brought these gliders in and landed the troops.'

" 'Yes, I said I would.'

" 'And you have!'

"This bit of talk gave him away. I knew then how much he had doubted, all along, that we could make good on the glider idea.

"It was only natural, I suppose. Our people tended to talk a little too much, and I think Wingate felt that. That's the way the British usually feel about Americans. They say we brag. It really isn't bragging. It's just enthusiasm. But we oversell."

Wingate staff officers crowded around, astonished, excited. Cochran was off, supervising the pathfinding job. The Man and his staff waited tensely for the second phase of the landings, the gliders of the main force.

These came in on schedule, half an hour after the pathfinders. The radio of the communications pathfinder guided the tow planes. The field markings, a diamond pattern, brought in the gliders. Only one failed to arrive, having gone astray and come down in a wrong jungle clearing for a safe landing.

Soldiers of the Black Watch were piling out of gliders, forming up in patrol parties and moving out into surrounding thickets. In a jungle glade two miles away, a force of Wingate's West African troops were stationed. They had not been told about the gliders. It was left to them to spot the air invasion and stop it as best they could. They sent out patrols. These encountered the glider-borne Scots, who made a sham battle defense of the seized jungle clearing.

Out of the gliders heavy equipment was unloaded, and mules. These gave no trouble. Airborne supplies and armament were packed on the backs of the airborne mules, and transport parties moved into the thickets to support the defense.

The Man watched gliders go by. He noted no flaw in the arrival and deployment of his jungle columns. Mule-conscious, he saw the air-invasion handling of his typical Wingate system of transport as sheer miracle.

The gliders were to be taken out by snatch pickup. Crews tried to push them into position, but they were stuck in the mud and couldn't be budged. They'd have to be picked up where they were, out of the mud, snatch mechanism placed in front of each. Radio word was sent to the tow planes to set their pickup reels for a harder pull. It was like snatching off a heavier load. The tow planes came over, flying low.

THE FLYING MULES: Three mules in a glider just before a pick-up in the maneuvers which happily proved that mules, too, were air-minded.

It meant hard pulling, but gliders were picked up out of the mud, one after another.

Wingate turned to Cochran and asked, "Which one do I ride in?" The Man had never been in a glider before.

Cochran told Bill Taylor to fly the next one out, entrusting Wingate to the flying skill of the commander of the glider section. Cochran rode as Taylor's co-pilot.

The Man called to his aide, "Do you want to go with me?"

The aide stammered, "Ah—ah—somebody will have to take the car back."

Wingate repeated, "Are you going with me?"

The aide went.

In the glider, the two passengers were strapped into their seats, so they wouldn't be thrown around when the tow plane hit the pickup rope. The tow plane was coming, when Taylor, at the glider controls, looked back.

Wingate had unfastened himself and gone to the door at the back of the glider, where the jolt of the pickup might have hurled him out. There he shouted to one of his officers on the ground, "Tell the R.A.F.," he yelled, his gurgling voice going shrill, "that I not only have seen it, I have done it."

With seconds to spare they had him back in his seat, and strapped, when the tow plane snatched them into the air.

"Once we were off the ground and flying behind the tow planes," relates Taylor, "Wingate reached in his pocket, pulled out a book and started to read, as unconcerned as if being snatched off in a glider were the most ordinary thing in the world. By now I had turned the controls over to Cochran. I said, 'Phil, let me have the controls and I'll make this glider do some tricks on the end of this rope that will make The Man forget all about that book!' But Cochran wouldn't let me do it."

"YOU LONG-EARED OLD DARLIN'S!"

As they approached the landing field, Wingate closed his book, put it back in his pocket. Down on the field he could see his automobile, which had gone over to meet him. Taylor was at the glider controls. "I put the glider down so that it rolled up and stopped right beside the car. Wingate had merely to step out from the glider and into the automobile. And The Man thought this was quite something."

The day landings were the first half of the maneuver. Night landings were to follow. The actual air invasion in Burma would be staged at night, they planned, glider landings behind Jap lines under the cover of darkness. In the maneuver at night the seizure of the jungle clearing in the darkness would be the replica of the real thing.

Mountbatten came down for that, Wingate having reported to him the success of the daylight landings and pickups. Mountbatten was received with suitable ceremony. The British were stuffy about that. He had a laughing chat and some serious talk with Cochran and a conference with Wingate.

It was part of the ceremonial aspect for Lord Louis to make an address to the Americans, an address on the flying field. To give him a chance to be heard, Cochran ordered all planes grounded—no roar of motors to drown out the cousin of the King. The Americans gathered round, and presently Mountbatten, standing in a jeep, was making his address. He was in the middle of it when there was a roar in the sky.

"I had forgotten," Cochran says, "that R. T. Smith was out in his P-51. When he came in he didn't know that Lord Louis was there. All he saw was a crowd gathered around a jeep on the flying field, somebody making a speech. He assumed that probably I was delivering the oration, and he thought, 'Here's where I mess up that old fool.'

"Down he came, buzzing the speaker standing in the jeep.

135

"YOU LONG-EARED OLD DARLIN'S!"

Diving at four hundred and fifty or five hundred miles an hour, he swooped over Mountbatten's head and practically took his hat off. It was a beautiful show as stunt flying, but it was tough on the dignity of the King's cousin. Mountbatten stood without flinching as the P-51 dusted his head. I nearly collapsed.

"I said, 'That damn fool just arrived, Lord Louis. He was away and didn't know you were here.'

"Mountbatten replied, 'That's all right. I shouldn't be talking on a flying field.' But he was awfully mad, not mad at us, but at the situation. He said his aide should have had more sense than to have him speaking there."

There was worry about the weather for the night operation. The rain had stopped, but the sky was cloudy. The moon was at about half, and partly shrouded by clouds it might not provide enough light, even the faint moonlight needed. As evening came, they had a 50 per cent overcast. The half-moon was shining between drifting clouds. Cochran was nervous, anxious. If they didn't go ahead, they wouldn't know where they stood, With only half of the maneuver accomplished, the daylight half, the air invasion might still be called off. Project Nine might still be abolished. Wingate was tense, Mountbatten waiting to be shown. Cochran decided to chance it, figuring that it was better to risk failure than to stand on half a maneuver.

Mountbatten and Wingate proceeded to the landing area. Cochran flew by small plane to be with them. The blackness of a tropical night came quickly. Mountbatten, Wingate and staff officers gathered at the place the gliders would come in. At the scheduled time they heard the hum of airplane motors in the dark sky; then they could see vague shapes coming down into the clearing, the two pathfinders. The first landed with precision just in front of the gallery of spec-

MOUNTBATTEN speaks from a jeep. Note interested listener, standing at the right.

tators. Assault troops piled out. The second pathfinder followed, and lights were brought out, landing lights for the main force. Bill Taylor and Neal Blush, running in the darkness, placed a diamond-shaped pattern of lights in the landing area. A mile in front of that a cut-loose light was set, to signal the point at which the gliders of the main wave should drop tow lines for the glide in.

Cochran hurried to Taylor, querying him. Was he sure the lights were right? It was anxiety, nerves. Taylor replied with grim philosophy that, if he had done anything wrong about the lights, it was too late now. The main wave of gliders was coming in.

Off to one side of the dark jungle clearing the gallery watched tensely, as dim shapes one after another swept in silently with no more than faint sounds of bumping and landing. All the gliders arrived except two. These, in a double tow, had encountered difficulty as they had taken off and had been compelled to release for landing at the home base, their starting place. They came down safely.

Twenty-two gliders had come in. Mountbatten, peering in the darkness, could not believe so many had landed. He was incredulous. They took him around over the field to count the gliders, each one individually, twenty-two in all. Only one was damaged. Vincent Rose had come in a little too far to one side, had hit a boulder and knocked the wheels off his glider.

Troops of the Black Watch, having piled out of gliders, were playing their part in the ground phase of the maneuvers. Their patrol parties tangled with West Africans, who moved to oppose the aerial invasion. The sham battle became enthusiastic, violent. Scots and West Africans got into fist fights, knocking each other out, eyes blackened, noses bleeding. It

MOUNTBATTEN AND WINGATE watch, willing to be shown.

COCHRAN AND ALISON look on with confidence that in the end turned into triumph.

got so bad that the referees had to stop the fights. They ruled that the air invasion forces had won.

The night pickups were being made. The first transport came roaring over in the darkness, and snatched the glider off cleanly. Mountbatten and Wingate were as excited as kids with a new toy. The crowd of staff officers waxed so enthusiastic they got in the way, the gallery piling out into the field. The Americans had to chase them back, afraid they might get hit as low-flying transports swooped down and snatched the gliders. Staff officers wanted to get in on the novelty occurring before their eyes, wanted to ride in snatched-off gliders. Presently passengers were being flown out in each pickup.

Off to one side, Mountbatten, Wingate, Cochran and Alison lay down in the wet weeds with a light and a map, and hastily talked over their plans, developing and expanding them. All the Mountbatten-Wingate doubt was gone. "They were now willing to believe anything we said. If we had told them we could shoot airplanes into the sky with rubber bands, they'd have believed it."

The original air-invasion plan had called for one Wingate brigade to be landed by glider. They hiked that up to two. They wanted to make it three, but later General Stilwell insisted on having one Wingate brigade attached to his ground campaign.

About two o'clock, the planning conference in the wet grass adjourned and went to Bill Taylor. Could he have his glider force at the India-Burma border by February 1, at the base from which the air invasion would be launched? Taylor thought he could, although the time was short and the job big. Cochran snorted, "You know damn well we'll be there."

They left Taylor on the field, where he remained to repair the one damaged glider in the morning and fly it out. Some

British soldiers broke out a bottle of Scotch. He had a drink with them, then rolled up in his blanket.

"When I awakened in the morning, there was a jackal staring at me, trying to decide whether I was dead and he could start eating me."

Cochran flew Mountbatten from Gwalior in a Project Nine light plane. Lord Louis said, "You know, I haven't flown for seven years, but I used to fly a small plane." At the first stop he asked, "Do you suppose I could fly this plane?"

"I told him to get in the front seat, I taking the back seat, and then I wondered why I did it. Taking off, the first thing he did was a ground loop. He had big feet and got them all over the pedals, and the plane went spinning around. I yelled at him, 'Get your feet off the brake.' I didn't have the guts to say, 'Look here, Lord Louis, get out of that seat and let me take over.'

"He said, 'Which is the brake?'

"He got the plane going on the runway, but ran off to one side, and a wing went down and scraped the ground. I thought, 'My Lord, here we go! If we could only get it in the air, it would save our lives.' I reached forward and grabbed at the controls and took it off, then gave the controls back to Mountbatten.

"He flew around for an hour and a half, and every once in a while he would turn around to me, nod and grin, congratulating himself. All the time I was wondering, 'How is he going to land it?'

"We approached the flying field for which we were bound, he leveled off, and flew in. He didn't quite get the tail down, and I thought we were going over on our back. I could see the newspaper headlines: 'Lord Louis Mountbatten, Supreme Commander of the Southeast Asia Theater, injured in American plane.'

"Finally he got straightened out, and was much ashamed at the sloppiness of the landing. He kept saying, 'I haven't flown for seven years.' Afterward, he wrote me a letter apologizing for the way he had handled my airplane and for nearly dashing us into the ground."

The acquaintance of Mountbatten and Project Nine once made, a lasting friendship was formed. The American airmen liked the good-looking, good-natured Commander-in-Chief. They called him "Louie the Lord."

Cochran and Alison acquired a Mountbatten document which they used with ruthless effect. They called it the "Dear Dickie" letter. It was from General Arnold to Mountbatten and began "Dear Dickie," the name for Mountbatten used by his familiar friends. In the letter the American Air Force commander affirmed the official status of Project Nine as an autonomously operating Air Force unit. A copy of it worked wonders in settling disputes, and it supplemented the previous letter signed by General Arnold and initialed by General Marshall. Here was the highest authorization, when Cochran and Alison needed to declare their independence and resist raids on their equipment and supplies.

11. "We've Fought With Many Men Across the Seas"

THEY HAD TWO BASES for the air invasion, two flying fields in Imphal Valley, the Assam hill country along the India-Burma border. These they had flown to inspect on Christmas Eve, Cochran, Alison and Bill Taylor, who said nothing about the 103° temperature he was running with malaria.

The bases were twelve miles apart. Landing at one, called Lalaghat, Taylor said it would do for gliders and tow planes, if the runways were extended. Cochran and Alison flew on to the other, Hailikandi, leaving Taylor behind. He said he wanted to rest. "I spent the night in a deserted hut with a fever of 104° and with monkeys and crows looking in at me. I was too sick to care." Cochran and Alison returned for him the next day, saying the Hailikandi field would serve for headquarters, fighters, and bombers, though it would need much improvement. The light planes could use both bases.

In January they moved to the bases. The Assam railroad was overtaxed with supplies for the Stilwell campaign in the north and for China over the Hump. The railroad people were reluctant to believe that the aerial task force delivery job was in earnest. Transportation Officer Ed White learned the Calcutta way of moving things, how to manipulate equipment off a boat and onto cars that they sometimes had no right to use. They stole empty cars.

Freight started north out of Calcutta on standard gauge tracks. Then forty miles north of Calcutta it had to be transferred to a railroad on another gauge. There was a similar transfer farther on. Next the freight had to be ferried across the Brahmaputra River. By the time a trainload got to base it might turn out to be supplies for the Chinese Army.

The boys told tall stories about the railroads in India, how a locomotive engineer would stop a train at a place where some friends were, and they'd make tea of hot water from the boiler of the engine. They'd have tea together, and if your carload got to you tomorrow or the next day, it didn't matter. The railroads were intended to transport tea, one train every three or four days. Time meant nothing.

They flew equipment in their own transport planes and in gliders. These, being transferred to invasion base, flew loaded. Slowest of all were cargoes that went by barge up the Brahmaputra.

The flying fields at Hailikandi and Lalaghat had been constructed by the British, but the bases were primitive. There were no dispersal points for the heavy planes. The ground wasn't prepared. You put a plane on unprepared ground, and it sinks in, especially a heavy bomber. They had

INTO ASSAM: Towing a glider to one of the new bases.

"WE'VE FOUGHT WITH MANY MEN ACROSS THE SEAS"

a swarm of native workers with elephants cut down trees and make spaces in the jungle to hide planes. They had no roller to make the ground hard for an airplane to stand on. One of the boys got an elephant. He hired a mahout to have his elephant walk around on the ground all day long. The mahout thought the white man was crazy, paying him six dollars a day to do that.

They built twenty-four strips on each field. The landing strips were six thousand feet long and three hundred feet wide, with ditches on either side to drain them. They were laid out on flattened rice paddy fields. Camouflage was difficult. They tried to get concealment by using local foliage. They were afraid the Japs would come in and burn them out when the planes were assembled at the bases.

The British had set up a few huts for housing. More were needed. Called *bashas*, they were made of split bamboo, matted, with windows. The local natives could put them up quickly.

They dealt with a tea planter, "Sandy" Greeves, who ran affairs in the valley, a Scot who had been out there for thirty-three years. Affable and cooperative, he profited richly as a labor contractor for the aerial task force. He was a jolly fat man, with an Indian wife who was very dark. He had two daughters, one dark and one light. His Indian wife wore a ring in her nose. Oley Olson said, "What's wrong with that? It's a gold ring."

Sandy Greeves had a myna bird, supposed to be a great talker. Cochran was interested. The myna is a weird bird that imitates all the sounds of the jungle but has no call of its own. "We were paying a social call at the tea plantation, and all I saw was a crow that wouldn't say a thing. Sandy would lean back and call, 'Myna! Myna!' That was supposed to make the bird talk, but nothing happened.

GLIDER OPERATIONS OFFICE: One of the thatch-roofed shacks at Lalaghat.

Sandy said, 'Well, he's upset with all you people around. He is very independent.' The myna would have none of us. Later Sandy was telling us about something, and the bird suddenly called out, 'What do you want?' It could talk all right but it was like the British staff people, had to have time for a double-take."

They never could get enough native labor to save themselves from brutal overwork. Everybody pitched in. Fighter pilots, lieutenants, captains ran scrapers or tractors, leveling ground, the cream of the fighter squadron in the dirt. Medical and administrative officers toiled like coolies, rolling gasoline drums, wrestling with heavy stuff, pushing small freight cars around. That was the story from beginning to end, killing overwork.

General Bob Old, head of the American Troop Carrier Command in the India-China area, came to confabulate with Project Nine. The general was shocked. At Lalaghat, the glider pilots, having worked day and night unloading supply trains, building gasoline supply dumps, and marshaling gliders, were a disreputable outfit, dirty, greasy, in need of shaves and haircuts. They failed to look the part of soldiers of the United States Army. So it appeared to General Old, when he saw them falling in, officers and enlisted men in the same line, to get their handouts of food. Bill Taylor was put on the carpet and got the proverbial skinning.

"The general told me that my men looked more like hobos than army personnel, which I couldn't deny. Nor did I try to explain the reason. You don't argue with a general."

Phil Cochran was reminded how he had been bawled out because of the appearance of his cave-dweller pilots in North Africa. He produced a classic directive, surely one of the most curious ever posted by a commanding officer to an army group:

"To: All Personnel and Attached Organizations.

"Look, Sports, the beards and attempts at beards are not appreciated by visitors.

"Since we can't explain to all strangers that the fuzz is a gag or 'something I always wanted to do' affair, we must avoid their reporting that we are unshaven (regulations say you must shave) by appearing like Saturday night in Jersey whenever possible.

"Work comes before shaving. You will never be criticized for being unkempt if you are so damn busy you can't take time to doll up. But be clean while you can.

"Ain't it awful?

P. G. COCHRAN
Colonel, Air Corps,
Commanding."

But it didn't take General Old long to become an air commando. In a couple of days he too was dirty, working hard. He told Bill Taylor that the skinning he had given him had been premature and out of order. Whereupon Bill took the general to a bonfire singsong held by the glider boys.

The glider pilots kept up their music. At Karachi they had been able to talk a service officer out of a supply of harmonicas, ocarinas, and other instruments of uproar. Then the glider pilot who could play the piano had discovered a purchasable piano in Calcutta. The glider section pitched in and bought it for eight hundred rupees, about $250. In Calcutta, Comedian Joe E. Brown borrowed it for a USO show he was putting on. "My boys in the audience," Bill Taylor relates, "had murder in their eyes, because, as part of the Joe E. Brown act, his accompanist kept slamming down the top of the piano. My boys thought he was going to tear the piano apart. They were mad about it. The act fell flat, so far as they were concerned. As soon as the show was over they grabbed the piano and hid it. Later, they flew it to Lalaghat in a glider. Everyone drew straws to see who would fly the glider, because it was decided that, if the pilot wrecked the piano, he'd have to pay for it.

"Two of the boys composed a song called *Basha Blues*, and had a record made of it by a Calcutta native band and the Bing Crosby of India. Later, *Basha Blues* was on the radio in the United States."

One night a glider pilot came home with a bear he had bought. Some of the boys were asleep. He put the bear in bed with one fellow, who woke up with the bear hugging him. He yelled and reached for his gun, but the bear held him fast, until the others pried loose the hugging arms. After this they tried to slip the bear into the bed of their commanding officer, but Bill Taylor got out before the bear got in.

They flew the bear in a glider, tying him down to keep him from ripping the glider apart. The bear got airsick, and on the ground staggered and stumbled. That line of amusement ended when they found that the bear had broken loose and ripped their beds and bedding to shreds, leaving them with nothing to sleep on. One pilot was so angry he shot the bear with his forty-five, and they had bear meat next day for dinner.

They had monkeys and parrots and all kinds of animals for pets. The Lalaghat flying field was infested with baboons. They had to drive them off the runways before they could take off. One Texan of the cowboy tradition spent hours trying in vain to lasso a baboon.

Back in Washington Project Nine had received a long-distance call from a dock at Los Angeles: "We have thirty

GURKHAS ARRIVE AT LALAGHAT: Their American plane shows scars after an enemy plane intercepted it, scored several hits en route.

thousand pounds of hypo for developing films. It's for you fellows. What'll we do with it?" Thirty thousand pounds of hypo! How had that got on their list? They couldn't guess. To this day they don't know. They told the people at Los Angeles, "We don't need any large amount of hypo." The reply was, "You have a whole dockload out here. There are barrels as far as you can see. We just wondered what it's going to be for. We'll ship it, but nobody gave us a boat to ship it in."

It was one of those twisters of routine. They had the hypo, and were compelled to accept half of it. They shipped fifteen thousand pounds, enough to develop all the photographs made in America in three months, enough developing material to last the whole India-Burma theater for a year. They used three or four hundred pounds in the development of pictures. The hypo, however, came in handy in other ways. "Rush," the cameraman—his name was Russhon—knew what to do with it. When hypo is put in water, the chemical reaction cools it. Rush used it to chill beer.

Wingate's troops were stationed at a base nearby, in Imphal Valley. They had no trouble with beards. Wingate always grew one on a campaign, and so did most of his officers. Many of his Indian troops, of course, already had them. But it was not the wild appearance of Wingate's fighters which gave him the "Tarzan" nickname he had for a time enjoyed at Delhi headquarters; it was his tough training system for men destined for jungle fighting.

In his successive campaigns he had developed different techniques for dealing with different nations under arms, but toughness was always a requirement. The Special Night Squads in Palestine had been given a commando training that combined the fighting methods of the American Indian with use of a certain amount of modern equipment, all that

SOME OF WINGATE'S CHINDITS clean their guns at the Hailikandi base.

was available for issue or that could be captured from the Arabs. They took training eagerly because their hearts were in it.

After Wingate trained the Night Squads and the Jewish auxiliary unit, Ben-Gurion said, "There was not a man who would not have gone through fire and water at his bidding." Wingate in turn lost no opportunity to testify to the bravery of young Palestine farmers turned soldiers. Speaking to their own people, as his Jewish boys must not be overpraised to their faces, he said temperately, "They make fine soldiers. They do drop off to sleep sometimes during night watch. And they do talk a great deal for soldiers. But they are excellent pupils and doing a good job." In London, later, he was to boast, "There are no better soldiers in the world than the Jews."

The Ethiopian campaign had been a different matter. There, he had to accustom highly divergent groups to working together and persuade the Ethiopians to use European arms. In Burma he had somewhat the same problem.

His Burma contingent, this time, included Scots of the Black Watch, West Africans, and Indian troops who were mostly Gurkhas. The West African blacks were big, ebony fellows, of magnificent physique, broad shoulders, small waists, tremendous arms and big heads. They were shiny black, had huge muscles, and were very gay. They couldn't speak English, except for two words, their greeting. This was "Hello, Johnny." Any American they saw, even if he were a full general, they'd greet with "Hello, Johnny." They knew the British ranks, but not the American, and would shout "Hello, Johnny," at anyone in an American uniform.

The Air Commandos practiced glider flights with Wingate soldiers they were to carry in the invasion. One West African went to his commanding officer, and said, "Sir, I am not afraid to fly, but I must tell you that those airplanes have no motors!"

They had one bad accident. Back at Wilmington, Ohio, a glider pilot had been killed in the pickup. Now at Lalaghat, a crash killed seven men, including four British soldiers. Something went wrong after a night take-off. Flying double tow, one glider got in the propeller wash of the plane ahead, and went out of control. Both gliders released. One made a safe landing. The other crashed.

The fatalities threatened to have a bad psychologic consequence. They had to use glider pilots for the coffin-building and funerals. That could have had a bad emotional effect on the glider section. Still worse, the morale of the Wingate troops assigned to gliders might be impaired. In these they had built confidence in gliders, and wondered whether the casualties might not affect their will to fly at the end of tow lines. They received a note from the commander of the Wingate unit to which the men who had been killed belonged. He stated that after a talk with his group, he had been asked to convey the following: "Please be assured that we will go with your boys any place, any time, anywhere."

Wingate's troops were called Chindits. This was a mispronunciation of the Burmese word *Chintha*, the grotesque mythical animal that guards Burmese temples. Cochran considered the name a symbolism of Wingate's own aspiring. "The Man had a sort of mystic attitude. He knew he was going to be 'Wingate of Burma,' like 'Lawrence of Arabia.' He took the attitude of being a great Burmese, but I never heard him give a command in Burmese or ever say a word in that language. He had a way of dramatizing himself. That was his approach to native peoples. He seemed to say to the Burmese: 'I am Wingate, I am your protector. You are a wonderful people with a wonderful civilization. The Japs have come in to oppress you, but I, with the Chintha that guards your temples, will release you.' He called his flag the Chintha Emblem."

Wingate, an introvert by nature, possessed deep convictions which bade him try to achieve sympathy with subject peoples. Before he had left Delhi on the first campaign, while he was in the planning stage, he had read extensively about the religion and customs of the Burmese and even of the Japanese, whom he was to fight. He wanted to understand even the enemy mentality.

If he did not talk readily in Burmese it was because his gift for languages was primarily for reading. He had the introvert's shyness until discussion, the need to make a point, carried him into a long argument, when, as Cochran said, he would make a speech. Nervous excitement could make him talk; in the tension at the end of the first Burma campaign, he was said to have talked for a week. But his talk ranged over a wide area—history, literature, and the soldier's favorite subject, "What will you do when the war is over?" Wingate's own plans ranged from settling in Burma to becoming a literary critic.

As for the Chintha Emblem, it was like Wingate's insistence, in the Ethiopian campaign, that the Ethiopian soldiers serving under him be called "Patriots." He wanted the African and Asiatic peoples to value their own importance and cling to their own cultures. In Palestine he had no trouble, of course, appealing to national pride, but even there, on one occasion, he had gone farther with history than his young followers were prepared to appreciate. This was when, applying Bible tactics to Bible terrain, he seriously undertook to carry out Gideon's maneuver with the trumpets as related in the seventh chapter of the Book of Judges.

A sergeant was sent into Haifa to obtain rams' horns, the

THE CHINTHA GUARDIAN at the temple gate.

trumpets used by Gideon; but whether the mission was wholly uncongenial or merely difficult, the sergeant reported back without the horns. Try again, said Wingate inexorably, and on a second trip the sergeant was able to find one ram's horn, which no one could blow, and to borrow several modern metal trumpets from the fire brigade. They weren't at all what Wingate had in mind but he did his best with them, calling for them to be sounded by embarrassed noncoms who all too plainly lacked their leader's familiarity with Bible precedent. An issue of Bren guns, which were highly acceptable as substitutes for the swords of Gideon's band, saved the day.

Had Cochran been present on that occasion he might have failed to appreciate the flavor, the symbolism of Wingate's idea. Alison, born in the Bible Belt and more familiar with Gideon, might have understood better. Maybe the improved relations between Cochran and Wingate, as they worked together, were in part due to the intervention of the soft-spoken Southerner, who never failed in loyalty to Cochran yet had a much different background for understanding Wingate.

Cochran, with his own energetic nature and frank ambition to excel, saw ambition as the guiding force in Wingate, just as he had considered it competition in drinking when Alison joined his Russian or his Chinese hosts in their national drinks. Wingate's own explanation of his effort to adapt himself to the customs and culture of his brothers-in-arms went back to Palestine, where, as the Jewish soldiers noticed, he always said "we," not "you." At that time he explained that to ask people to fight for you without joining in the battle on equal terms was an insult both to the ally and to oneself. He proposed to fight with the Jews, not merely to arm them, as the Axis was arming the Arabs.

LOCAL TRANSPORTATION:
Bullock carts are still the thing on Burma roads.

"WE'VE FOUGHT WITH MANY MEN ACROSS THE SEAS"

So, with regard to the Burmese, Wingate had said during his first campaign: "I am convinced that the method of going in with a bag of gold is all wrong. Don't pay people to fight for you. They won't respect you. They'll say to themselves, 'If they've got rifles, why don't they use them?' My method is to tell people, 'We've come to fight a common enemy. We don't need you to fight our battles for us. But if you want to help, show us what you can do and we may give you arms.' To raise a real fighting revolt, you must send in a *corps d'élite* to do exploits, not peddlers of cash and ammunition."

In Burma, for the first time in his war experience, Wingate faced almost insurmountable obstacles in organizing the native population. The white man's record had not been consistent enough to make clear his present purpose, and to the Burmese it was difficult to explain why soldiers under the British or the American flag should be welcomed rather than soldiers under the flag of Japan. The Chintha Emblem was Wingate's only answer to the Rising Sun, when his translators with their multigraphed broadsides proved ineffective.

In the fabulous lands of India and Burma, the young Americans with Cochran and Alison discovered many fascinating things to see and do, when they could take time off from the war. Their leaders, of course, were always busy. Cochran saw India's wonder of the world, the Taj Mahal, only when he happened to fly that way.

He had, however, a story about it. "They tried to sell one of our kids from New York the Taj Mahal. He said, 'Have you ever seen the Empire State Building?' Later, when I got home, I stole that idea. At the Erie Club I was talking with my Dad and the owner of the Erie *Times*. They asked, 'What did you think of the Taj Mahal?' and I said that, as far as I was concerned, the Erie Brewing Company building was

BURMA GIRL with the "whackin' white cheroot" of Kipling's *Mandalay*.

a majestic edifice. The owner of that brewery sent me a case of beer for that remark."

What about the Burmese girls? Kipling thought enough of them to picture one sitting and thinking by the pagoda in his famous poem. Well, they noticed the women in Burma and India, naturally. "The first thing that amazed me," Cochran said, "was the graceful walk of the women in India. They get that from carrying heavy loads on their heads. We saw them first in Karachi, where they were carrying crushed rock. Two men would lift a basket of rock onto a woman's head, and she would climb a ladder with it. She would move her head to balance the load.

"We saw them carrying bricks, and watched to see if there were any champions among the women. No, probably because they belonged to a union. Ten was the number of bricks each carried on her head. We were hoping that some doll would take twelve, but none ever did.

"While carrying loads on their heads, they were skillful in keeping their clothes around them, loose clothes, wrapped around, nothing tight. If the wind blew, they would move dextrously, keeping covered. If we went up and looked at them, they'd draw the veil over their faces, while carrying bricks on their heads.

"The people of the villages near the bases in Manipur, on the Burma border, were different. They were of a Mongolian type, akin to the races of the nearby Himalayas, like the Gurkhas, and the Tibetans. They had beautiful skin, much fairer than the dark Hindus of Bengal. In Hindu sections, if we came along in a jeep, the women would run away, covering their faces, but not in Manipur. There were women all over the place, and they weren't frightened when we came near them. The people there had a different attitude. They smiled. They were a gay people. They were more like the Chinese. The Chinese, when you go by, grin."

The thing they had to deal with eternally was the jungle, flying over it, landing in it, surrounded by it, living in it, in *bashas* among the trees. Cochran expresses the hostility: "We tolerated the jungle, but we would have nothing to do with it. The only thing I remember about it is the sound of peculiar birds. There was one bird that called, 'Ora! Ora!' all the time. He would wake us up in the morning, 'Ora, ora.' We'd hear Oley Olson call back, 'He isn't here!' There were big frogs, one of which, in a pit near our *basha*, kept saying, 'Schedule.' That was John Alison's cue. When the frog started croaking, 'Schedule, schedule,' John would go to the door and shout back, 'The schedule isn't ready.'"

"We heard of tea planters in the neighborhood going tiger hunting, how so-and-so got a big tiger twelve miles away. But we never saw any. There were cobras, kraits and vipers, all very poisonous. The Russell's viper is a green snake, beautiful in color, with a triangular head, small, fast and dangerous."

John Alison liked the jungle. He lived much in the tropical forest at Broadway—one of their bases later in the campaign—and recalls it sentimentally. "The jungle, which had seemed so terrifying the night we landed, was not nearly so uninviting when daylight came. I was surprised to see that it didn't have dense undergrowth. It was just a big forest, pleasant, with beautiful trees. The jungle wasn't really unfriendly, except that it was hard to find anything to eat in it. We lived among the trees on the edge of the airfield. It was the dry season of the year, the ground dry and hard. There were no insects. I enjoyed it.

"Hailikandi was a beautiful place, like a movie set. It was rolling country, the flying field set in rice paddies between low hills. The *bashas* in which we lived were grass huts, pleasant, sweet-smelling, clean. Hailikandi was delightful. Until the rains came, the skies were clear and blue. The jungle was an impressive thing, with a tremendous amount of beauty. At Broadway, the woods were open and parklike, though when you penetrated deeply there were dense vines and underbrush. Our camp site was one of the loveliest

CHINDIT EMBLEM: Insignia derived from the Burmese temple guardians. Here Lt. Col. Clint Gaty presents a plaque bearing the emblem to T/Sgt. Paul H. Abernathy, receiving it on behalf of the enlisted men.

places you could think of, under tremendous teakwood trees. The weather was ideal, hot in the middle of the day and cold at nights. If we hadn't been fighting a war, it would have been a perfect outing, until the rains came. Then you forgot how beautiful it was, and you thought only of the mud.

"We could see traces of elephants. There was a tribe of baboons. We could hear them screaming. They would whoop it up for about an hour every day. There were tigers in the jungle, but we never saw one, only tiger trails. There were very few birds, no flowers, just creepers and vines. There were leeches in some parts but not where we were, Broadway being in a comparatively dry stretch of jungle.

"I should like to go back some day, build a shack among the trees and live in the jungle for a vacation." When Alison talked that way, Cochran just looked at him. Even between the Americans there were differences of opinion that could not be bridged.

But Wingate, with his Chintha emblem and the universal language of the cartoon, made at least one successful gesture of international accord. With the drawing of the mythical animal which became part of the Wingate and the Air Commando insignia, also made by Milton Caniff who had drawn the winged mule, Wingate paid a compliment not only to the Burmese but, at the same time, to Flip Corkin of the funnies.

12. "Gentlemen Unafraid"

TWO JUNGLE CLEARINGS were to be seized by air invasion. They were selected by Wingate for maximum effect against the Japanese army in northern Burma. The Man had in mind the strategies of the military situation at their largest. The clearings were at a vital spot for the Japs.

In the extreme north of Burma, General Stilwell's American-Chinese army was advancing through jungle country. Stilwell had annexed Merrill's Marauders, the ranger outfit that General Marshall had intended for Wingate. He had, moreover, one Wingate brigade which was pushing south in advance of his right flank. The air invasion was designed to strike behind the enemy forces opposing Stilwell, disrupt their rear communications and cut off their supplies. The Japs, on their part, were planning a push westward into India for a threat against the route of supplies for Stilwell's army. The strategy on both sides was one of thrusting at supply lines, with the Wingate thrust to be through the air.

"GENTLEMEN UNAFRAID"

Supplies for the Japs facing Stilwell moved north on the Irrawaddy River and along a rail and highway route. This was their life line. At Katha, on the Irrawaddy, a rail spur ran westward and above Indaw connected with railroad and highway, a junction of river and land routes. This was the Indaw-Katha bottleneck, where the life line of Jap resistance against Stilwell was the most vulnerable. Wingate planned to cut the bottleneck. The two jungle clearings to be seized were in the Indaw-Katha area. They were forty miles apart, each situated well within striking distance of strategic points along the bottleneck of the Japanese life line. From the two clearings, established as air bases and strongholds, Wingate's long-range penetration columns could operate against the river, rail and highway supply routes.

The Man still called the campaign long-range penetration. "But," Cochran insists, "it had become the opposite of that. It was really short-range penetration. The long part of it was to be done through the air. The seizing of bases in the jungle would eliminate the long trek of troops through the wilderness. From the bases Wingate columns would be able to reach vital objectives in a short time and with short jungle marches. But Wingate stuck to his original name."

He flew with Cochran and Alison to inspect the clearings. He knew them from his campaign of the previous year. In one, an R.A.F. transport had been able to land and take out injured soldiers during Wingate's tragic difficulties with his wounded. As they flew over the jungle, Cochran and Alison were surprised by the many clearings that gliders could use. From two thousand feet they could note details, see the grass, brown grass. At the two suggested by Wingate, they said yes, they were suitable for glider landings.

Names were given, names appropriate to the British-American character of the air invasion. One they called

Piccadilly, the one out of which Wingate wounded had been flown the previous year. That was to be the principal base. They called the other Broadway.

The jungle clearings were photographed, camera studies made for a detailed planning of the landings. Pilots who were to fly in the invasion were taken over Piccadilly and Broadway to familiarize them with the route and the contours of the forest glades. Then Wingate ordered planes to stay away from the invasion area. This was a precaution for secrecy. Wingate was afraid that, if the Japs saw planes flying around Piccadilly and Broadway, they might suspect something was planned in that direction. It might be a tip-off.

They now had achieved fulfillment of Hap Arnold's hope of collaboration. Gone was the poor impression that Cochran had made on Wingate in London. "He seldom showed any affection toward anybody, but he did to me. And John Alison tickled him. He liked John." The Man's campaign whiskers were long enough now for his soldiers to call him "The Beard." To a habit of running a comb through his hair was added a further maneuver of combing his beard at odd times. One Air Commando says: "I was always fascinated by Wingate's curious mannerisms, little things like folding the lobe of one ear forward and then letting it pop back. His way of combing his beard was curious too. He'd pass the comb down through the whiskers time and again in a slow and gentle way. Then, for a finisher, he'd whip the comb up roughly through the hair on his jaws the opposite way."

To Cochran and Alison, The Man made the long speeches to which he was addicted. At first they were baffled, as Cochran had been when he met Wingate in London, by the gurgling tones and the English idiosyncrasies of speech. "He

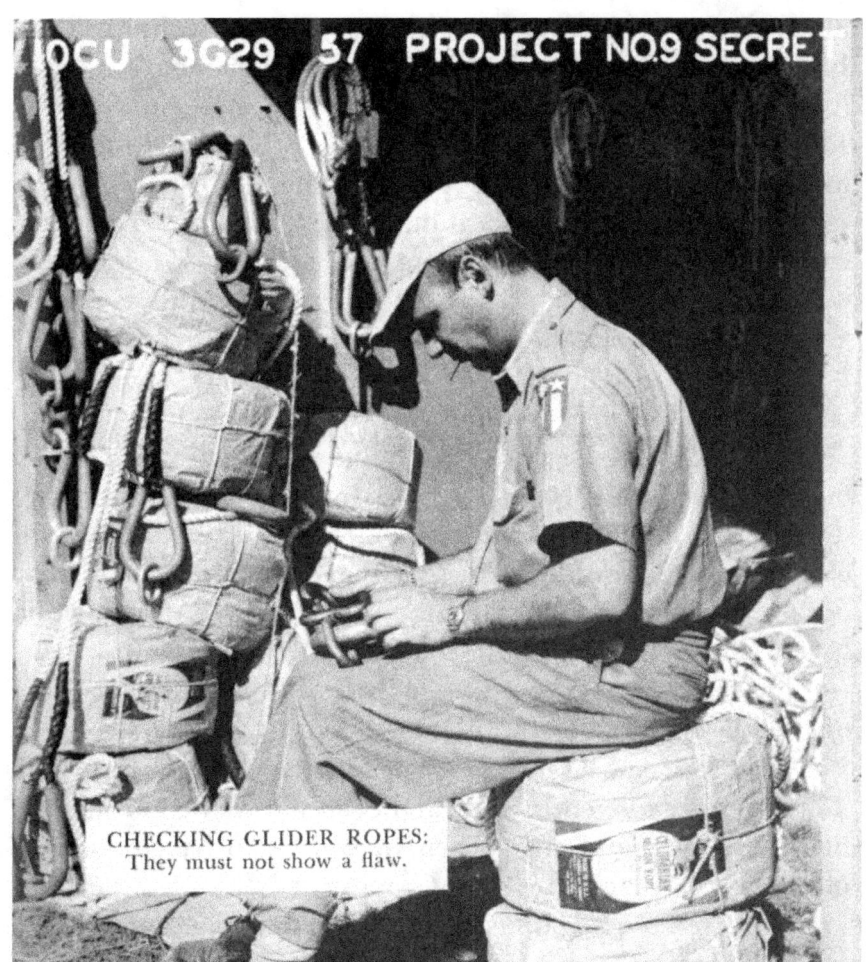

CHECKING GLIDER ROPES:
They must not show a flaw.

talked clearly when you got used to it," says Cochran, "but that was difficult. I cured him of his habit of mouthing and dropping last phrases. I asked him to repeat them so often that he quit it. He got tired of saying the same thing over and over again, and talked clearly. The English build up terrible habits in their speaking. They will say, 'Doncherknow, haw, haw,' and then drop the last part of what they are saying. We found that some Britishers didn't understand that kind of talk either, and didn't much care.

"The Man had a habit of walking up and down while talking. He was very nervous. He would soon have me up beside him, while he paced back and forth with that short, buoyant gait of his. He looked old, but he had the springing step of a boy. If Prime Minister Churchill started to talk with him, Wingate would pretty soon have him interested, and both of them would be walking up and down. After a while I refused to let him pull that walking trick with me. I wouldn't get up. I knew that as soon as he started walking he would go into an oration, and waste time."

There were never-ending surprises in the topics on which The Man would embark, and never mind the business at hand. One day at lunch, when they were to have conferred on invasion plans, he told Cochran all about pineapple. "He told me the advantages of good pineapple, and why he loved it. He made a long address about that, about food in general and pineapple in particular. Another time he informed us that if a man ate enough onions, he would never be ill. He believed that old wives' tale, and he had a lot of arguments to prove it.

"He always carried a book with him, something deep. Sometimes he would give it to me to read. I would take the book, put it aside, and give it back to him, never reading it. The tome would be about philosophy, something profound.

There was one book that intrigued him no end. It was by Damon Runyon. He told me that Damon Runyon was really something as an author."

Cochran found a book he liked and told Alison was funny. Alison started it and told Olson it was funny. The book passed from hand to hand, Gene Fowler's life of John Barrymore, *Good Night, Sweet Prince.* Cochran says: "We'd be having a meeting to discuss plans of operation. Somebody, probably Oley Olson, would start reading aloud passages from the book, like the place where John Barrymore, when a young actor, loused up the performance of a famous star. Supposed to bring a message to the great actor, Barrymore appeared with a piece of paper the size of a postage stamp, and said, 'Here's your message.' The star, upset, told Barrymore to get the real message. Barrymore went out and came back with the same postage stamp, saying, 'The telegram was written by the fellow who engraves the Lord's Prayer on the heads of pins.' We howled over Barrymore's gags, thinking what a crazy guy he was."

On the first Burma campaign, Wingate and his officers had formed a reading group. They found relaxation in literary discussion on a level surprising to Americans. Their commander-in-chief, Wavell, was of course to compile an anthology of poetry remembered in the midst of war. Wingate's officers not only wrote readable accounts of the campaign, they set down the range of reading covered and discussed in training and, later, in the jungle. In training, due perhaps to Wingate's insistence on Tarzan stunts and the methods of American Indian attack, there was a wave of enthusiasm for stories of the American West, and officers schooled at Eton greeted each other with "Howdy, buckaroo! Which way you ridin'?" or reminded each other that "There's Japs in them thar hills."

When actual jungle penetration began, it was a case of choosing books to carry or to receive with rations sent by air (there were no supply lines). Such a selection had to be limited. Poetry and *Punch* could be expected to appear on the list. But one officer had Shaw's plays, and Wingate agreed that Shaw and Wells were the only important British writers of the era. One specialized in Trollope, while another argued with Wingate the merits of a new biography of the Brontës. On the last lap of that journey, Wingate himself still had, besides his Bible, Plato, Xenophon, and Mark Twain's *Innocents Abroad*.

Walking through the jungle, they played what they called the "cliché game"—the undergrowth was "lush," the orchids were "exotic," and so on. They were also able to communicate in terms of the Bible that was Wingate's mother tongue. Their rations dropped from the air became "manna from heaven," for instance. Once, when supplies got low, an officer after Wingate's own heart wirelessed wistfully, "See Psalms 22:17" (*I may tell all my bones....*). Wingate wirelessed back, "John 11:50." (*.... it is expedient for us, that one man should die for the people....*).

Cochran, as he came to know Wingate better, played some droll tricks on him. Once, as Cochran recalls, he and Oley Olson flew Wingate to his base in an ancient Lockheed that might have been a relic of World War I. "So we put on an act for him. I would say, 'Hey Oley, how do you start this thing?' Then we would ask the sergeant of the ground crew, 'How do you start this?' Wingate could not quite bring himself to say, 'Look here, can you fly this?' We told him we had never been in a plane of that type before. The Man was badly worried, but never gave a sign of it."

Cochran's anti-British prejudice relaxed when he discovered that Wingate was disliked by his own army. Gold

RIGGING COMMUNICATIONS: Pilots string phone wires from glider to tow plane.

braid above him was hostile. His command went straight to the top. That is, he was there by the mandate of the Quebec Conference, Roosevelt-Churchill. The Indian army didn't like that. Also he was famous for telling off the R.A.F.

Not only did he have the right to go straight to Churchill, he often did. He'd grow angry, call a stenographer and say, "Take a screed to the Prime Minister." Then he would send to Mountbatten, and to people about whom he was complaining, copies of the screed.

He said, "Don't be frightened, Phil, we'll get our way. I will resign, and they know I will."

"And they did know," comments Cochran, "because he was the fellow who had cut his throat once, in protest. They didn't dare let him resign. If they did, the Prime Minister himself might come out and start looking things over."

Cochran saw this, however, in terms of personal ambition and power. At one time, he remembered, Wingate told him not to be disturbed because he saw double-dealing going on in high places. "Look, Phil, don't be upset. War is a terrible thing, a thing men build fortunes on. Many fellows out here will rise high through the war, and many fellows in Britain will make great amounts of money. That is the kind of people we are dealing with." Recalling this, Cochran adds that he thought it odd to hear such sentiments from a man who had made war his lifework. But it was not so odd. Wingate had become a soldier only because the world lacked adequate organization to keep the peace.

Wingate's conviction that war could be waged most effectively by men who knew what they were fighting for, Cochran also interpreted in terms of ambition: "Wingate had a great sense of publicity. To him it was power. He used publicity to push himself along." Besides the correspondents attached to Wingate's headquarters, of whom there were several because he was always good "copy," and besides the staff he maintained for issuing broadsides to native populations in the fighting area, he always took great pains to inform officers and men of what was ahead of them. He believed it gave you more confidence to know where you were going, what was to be done. Wingate's troops were given frequent briefings, with maps, to convey a knowledge of the position and a sense of direction in their movement over streams and new country. Also, he now got his officers together to hear about the new air-invasion plans.

Cochran and Alison divided the task of explaining. "They knew nothing about airplanes," Cochran said, "and I don't think they thought we were telling the truth. We would explain what our planes and gliders were going to do in their campaign, and they just simply didn't believe it.

"The Wingate officers varied from people who talk pretty much as we talk, with hardly any accent at all, to traditional theatrical Englishmen of the stage. I used to think that vaudevillians were burlesquing an English lord when they talked in that gag way, but actually Wingate had an officer who was even more so. He had so much of this haw-haw business that it would take him hours to come out with something. He drove us crazy. Some Englishmen made long speeches, and we didn't know what they were talking about.

"In making an hour-long educational address I would use American expressions, and they would laugh. That amused them no end. I have a habit of saying 'dream up.' I'd remark, 'Well, I'll dream up something.' They'd say, 'Dream up, ha, ha, ha.'"

13. "Their Lives Are on My Head"

THE LEADER OF THEIR FIGHTER SQUADRON had a personal grudge against the Japs. He was Grant Mahoney, who already had behind him enough war records for several men. He had been in the Philippines when the Japs invaded, one of the airmen who performed wonders with pitiful equipment. When the Philippines were falling he was moved to Java, and did more than his share of the fighting in that hopeless battle. He carried on an individual campaign against the Japs in Java until the island fell, then went to Australia. He thought he would continue in combat, but was sent to India as an aide to General Brady. He hated that, though he liked the general. He wanted action, and General Brady allowed him to go to China and join Chennault. There he continued his battle against the Japs, and emerged with a record of fourteen enemy planes, not including those destroyed on the ground.

In China, Mahoney met John Alison. They became fast friends, and when Project Nine selected a commander for its

LT. COLONEL GRANT MAHONEY didn't like Japs.

fighter plane unit. Alison said automatically, "Mahoney." They never considered anybody else. Alison called him by long distance, and Mahoney could hardly wait to join them.

"He considered it a personal war," Cochran says. "First, because so many of his close friends had been killed and captured by them. Second, because the Japs had kicked Mahoney himself out of so many places. He was sick of being pushed around by Japs, shoved out of the Philippines, driven out of Java. His one big idea was to push Japs around."

Mahoney was tall and slender, with thick, black curly hair, and a face that shone with Irish good looks. He had an Irish temper, and a determined Irish jaw. He was black Irish, and John Alison sometimes said to him, "Mahoney, what kind of an Irishman are you? You're not a Catholic and you don't drink." "John," explains Cochran, "meant that he was so different from me. John was used to my kind of Irish."

Mahoney had piercing blue eyes, was soft-spoken, and lisped. He had a peculiar manner of delicate speech, was shy, reticent, and self-effacing. "You would never dream," says Cochran, "that he was a terribly ferocious fellow, but actually he was. He was obsessed with a fanaticism and a mania for fighting Japs. He was a Jap-killer."

In the recruiting of Project Nine Mahoney had picked fighter pilots after his own heart, killers of the air. For a second-in-command he selected Bob Pettit, a veteran of Guadalcanal. Pettit had flown and fought in the Guadalcanal air battles for eighteen months, with hundreds of combat hours, and had won a string of decorations. When rumors got around that fighter pilots were being enlisted for an assignment of especial adventure and hazard, applications poured in. They phoned from Chicago, the West Coast, Florida, begging for the chance to go overseas. "You don't have to hunt for fighter pilots in the United States, not if you have a combat assignment for them. They were on our neck all the time."

They got two test pilots from Wright Field, another who had flown with the Royal Canadian Air Force, and still another who had been in the Aleutians. In Florida was stationed a group used to test new tactics. Whenever an original maneuver was thought of, it was sent to them to be tried out. They were superb fighter pilots, who had never had a chance to get into the air. Mahoney went to their base, and lined up all he needed.

Project Nine had brought to India no bombers, Wingate having promised Cochran in London that the R.A.F. would provide a squadron. This promise failed, there were no bombers from the R.A.F. Cochran and Alison fell back on their letter of authorization from Chief of Staff General Marshall and Air Force Commander General Arnold. Armed with this they went to General Stratemeyer, American Air Force commander in India, and asked for an entire B-25 squadron, medium bombardment. The general got in touch with Washington, and explained the situation. Washington replied with an okay. "We got the B-25s."

They had neither bomber pilots, gunners nor crew men. They got what they could, pilots and gunners, in India, and from China. They had to have a leader for the bomber squadron. They knew nobody in the India-China area, and anyway wanted a leader who would organize a bomber force according to their way of doing things. What they needed was one of their own outfit who was a bomber man, only none was. They had to draft a fighter pilot.

"We solved the dilemma by going to tall, long-drink-of-water R. T. (Tadpole) Smith. He had fought the Japs with Chennault in China, and had a great record, eleven Japs shot down. He was an enthusiastic fighter pilot, but had never been in a B-25 in his life. We told R. T. he was going to be transferred to bombing, which is almost an insult to a fighter pilot. But R. T. Smith was an amiable fellow. He understood. We promised him, moreover, that while running the bomber show he could have his own fighter plane and go on Jap fighting missions whenever he wanted to.

"R. T. Smith was so competent that he could plunge into bombardment aviation, to which he was a stranger, master it in a hurry, and do a job of organization immediately. He took, moreover, the fighter-pilot spirit into bombing. He would handle those B-25s as if they were fighters."

On February 3 the fighters and bombers began an offensive. It was a prelude to invasion, a thundering campaign to disrupt opposition they might encounter in the seizure of jungle bases. This they regarded as the real beginning of the Air Commando operation. They were now under their proper name, the First Air Commando Unit. It was striking violently at the Jap, and the anonymity of Project Nine was no longer needed. In Washington, Cochran and Alison had promised General Arnold that the operation would begin on February 1. They were two days late.

Grant Mahoney's fighter planes began the offensive with strafing, bombing and rocket fire against enemy air bases to the south of the invasion area. Japanese air power that might be thrown against the air invasion was concentrated down that way, near Mandalay. Day after day the Japs were harried from the air, Mahoney's fighters and R. T. Smith's bombers were on a ferocious campaign, fighting air battles with the Japs, burning their planes on the ground. They blasted airdromes, smashed gasoline supplies. They burned warehouses, shot up concentrations of troops, blew out bridges.

PRELUDE TO INVASION: Bombs drop from B-25 toward Jap base below. Inset: R. T. Smith.

The offensive, pounding to the south of the area they intended to invade, had likewise a purpose of misdirection. They made it appear that they were striking at the communications of the Jap army facing Imphal Valley for a drive into India. "We did everything to pretend that our purpose was to break Japanese communications with the Imphal front, a supply line all the way back to Mandalay. We never missed a day sending our planes down there to keep their minds on the wrong idea.

"The Japs knew that we were established at our bases. They sent planes over and took pictures, and the Indians around the bases were giving them stuff a mile a minute. They knew we had gliders, a tip-off that something unusual was afoot. But they didn't think we were as big as we were. They underestimated, and our offensive was calculated to give them a false idea why we were there, to hit the communications of this Imphal army instead of the real thing, the air invasion.

"At the same time our pilots were learning the district to the south of the invasion area, the district from which trouble would come after we were at Piccadilly and Broadway. We insisted that the leaders should learn the district from A to Z, so that when talking we would be talking about things we had seen. That's a habit a fighter pilot picks up. Then you can say, 'You know where the Chindwin branches off and the Salween makes that funny right-hand bend?' Everybody says yes. 'Well, about forty-five yards from there there's an opening in the jungle.' "

They were running an offensive that was actually a defense. Cochran had seen that kind of strategy at close range in Tunisia. "It was the German way. When their air force came at you hour after hour, you knew something was going on back there that they were defending."

"THEIR LIVES ARE ON MY HEAD"

They had one hard time near Mandalay. They lost two fighters, and Cochran was reported lost. "We were on a dive-bombing mission, but before we came up from our dive-bombing run, the Jap was above us with more than we had. He was tired of the hell we had been raising and had brought up a lot of fighters. We lost two boys and most of us were shot up. The Jap caught us in a bad position, and gave us quite a beating.

"I was reported here in America as having been killed at Mandalay. My picture was in the home-town paper with an obituary. I knew nothing about it. How the report got out I don't know. Evidently somebody heard a radio conversation in which R. T. Smith said my fighter plane had been shot down and I was a goner. They heard R. T. Smith, but not my answer, 'The hell I am!'"

Wingate put a stop to Cochran's fun. The Man went to the United States Army authorities in India and got an order that Cochran was no longer to fly over Burma. Neither was John Alison nor Oley Olson. As top officers of the aerial task force, they knew the whole plan for the campaign, and if the Japs caught them it would go hard for them. Wingate said, "You probably would be smart enough to tell them a lie, but they would give you no peace."

While the fighter-bomber offensive was on, the prelude to invasion, the gliders were active. The Wingate brigade attached to Stilwell's army was having difficulties, as it pushed southward through jungles. Its commander, Brigadier Ferguson, called for Air Commando help. In the path of advance was a Jap radio station used to warn and coordinate enemy troops. Air Commando planes bombed the station, but failed to knock it out. Cochran and Alison decided to eliminate it with a glider blow, a patrol of Chindit troops to be

"THEIR LIVES ARE ON MY HEAD"

landed by glider, then to attack and destroy the Jap radio station, and finally to be picked up in their glider.

The landing place was on the upper Chindwin, a sandbank. This had been scouted from the air, but aerial photographs failed to show a trench in the sand. The glider, with flight officers John Price and John Gotham as pilot and co-pilot, hit the trench. The landing gear was knocked off and one wing collapsed. Three Wingate soldiers were injured. Japs were near, and bullets soon were flying. Minus their means of flying back, the commanding officer of the Chindit patrol decided to push on and attack the radio station, and, after destroying it, to march northward for a junction with Ferguson's brigade. The two glider pilots and the three injured British soldiers were to walk back to the base whence they had come.

They made a trek of 130 miles through the jungle, including a swim of seven miles down the Chindwin River to escape Japanese patrols. They ate what food they could find in the jungle and drank water from buffalo holes. They returned safely, the American airmen reporting that the jungle was a friend which had provided food and shelter from the Japanese, shelter also from the local natives. They had carefully avoided tribal villages, because they had passed through the home grounds of the Naga headhunters.

Ferguson's brigade, pushing south through the jungle, came to the Chindwin, and that brought a crisis, the crossing of the river. In the previous Wingate campaign a similar crossing of the Chindwin had been a formidable task. This time the river problem was complicated by a ticklish military situation. Stilwell's army, on the right flank of which Ferguson's brigade was advancing, got into a fight with the Japs. There were Japs all around. Ferguson's brigade didn't want a battle just then. They wanted to get farther down into

THE BLACK WATCH BOARDS A GLIDER with jaunty step and cheerful grin.

"THEIR LIVES ARE ON MY HEAD"

the jungles. They had to cross the Chindwin, and do it in a hurry, before the enemy realized what was happening. A few Japs on the opposite bank could have wrecked the river crossing. They picked a place for a crossing. The river was wide, deep and turbulent. They needed boats, efficient boats with motors. Assault boats were flown by glider. This was the kind of job that Cochran and Alison had envisioned for their gliders before the plan had been changed to air invasion, the delivery of heavy equipment to Wingate forces.

Twelve folded boats with outboard motors were loaded into gliders. Taking off before dusk, transport planes towed the gliders over the mountains, and after dark arrived at the point of the Chinwin River where Ferguson's brigade was waiting. They made landings on the sandy banks. Boats and motors were unloaded and delivered by Ferguson. One glider had its wheels torn off by landing in the soft sand. The other was picked up, but not before there had been a tangle of error.

The towing planes were circling overhead, waiting for the pickup. The transport pilots spotted other planes, thought they were Japanese, and headed for home. There they learned they had seen supply planes, their own light planes flying provisions to Ferguson's troops. They were sent and motors were unloaded and delivered to Ferguson. One of Ferguson's soldiers had been seriously injured, his leg broken. They took him out too, the first time a casualty had ever been evacuated by glider. When they landed, Vincent Rose found that only one strand of his tow rope was left. He had flown 250 miles over mountains with a breaking tow rope.

Ferguson's brigade crossed the Chindwin with loaded assault boats towing loaded rafts. In fast time they got troops, equipment and mules across, undetected by the Japs.

"THEIR LIVES ARE ON MY HEAD"

There were complicated Chindit-Air-Commando devices to fool the Japs and keep them from suspecting that air invasion was afoot. Wingate sent patrols to the Chindwin, into

GALA DAY AT LALAGHAT:
Red Cross girls, doughnuts, and
plenty of coffee.

a sector where his long-range penetration columns had operated the previous year. His plan was to throw the enemy off guard by giving the impression that this year's operation was to be much the same as last year's. Dummy paratroops were dropped. Soldiers were landed and picked up by glider. Equipment was tossed around so the Japs would find it and think a large Wingate force was moving across the Chindwin. Patrols went into villages, and asked where they could get food for six thousand troops and fodder for six hundred mules. The Japs picked up the wild tip. All this was stage play to draw the enemy's attention away from the place where the blow would fall.

Meanwhile, an enterprise of another kind, also requiring secrecy, was happily managed. Bill Taylor and Clint Gaty heard of American Red Cross nurses at an Army center near Calcutta. As D-Day approached they decided to provide a wonderful surprise. "We'd give the boys a final look-see at American beauties before they entered the campaign in the dark jungle."

They flew the girls down. Great baskets of doughnuts came too, and a garbage can full of coffee was made. At Lalaghat the nurses presided over a doughnut and coffee feast, a nostalgic American prelude to air-jungle war.

"We kept it all a secret from Phil and John and the boys up at Hailikandi," the plotters recalled. "We knew that if they heard anything about it, we wouldn't have a chance of bringing the girls down. Not until a month later did Phil and John run across the photographs we made while they were serving the doughnuts and coffee, and learn how we slipped one over, just before the D-Day."

14. "Good Hunting, All That Keep the Jungle Law"

THEIR BURMA D-DAY was set for March 5, during the first full moon after the monsoon rains. Cochran called it their Ides of March. The glider trains were to take off at sundown and proceed into the night. They would fly most of the way and make their landings under the cover of darkness, in the glimmer of the tropical full moon. The schedule called for the landing of eighty gliders loaded with assault troops and equipment on the first night, forty gliders for the seizure of Piccadilly, an equal number for Broadway.

They had expected to launch the invasion from a secondary base. East of Hailikandi and Lalaghat was a range of mountains, up to eight thousand feet in height. Their secondary advance base was to have been beyond this, at Tamu, on the other side of the mountains. Beyond Tamu were only low hills. Thus they planned to avoid the necessity of taking heavily loaded glider trains over the high range. They would fly the gliders empty to Tamu and load them there for take-offs on a route unimpeded by lofty summits. Tamu, moreover, was a hundred and twenty miles nearer to Piccadilly and Broadway, shortening a long haul. At Tamu they cut down trees, and lengthened the field, so that the double-tows of heavy gliders could take off.

Then information came that the Japanese were infiltrating across the Chindwin into the Tiddim area and were approaching the Tamu base. This was the beginning of the enemy invasion of India, the drive into Imphal Valley to threaten the supply line for Stilwell's advance in northern Burma. The Air Commandos hoped to use Tamu before the Japs got there, but the plan had to be abandoned. The Japs were too close to Tamu. They captured the base the day before the air invasion was launched. This meant that the glider invasion would have to climb over the mountains. The heavily loaded glider trains, upon taking off, would have to ascend to above eight thousand feet to clear the range before they could head for Piccadilly and Broadway. The route to these, moreover, was now 120 miles longer, extra flying time for tow planes and gliders.

There was a crescendo of planning, an excess, according to Cochran and Alison. "The British went into mazes of detailed scheduling. There was too much planning. We would have done it by saying, 'What do you want and where?' The British planned down to every tin can, where it was going, at what time, where each plane went, where each mule went. The British had operations tents, where they piled up an amount of detail that was a terrible effort. Being against paper work, we shied away. We knew that in actual operations the plans would have to change, but the British habit was to schedule everything. Wingate, in his report afterwards,

IT'S SHAPED LIKE A FISH: Cochran briefs glider pilots on the geography of Burma.

laughed at his own people and himself for making all those schedules. In his wry way, The Man commented that there was one thing the schedules did do, if anybody called upon his people for a new schedule, they could get it up in record-breaking time. They had had the practice."

The briefings were long and complex. All along, they had been given orientation lectures, imparting information about the country they would fly over. Routes had been laid out with a view to the best altitudes and the avoidance of enemy strong points and of sections occupied by hostile natives. Rendezvous points had been selected for such as might be forced down in the Burma jungle. All of which was hammered into pilots' minds with intense briefing. Because of the lack of better equipment, they used bedsheets for making sketches instead of the sand-table models and large photographs that were customary.

Cochran and Alison planned to fly in the invasion as glider pilots, each having qualified back in the United States. They were eager to be in the forefront of history's first all-air invasion. The honor of taking the first gliders into Piccadilly and Broadway respectively belonged by custom to the leaders of the glider section, Bill Taylor and Vincent Rose. They would lead the way in. Cochran and Alison, piloting gliders, each would take command at one of the clearings, Cochran at Piccadilly, Alison at Broadway.

This arrangement was countermanded by The Man. Wingate was to remain in command at headquarters, staying behind to direct his troops by radio. He considered it military folly to let both of his air commanders go adventuring, with a chance of losing both. One would have to remain behind. Cochran wanted to shoulder the stay-at-home command assignment onto Alison. "But little Johnny," says Bill Taylor, "outtalked Phil for one time. Back in the United States both

"GOOD HUNTING, ALL THAT KEEP THE JUNGLE LAW"

had taken glider training, but Johnny had had more experience at double-tow flying, and this was to be a double-tow job. Johnny talked that up, and Phil was stuck." That gave Alison the command at one of the jungle clearings. The command at the other went to the officer next in rank, to Executive Officer Oley Olson. Alison would take Piccadilly, Olson would have Broadway.

The task of towing the first gliders went to the leaders of the transport squadron. They would have a tricky job, that of flying at night over black jungles and of picking out the assigned clearings in the moonlight. They had been given little opportunity to familiarize themselves with the route and the appearance of Piccadilly and Broadway, because of Wingate's order forbidding planes to fly near the landing areas for fear of exciting Jap suspicions. The night before Burma D-Day, the chance was taken of flying tow-plane and glider pilots under cover of darkness for a look at the route and the jungle clearings. This had to suffice.

The leader of the transport section was Bill Cherry, who had been Eddie Rickenbacker's pilot on the ill-fated flight over the Pacific. He had gone through the ordeal of the forced landing and weeks of drifting at sea on rafts, the ordeal that Rickenbacker had so well described. Some had censured pilot Bill Cherry for the way he handled the flight. "In the Air Force, a lot of us couldn't figure whether Bill had been right or not. Some felt he had done the best he knew how. Some thought he had been bullheaded and made a bad mistake. There was a feeling that he had not quite deserved the beating he took as a result of the thing, and we thought, 'There is a fellow who will be looking for a chance to redeem himself.' We didn't know what his trouble was, nor did we care. We thought that he'd be eager to do a whale of a job as the head of our transports.

"GOOD HUNTING, ALL THAT KEEP THE JUNGLE LAW"

"Bill was a bundle of nerves. He talked so fast you could hardly understand him. He was always smoking a cigar or a pipe; he went in for odd pipes. He let his light hair grow very long. Bill's idea for jungle flying was to load himself down with enough supplies and gadgets for ten people. He referred back to the Rickenbacker flight, and the hunger and thirst, drifting for weeks. He said, "I got caught short once,' and by God he was never going to get caught short again. If he went down in those damn jungles, he was going to be prepared; he was going to load himself with everything he could think of."

The second-in-command of the transports was one of John Alison's friends. Alison had known him in China, and told Cochran about the transport pilot who had flown down the main street of Lashio, the important Japanese base in northern Burma, while his crew chief tossed hundred-pound bombs at the Japs out of the back door of the ponderous cargo plane. He had taken more people out of Burma than any other transport pilot during the frantic, pitiful days when desperate tens of thousands were fleeing the invading enemy. On one flight he had carried seventy-three in a D.C. transport. "And so," relates Cochran, "we got big Jake Saartz. He was teaching instrument flying at an Army air base in Michigan. We said, 'Do you want to go to war?' He answered, 'When do we leave?' "

Saartz recommended Dick Cole, who had been Jimmy Doolittle's co-pilot in the bombing of Tokyo. Cole had sat beside Doolittle as the great old-time speed and stunt flyer led the American bombers which, early in the war, hurled explosives on Japan's capital. Afterward, bomber pilot Dick Cole had somehow been put in transport work. He was eager to go on another exciting job. "We found him a quiet, unassuming fellow. We would talk with Dick Cole, and he would say yes or no. If we said it was a nice day, Dick might grow so talkative as to nod."

As Burma D-Day approached, the air assaults against the Japs to the south of Piccadilly and Broadway rose to a crescendo. The night before the invasion the Japanese airfields nearest to the landing areas were heavily bombed, a culminating effort to knock out Jap air power that might be used against the seizure of jungle bases by glider.

That night ammunition was issued and knives were sharpened. Beards were shaved off, to make it easier for the doctors to treat wounds. Visits were exchanged between glider pilots and the officers of the Chindit detachments they were to fly.

The take-offs were to be from the glider base at Lalaghat, and there transport planes poured in a stream of British and American staff officers of the Allied command. They came with good wishes for the success of the first aerial invasion, although more than one seemed prepared to say, "I told you so." Wingate's superior was there, British General Slim. So was the superior officer to Cochran and Alison, General Stratemeyer.

The Man was everywhere, supervising with an icy calm, yet capable of taking those meditative strolls of his. Cochran was affected by the strain: "I had stage fright. I did a peculiar thing. I griped all day long that we had not done it the night before. I kept beefing to General Wingate that we wasted one good night. This was March fifth, and I was sorry we had not done it on the fourth." Alison was busy and placid.

Gliders and tow planes were marshaled in the field, in position for take-offs. Wingate troops were assembled with equipment and suppies, the assault detachments that were to be flown for the seizure of the jungle clearings. The field, jammed with aircraft, would have been a remarkable target for the Japs to shoot up. Through the late afternoon, Air Commando fighters kept a vigilant patrol for protection against hostile planes. The take-offs were to be at sundown.

Wingate had posted again his famous Order of the Day issued at the start of the first Burma campaign. It read:

"At this moment we stand beside the soldiers of the United Nations in the front-line trenches throughout the world. It is always a minority that occupies the front line. It is a still smaller minority that accepts with good heart tasks like this that we have chosen to carry out. We need not, therefore, as we go into conflict, suspect ourselves of selfish or interested motives. We have all had the opportunity of withdrawing and we are here because we have chosen to be here; that is, we have chosen to bear the heat and burden of the day. . . .

"The motive which has led each and all of us to devote ourselves to what lies ahead cannot conceivably have been a bad motive. Comfort and security are not sacrificed voluntarily for others by ill-disposed people. Our motives therefore may be taken to be the desire to serve our day and generation in the way that seems nearest to our hands . . . to do the right as far as we can see the right.

"Our aim is to make possible a government of the world in which all men can live at peace and with equal opportunities of sacrifice. . . .

"Finally, knowing the variety of man's effort and the confusion of his purposes, let us pray that God may accept our services and direct our endeavours so that, when we shall have done all, we may see the fruits of our labours and be satisfied."

In this proclamation, often quoted because it is so characteristic of Wingate and what he stood for, there is an echo

"GOOD HUNTING, ALL THAT KEEP THE JUNGLE LAW"

of the young Orde Wingate's resolve to be a soldier because there was still a need for soldiers in a warring world. There is a thoughtful statement of the soldier's aims at their best. But there is also a prophetic mention of the United Nations, and more than a verbal echo not only of Churchill but of that famous speech in which an American President, at Gettysburg, apologized for war and offered a high resolve for peace.

Issued to Wingate's Chindits, the proclamation was posted also on the side of an American glider, and when it blew away it was pasted back again. Cochran and Alison issued no papers but Cochran did make a last-minute pep talk to the invading Air Commandos, that ended: "Nothing you've ever done, nothing you're ever going to do counts now. Only the next few hours. Tonight you are going to find your souls."

ALL ABOARD FOR BROADWAY: Troops board a glider just before the take-off.

15. "In Jeopardy We Steer"

AT THE LAST POSSIBLE MOMENT before the great take-off, photographs prevented a disaster. An act of disobedience saved the campaign at the start.

The Air Commandos had a cameraman, Captain Charles Russhon, whom everybody called Rush. Really he was no cameraman at all. He was a sound man. He had been a sound technician with the N.B.C. in New York and then in Hollywood motion picture studios. The Army had sent him out to India to do sound work with a photographic crew. In India his elaborate sound equipment had been ruined by bad handling. Parts were broken, the mechanism invaded by tropical fungus. It could not be repaired. Rush, a sound man without sound equipment, had tried to justify his existence by resorting to the motion picture camera, although photography was not even a hobby of his. He had shot pictures on bombing missions, and had been wounded.

Rush, prowling around for something interesting, saw

gliders. He looked up Cochran, and asked to fly in a glider and take some pictures. Project Nine was in its secrecy stages, Cochran and Alison were reluctant, but Rush talked himself in. He told them he had worked in Hollywood studios, never mentioning that this had been as a sound man. They thought he was a Hollywood cameraman, which impressed them as the height of photographic prestige. They ended by commissioning Rush to make a motion picture record of the Air Command campaign. Shortly afterward an order from Washington, from General Arnold, directed them to have a motion picture record made of the operation. Cochran and Alison had obeyed the order in advance.

Rush got worried. He felt he had better not fool Cochran and Alison any longer. He went to them and confessed he was not a Hollywood cameraman, but a Hollywood sound man. They blinked. This was unorthodox even for Project Nine, but then Rush was making first-rate pictures. Cameraman or no cameraman, they kept him. Rush was a tall, awkward fellow with a black mustache, abundant loud talk and laughter and no lack of self-assurance. "Rush" was an apt name for him. He had boundless energy. He not only made a motion picture record, but did military photography for Project Nine, speedily mastering the technique of reconnaissance camera work. He set up a laboratory where pictures were developed, printed and enlarged with the skill and speed of a professional establishment.

Air reconnaissance is the eyesight of a flying unit, and its importance increases when the flights must be made over an unknown country. Early in the Burma adventure a light-plane pilot took off for a trip he should have made in twenty minutes. Picked up by the British a week later, sixty miles north of the route he should have taken, his excuse was, "I just ran plumb out of map." But before maps could be made, much of this terrain had to be photographed from the air.

Rush made the air reconnaissance pictures of the Piccadilly and Broadway jungle clearings, the photographic studies for planning and briefing. He would have made more, save for the Wingate order forbidding planes to fly near the landing areas, lest the Japs get a tip. As Burma D-Day approached, Rush was concerned.

"Three days before the date of the invasion, March 5, Colonel Cochran came to my laboratory, and I said to him, 'Wouldn't it be a good idea if I flew over the jungle clearings and made pictures again on the afternoon just before the take-offs?' He reminded me in his very straight and direct way that General Wingate had given positive orders that no planes were to fly anywhere near Piccadilly and Broadway until the gliders had actually landed.

"I put up an argument. My real reason was that I wanted to have last-minute air pictures for my photographic record. As a sales point, I contended that it was a reasonable precaution. If the Japs were there, we'd have pictorial evidence and be able to do something about it before it was too late.

"Yes, it was a good idea, agreed Colonel Cochran. But he added that orders were orders, and when General Wingate gave them it was no fooling.

"However, the way he said that gave me some little encouragement. So I got him alone on the following day, and continued the argument. This time he agreed, but it must be a secret. He said I should fly to Piccadilly and Broadway and photograph the clearings on the afternoon before the takeoffs, but no one must know that we had violated General Wingate's orders."

The pilot for the trip was bomber leader Colonel R. T.

Smith. At eleven o'clock in the morning of Burma D-Day, he and Rush took off in a B-25.

"We flew to Broadway first, arriving there about one o'clock. Everything looked normal, just as when I had photographed the clearing a few weeks before, open space surrounded by black jungle. We flew around it in a complete circle, and I made a dozen stills. Then we headed for Piccadilly, to the south.

"There the first glimpse was a surprise. From the distance, the jungle clearing showed numerous lines across it, parallel streaks. These grew more vivid as we approached. It was a crazy puzzle. There had been nothing like that the time I had flown near Piccadilly before. Then, flying low over the clearing, I saw that the lines were logs. Hundreds of teak logs lay in rows across the open space. They had been placed since I had photographed the clearing weeks before. Anything trying to land among them would have been smashed. There was one place free of logs, where landings could be made. There I noticed fresh dirt marks as if the ground had recently been dug up. This, I thought, looked as if land mines had been placed. Anything coming in and trying to avoid the logs might land in the clear space and be blown up. It seemed like a trap. My snap judgment was that the Japs had laid a snare for a landing in the jungle clearing.

"All the while R. T. was making a circle so that I could get pictures. I was so astounded by what I saw that I forgot to shoot any pictures. I told him to make another circle, and took a couple of dozen stills, and then said, 'Hightail it home.'

"I had a life-and-death warning. It was now midafternoon, and the take-offs were scheduled for sundown. I couldn't flash the warning by wireless. We were under strict radio silence. Anyway, it would have been madness to have wirelessed such a message with the Japs likely to pick it up. My laboratory for picture developing was at Hailikandi. The take-offs were from the other field, Lalaghat. I decided to fly to the laboratory, get the picture job going, and from there telephone the word to Lalaghat. My laboratory assistants were, as I had instructed them, ready for a quick job. They got busy. I telephoned to Lalaghat to give the warning, but couldn't get Colonel Cochran on the wire, or Colonel Alison or anybody to whom such a message should be given. At Lalaghat everything was in a turmoil of preparation for the take-offs.

"The photographic prints were soon ready. I might as well fly over with them. Then I realized that there was no plane to fly in—everything was over at Lalaghat. R. T. Smith's B-25 was of no use. Lalaghat was so crowded with transport planes and gliders, a bomber wouldn't be able to land there. I was in one fine confusion. The only thing I could think of was a jeep, and was about to start on a wild ride for the twelve miles, when a fighter plane landed. An American colonel, on his way to Lalaghat, hadn't been able to find the field and had landed at Hailikandi for directions. I gave him the directions, also photographs to deliver to Colonel Cochran. There was no room in the fighter plane to take me too.

"The colonel flew off, and I started by jeep again. I was halfway down the field, when I saw a light plane come and land. I turned back, and had the sergeant pilot fly me to Lalaghat. If you've ever ridden in an L-1 and know how slow it is, you'll understand how I felt flying those mere twelve miles, simply wanting to push the plane along.

"At Lalaghat, lined with gliders and tow planes, people scurrying around, I found Colonel Cochran and Colonel Alison studying the pictures, puzzled. I blurted my story, and we hurried to General Wingate with the pictures. He asked

THE PICTURE THAT SAVED THE DAY: Here is the photograph of Piccadilly field showing the log traps set by the enemy.

immediately who had told me to make the photographs? Who had permitted me to violate his orders?

"I said, 'General, I only thought it was normal procedure to take last-minute photos prior to an invasion.'

"That didn't seem to impress him. Phil spoke up and said he had had a hunch. That brought a huge smile to Wingate's stern, bearded face."

The conference they held was quick and tense. There was only one inference to be drawn from the photographs of Piccadilly, vivid with white parallel lines across the clearing. The Japs had logged the clearing. It later turned out that they had employed local natives with elephants to haul teak, and lay out parallel lines of long and bulky timbers. They had blocked the clearing against air landings, making it sure death. Any aircraft coming down in the rows of logs would be smashed to wreckage. Even the lightest glider, which could land almost anywhere, would have been demolished on hitting the logs, let alone the heavy air-commando gliders with their overloads of soldiers and equipment. The one open space with freshly broken earth suggesting land mines increased the surmise of a deadly trap.

The Japs had guessed something or perhaps knew everything. They may have been suspicious because Wingate had used the clearing during his previous campaign, having had a transport plane land in it and take out wounded. The Japs may have thought he might try some trick like that again. Therefore they had logged Piccadilly, but not Broadway. That open space in the jungle was clear.

Wingate gave his analysis, and stated that the worst contingency was that the Japs, aware of everything, had blocked off one clearing to lure the glider force into the other, with the enemy concentrating at Broadway to smash the air invasion as it came in. Then The Man, relying on his knowledge

CONSULTATION: Alison displays the Piccadilly photograph while Wingate weighs the odds.

of the Jap mind, concluded: "No, they are not capable of thinking that out."

Bill Taylor thought that they might still risk getting into Piccadilly, but was overruled. The alternative was to throw the entire glider operation to Broadway, or abandon the air invasion altogether.

Wingate took the decision on his own responsibility. He had his commanding general beside him, General Slim, who would have stopped him if he had thought him wrong. General Slim knew the abilities of Wingate. Cochran and Alison had their own American commanding officer to rely on. "We knew that if we did anything terribly wrong, General Stratemeyer would stop it. He made no move at interference, but just looked the thing over and then waited for what we decided to do.

"People gave us a lot of credit for being strong-minded, but actually we had only one decision that we could make. If General Wingate still wanted to send his men into Broadway, we would take them in. If he was willing to pour his people into that jungle glade, knowing there was a possibility of the Japs being there, he was taking the risk. It was really his decision, not ours." Cochran and Alison talked briefly by themselves. "We had been with each other for so long that we didn't have to say more than a few words. We said, 'We're ready to pour in on the field at Broadway.' "

The decision was to go ahead that night, with one blow, instead of two, one jungle clearing as the focus of air invasion. They would throw both forces of gliders, eighty in all, into Broadway, hoping to overwhelm the Japs by a mass landing, if any should be there.

Schedules had to be changed at the last minute on the flying field. Zero hour was at hand, and the rush of replanning was frantic. Cochran gave pilots a hasty rebriefing, using a map of Broadway drawn on a big sheet. "We knew there was going to be an awful jam. Glider trains, taking off at two-and-a-half-minute intervals, would all go crowding to one field instead of two."

John Alison, who was to have commanded Piccadilly, now had no command. Oley Olson had been assigned to Broadway. Alison insisted on going along as a glider pilot to serve at Broadway under Olson. Bill Taylor, who was to have landed the first glider at Piccadilly, took over the glider that was to be first at Broadway. Transport leader Bill Cherry, the onetime Rickenbacker pilot, would fly the first tow plane.

The take-offs were to have begun at five-forty. The change of plan caused a delay of about an hour. It was six-forty, just after sundown, when the first transport plane started down the runway with the first two gliders in double tow for the world's first all-air invasion behind enemy lines.

Four tow planes with the eight gliders went first, the pathfinder team. One after another they swept off the rapidly darkening field. There was a constant hum of motors on high, as the glider trains circled the field to get altitude for clearing the high range to the east. Heavily loaded, they had to circle repeatedly to make the climb to eight thousand feet.

Then there was a lull. The glider trains were under radio silence. Minutes went by, half an hour, the interval after which the main wave was to follow the pathfinders. The field was dark now, with only the needed field lights showing. No brilliantly lighted airport to attract hostile planes.

Now the main wave was moving, take-offs at rapid intervals in a long series, transports roaring down the dark field with gliders in tow, dim shapes flying off in the moonlight. Aloft there was an interminable roar of circling, climbing glider trains.

In getting over the mountains a couple of gliders broke loose, and came down near the field. That was a foretaste of a wave of bad news.

Next the tow plane piloted by Dick Cole, General Doolittle's old co-pilot in the first bombing of Tokyo, came back an hour ahead of schedule. Cole reported, "I lost my gliders." Halfway to Broadway his two gliders had broken loose and gone down in the jungle. In one of them had been Oley Olson, who was to have taken command at Broadway. Then another transport landed. The pilot reported, "I lost my tow over the Chindwin. It snapped."

Two more tow pilots came in, and announced they had lost their gliders, although the tow had been good. The bad news piled up into a fantasy of lost gliders, of aircraft and men going down into the black jungle at night.

The transport flyers reported that the moon had been bright until they got to the other side of the Chindwin. Then they ran into a haze. It was a sparkling night at the home base, but beyond the Chindwin the haze was thick. The moon was in the faces of the glider pilots. Cochran thought the glider pilots, bedeviled by the misty glow of the moon, couldn't see the planes towing them. That must be the trouble.

"The night before, I myself had been out in the night flight to familiarize transport and glider pilots with the route. The moon had been so bright that we had been able to see Jap airdromes below us. But the next night, up had come that haze, up into the full moon. Nothing ever happens the way we think it will, and it looked as if that haze was doing us in.

"By eight o'clock we were shocked. I knew we had lost

eight gliders. I didn't know how many, if any, had got into the jungle clearing. My decision was to keep pouring them in. I said to the boys, 'It looks like a lot of our people are going down, but we've got to support those that got in. Even if half of you guys are going down in enemy territory, I've got to send you.'

"I didn't send any more in double tow. They went out singly, a transport towing a glider. From then on, we didn't lose any.

"One returning transport pilot announced, 'I think they made it.' Another said, 'They cut loose, and I guess they got in all right.' One pilot reported that he had lost his glider tow about half a mile away from Broadway, but he thought they had been able to coast down into the clearing."

They waited for a radio message from Broadway. The glider invasion forces had been instructed to establish wireless communication at once, and flash a signal in code. Cochran waited for a message from Alison. Olson, the assigned commander to Broadway, having gone down in the jungle, Alison would take the command, if he got there. He would report immediately, if he was there. The radio was silent. No word came. They tried to establish communication with Broadway. There was no response.

Then, at last, a message crackled through in code, a message from Broadway. It read: *Soyalink*. Cochran collapsed internally. *Soyalink* meant the worst. Soyalink was a sausage made of soya bean sent from the United States to British forces. The British liked pork sausage, and hated soyalink. They had adopted the opprobrious word as the code signal to be flashed as a last resort—halt the operation, send no more gliders.

What was wrong? They tried to query back, but got no

response. The radio at the other end was dead again.

Cochran's imagination flared to suggestions of disaster. "I thought it signified the Japs had got at the fellows who had landed, and they were being shot up. I figured they were signaling, 'No more gliders can get in because of Japs.'"

Cochran's impulse was hot and impetuous. "My inclination was to put a bunch of assault troops into gliders and send them to the rescue, pour them in, no matter what. But Wingate said no."

Even in the moment of nerve-shattering suspense The Man was icily rational, continuing his habit of taking a walk while meditating and discussing philosophies. He said, "No, Phil, we must not attempt to snatch victory from a defeat." They must abide by the Soyalink message and send no more gliders. Cochran stopped those about to go. The operation was off, so far as the base was concerned. Of eighty gliders scheduled, fifty-four had been sent.

The radio remained silent all the rest of the night, and Cochran imagined the worst, the invasion force wiped out by the Japs. "I was utterly discouraged. I had hoped so much that I had never thought of defeat, and here something had knocked hell out of all our planning. But Wingate was not discouraged. With that mannerism of combing his beard, he said we really could not guess what had happened. When daylight came we would fly over Broadway to investigate."

In early morning there was a shout, "We're getting them. They're coming through on the radio." Cochran ran to the wireless shack, and on the radio telephone heard the voice of John Alison. A few quickly spoken phrases gave the first fragmentary report on a night of unparalleled adventure.

16. "The Rush Throughout the Mist"

THE STORY OF the establishment of Jungle Broadway was one of a singular mishap, a mad fantasy in the night.

Bill Taylor, in the first glider tow, was immediately astonished and disconcerted. The assigned course was to circle over the field to four thousand feet, and then strike out on a straight line, still gaining altitude to clear the mountains at eight thousand feet.

"I noticed that the climb was slow and sluggish," Taylor says. "My glider was acting unlike any glider I had ever flown. There was something strange about it. The only thing I could figure was that, with twenty Wingate Chindits aboard, the glider carried too much weight. Still, according to the schedule of loading, it should not have behaved as it did."

As they crossed the mountains, they encountered the haze that bedeviled the glider flights that night. Foggy moisture had blown in, mingled with the smoke of fires where natives were clearing fields on the hillside. The haze blurred the glider pilots' view of the tow planes ahead and the gliders in the double tow flying alongside. At first they could guide themselves by the lights the transports and gliders carried, but as they approached the Chindwin, beyond which was enemy territory, the lights were extinguished, according to orders. Then glider pilots could hardly see tow planes ahead or other gliders.

"We had reckoned with the chance of poor visibility, and I had instructed the gliders to fly in low tow position. Ordinarily they fly at a level above the tow plane. We flew at a lower level. This tended to silhouette the plane against the stars and moonlit sky, instead of blacking it out against the dark jungle below, and it permitted us to see the red-hot exhaust pipes. The great tropical full moon shone through the haze with a cloudy brightness. Glider pilots stared into the moon, with vision perplexed by strange light and shadow."

The air was rough. The gliders, with their cargoes of soldiers, were swinging and bouncing at the end of their tow lines. Pilots in a double tow, hardly able to see each other's gliders, had to maneuver sharply to keep these from swinging into each other. As they bounced, tow ropes would slacken, then suddenly become taut with a jerk and a jar.

"When you can see the tow plane ahead," Bill Taylor explains, "you note when it bounces in turbulent air. That gives you a tip of what's coming. You can compensate, and avoid too much slack in the tow line. This we couldn't do, being scarcely able to see the tow plane. A lot of slack would develop and then would be taken up with a violent pull. If that happened simultaneously to both gliders in a tow, the sudden double pull might break the single rope by which the double-tow line was attached to the tow plane.

"THE RUSH THROUGHOUT THE MIST"

"The glider continued to act strangely. After having been sluggish in the climb over the mountains, it responded reluctantly to the controls when we were in a slow descent on the other side."

In the glider flown by Vincent Rose, Rush, the cameraman, was riding. "I recall how at one point my heart stopped because I noticed directly to my right the flames of two engine exhausts. I was sure that a Jap plane had found us, a two-engine Betty. Our glider tow would have been dead meat for any Jap. Then I got a better silhouette of the plane alongside, and recognized it in the moonlight. It was the transport towing us. After crossing the high mountains we were descending, and our glider had picked up so much speed that it was flying faster than the transport, which now was beside us. Vincent Rose did a magnificent job of flying, in getting us back into our proper rear position without snapping the nylon rope."

Rush tells how they got off their course, and flew over a Jap air base at Katha. The Japs on the ground picked up the sound of the transport, and opened fire with antiaircraft guns. Rose and Rush saw tracers streaking up between the glider and the tow plane ahead. Rose remarked, "Fireflies sure fly high in Burma."

In the glider that was to be first to land, Bill Taylor saw they were nearing their goal. "We crossed the Irrawaddy below Katha," he relates, "and then turned northward, which again took us over the river, a bend of the Irrawaddy. We were descending now in a gradual downward course toward Broadway. The jungle below was pitch black with occasional patches of a lighter shade, glades and clearings.

"Ordinarily I should have been able to talk to the pilot of the tow plane ahead and with the glider on my wing.

But on the take-off, wire connection with the tow plane had been broken, and I couldn't talk to Bill Cherry out in front. It was up to him to find Broadway, and I shouldn't have minded being able to consult with him by phone or hear some of the jokes and wisecracks that you always got from him. The glider on my wing was piloted by Neal Blush. I couldn't talk to him, either. The wire connection between his glider and mine had been broken by the bouncing in the rough wind over the mountains.

"According to the time schedule, we must be approaching Broadway. I had studied the photographs of the clearing, and knew well its characteristic shape—one end looking like a fish tail, where an extension of the clearing reached into the jungle. Then, there it was.

"I noticed in the sky ahead the North Star. The landing was to be made going north, and the star was a guide. I cut loose. Neal Blush, in the glider alongside, would do the same, following me, while Bill Cherry, in his transport, flew back through the night.

"The moment I cut loose, my glider went into a dive, straight down. I pulled hard on the controls to level off, and found it almost impossible to keep from plunging on down into the jungle below. I couldn't imagine what was wrong, was puzzled again by the strange behavior of the glider. It took all my strength to keep a course.

"The lighter ground of the clearing was plainly visible against the black of the jungle, and I made the run to the ground, slowing the glider as best I could. But I couldn't slow it to anything like normal. That should have been at about sixty miles an hour, and I was going ninety. It felt as if the glider was dropping out from under me, something different, something wrong.

"At the level of the tall trees that surrounded the clear-

MAJOR BILL TAYLOR—left—was first to land at Broadway. With John Alison and two British officers, he's ready to celebrate.

ing I went from moonlight into black shadow, and lost all sense of horizon. I was unable to see the ground. There was a lashing sound of tall grass whipping the front of the glider. Then I saw a white patch coming up in front, and pulled back at the controls with all my strength. I was just able to get into the air for a hop over what was, as I found out later, a watering hole for elephants, big enough to put an ordinary house in. If the glider had plunged into the elephant hole, we would have been smashed to bits. As it was, I lost a wheel as I bounced down on the other side, coming to a stop within fifty yards of the point chosen weeks before in planning."

Taylor jumped to the ground, jungle earth underfoot. The British assault troops, directed by Colonel Scot, piled out in the moonlight, and went moving off through the tall grass to scout for possible enemies. Their task was to investigate the peril most to be feared, the chance that the Japs might be luring the air invasion into Broadway to destroy it.

A dim form came through the darkness with the whistling sound a glider makes, then a crash. It was Neal Blush having a crack-up landing, nobody hurt. Chindits scrambled out, and went scouting out into the jungle darkness.

The first pair of gliders was in, and the others of the pathfinder team soon followed, arriving by moonlight. John Alison, flying one, made a perfect landing. Others made crash landings. Lieutenant Seese came in crosswise on the field, and was headed for a crash with Taylor's glider. "He almost bodily picked up his own and jumped over mine. He was carrying Mad Mike Calvert, commander of the Wingate troops, and it looked like sure death. Mad Mike told me later that he had never seen anyone so cool as

"THE RUSH THROUGHOUT THE MIST"

Seese, who without a twitch of a muscle in his face jumped my glider and landed his passengers safely."

A shot rang out. "About twenty of us hit the dirt," Alison recalls. "You could hear bodies thumping on the ground all around. We thought it was Japs. Maybe, as we all feared, the enemy had lured us in to wipe us out. Then we found that the shot had been fired accidentally by a Wingate soldier in a détachment marching off to take its post. He was so excited his finger pulled the trigger."

Their big task now was to do a lightning job for the landing of the main wave of gliders. This they did with smoke pots as signals on the ground. They scurried around with flaming pots, laying a diamond pattern. Neal Blush went a mile down the clearing, and placed the release light, signaling the point where gliders were to cut loose from their tow planes.

The glider with the regular lighting equipment, to be used when the jungle clearing had become an airfield, failed to come in. It missed Broadway and crashed in nearby jungle trees. Later, it took the rescue crew sixteen hours to get through a brief space of dense forest to the wreck, to find all lives lost.

They waited for Oley Olson to come in and take command of Broadway. But Olson failed to appear. His glider, as they surmised, had gone down in the jungle on the way. That put Alison in charge, Alison, who, after luck had deprived him of a command at Piccadilly, was now in command of Broadway.

The communications glider with the radio equipment crashed. Nobody was hurt, but the radio was damaged. It wouldn't work. Major Bonham and his radio crew worked frantically, but not a signal could be got out of the wireless. They could not establish communication with their

SMASHED GLIDERS after the night landing at Broadway.

home base. Wingate's basic idea was radio direction, but they had no radio working, and Alison knew how Cochran must be gnawing his fingers with anxiety because of their silence.

Most of the gliders of the pathfinder team made crash landings, more wrecks than had been anticipated. The clearing, they found, was full of snares and pitfalls for gliders. The ground was lined with deep ruts, furrows where teak logs had been dragged. The local tribes in the logging season were accustomed to haul teak across the clearing by elephant, and this had worn trenches eighteen inches deep in the ground. Teak logs were lying around, left by the natives. There were, moreover, elephant and buffalo water holes. Hidden by tall elephant grass that covered the jungle glade, none of these hazards had been detected by air photography. They were concealed traps for gliders, especially the maze of furrows. A glider going into one was a probable wreck. This was the more likely as they landed too fast, at a greater speed than could be accounted for, that puzzling factor.

The main wave was coming in, one dim shape after another in the moonlight and black shadow. Gliders hit the teak-log ruts and crashed. Wrecks littered the clearing. Gliders crashed into wrecks.

Alison pictures it: "Before the crews could get out, another would be coming in. We would be trying to get boys out of a glider when another was landing. Getting the wounded out of the wrecks was a terrible job, it was so dark. I saw people nearly run down. If a glider hit a man, it would kill him. You'd hear a glider come in whistling in the wind. When you finally saw it, it would be two hundred feet away, and you'd start to run. You would just see a dark bulk.

"A glider is built like a drum. When one hits another—

well, you simply can't reproduce the sound. That sound was repeated time and again. We'd shout, 'Watch out!' And another would come in. We couldn't make ourselves heard over the boo.n of crashing gliders. The tension and apprehension were more than I can possibly describe."

Gliders kept coming. They had enough, too many. More gliders could only add to the wreckage, more wreckage for more gliders to crash into. They wanted to stop them, but it was impossible. They wanted to tell Cochran, back at the base, to stop pouring them in, but the radio wouldn't work. Bonham and his crew were laboring with desperation, but still couldn't get a signal out of the damaged set. And the gliders kept coming.

They were overshooting the landing field, with its diamond pattern of lights. The release light, signaling them to cut loose, was too far forward. Yet it was placed exactly according to plan, at the right place as proved by many tests. But the gliders were coming in too fast, at unexpected excessive speeds. It was necessary to move the release light to compensate for the too-fast landings. Bill Taylor ran the mile over the rough ground and through the grass to the light. Neal Blush was stationed there. They moved the light. They shifted it again and again, Taylor running the long hard mile five times during the night.

They moved the diamond pattern at the landing place so as to bring gliders in at places clear of wrecks. As one lane was cluttered with cracked-up gliders, they shifted the lights over to another lane. They moved the lights back, so that new landings would be made beyond the litter of wrecks.

"I ran around," says Alison, "like a chicken with its head cut off, and what running I couldn't do Rush did for me. He was a foot taller than I, and his legs a foot longer.

I'd shout to him to get men out of a glider that had just landed, get 'em out fast. I'd yell to him to switch lights. He and I were running around in the darkness with smoke pots in our hands. British Brigadier Mad Mike Calvert went dashing around with smoke pots. It was confusing and it was terrifying. Everybody pitched in. The British soldiers did an admirable job, but it looked awfully bad. The British were shocked. Our maneuvers had been so perfect, the timing had been so good. This was a shock to them. It was a hell of a shock to me."

Finally, after several hours, the radio worked, badly, erratically. They wanted to get the most urgent message through to Cochran—send no more gliders. They flashed the most drastic of their code words, *Soyalink*, meaning that everything was bad, stop everything. They hoped Cochran would get it. They would explain to him in subsequent radio talk. After that one flash, the radio went dead again.

More gliders arrived, as they would, even if Cochran had received the forbidding message. He couldn't call back transports and gliders near their goal. So the pandemonium went on, crashes and confusion in the moonlight. Forty-six gliders in all came in, and most of them were wrecked.

"Then," says Alison, "there was a lull. Apparently Phil had got the *Soyalink* message. No more gliders came in. Mad Mike Calvert said to me, 'Johnny, we've got that wave of gliders stopped. Come over and get some sleep until morning.' He could see how bitterly disappointed I was at what seemed like utter calamity. He added, 'With the sun shining, everything looks a little better.' We got under some brush, and an orderly fixed us some tea. I was utterly worn out after running around so much on that rough field.

"Everything was quiet for a while, and then we heard a noise in the dark sky overhead, the sound of a motor. Some-

PLASMA FOR THE WOUNDED: British soldier is given a transfusion at Broadway.

body yelled, 'Here come the Japs.' That was another thing we had been afraid of all along, that the Japs would discover what we were doing and fly over and bomb us.

"It wasn't Japs, but it was almost as bad. It was a tow plane with a glider, after having been lost for four hours. Mad Mike shouted, 'Send him home. Fire the red flare, to warn him away.' But we couldn't find the red flare. I yelled to Rush, 'Douse the landing lights, and maybe he'll go home.' But Rush couldn't put the landing lights out, couldn't smother the smoke-pot flares with handfuls of earth, not in time. The glider kid cut loose, and started in, whistling in the dark. We had seen a lot of dead and wounded that night, and now we sat tense. I said to Brigadier Calvert, 'Sir, he has no chance.'

"It was worse than we thought, because the glider coming in was the one that carried the bulldozer, the ponderous piece of machinery for laying out a flying field. We heard the glider whistle overhead and then the most awful, terrifying crash. It was a tremendous sound, as the glider with the bulldozer hit and crashed. Now Mike said, 'Oh my God!' with more feeling than I had ever heard before. Later I asked, 'How many men were killed in that glider?' The answer was, 'None.'

"It was the most freakish of all the freak events that night. The glider with the bulldozer flew too far down the field, cleared the wrecks and hit the trees. That had made the terrifying sound. The wings had been ripped off, and under the impact the bulldozer had been hurled forward. It pulled the strap that raised the nose of the glider, and up went the nose, cockpit, pilot, co-pilot and all. The two were hoisted suddenly out of the way of the plunging bulldozer, which ran out of the front of the glider and stopped among the trees, little damaged."

"THE RUSH THROUGHOUT THE MIST"

Brigadier Calvert had now come to the conclusion that the game was up, and said so to Alison. "He told me if we were licked we might as well admit it, and get out." Mad Mike thought the best they could do was to bring in light planes to evacuate the wounded. The rest could walk out. Calvert assured them that they could get through the jungle on foot and back to Burma. It would take weeks. Rush, the cameraman, was dismayed. He had come along wearing a pair of tennis shoes, appalling footgear for weeks of trudging through the jungle.

Alison demurred. He was persistent. "Let's wait till daylight and see how badly off we really are."

Daylight came. They looked at a scene of wreckage, smashed gliders everywhere.

Their commanding officer of engineers for air-strip construction, Captain Casey, had been killed in a glider that had cracked in the jungle near Broadway. All they had for an engineering officer was a lieutenant of the Airborne Engineers, young, small, frail.

Alison said to Lieutenant Brackett, "What do you think of this field?"

He replied, "Well, sir, it's pretty bad."

"We've got to get a small strip done for light planes."

"Yes, sir."

"Do you think," Alison went on with little hope, "that you can build a field to take care of the large transports?"

"I think so, sir."

"How long will it take?"

"Well, I think we can do it by this afternoon."

"And by God," shouts John Alison, "they did. It was a terrifying piece of labor. The engineers just worked their hearts out, constructing a long strip for big transports across the lines of teak-log furrows."

"THE RUSH THROUGHOUT THE MIST"

As the construction job began, Taylor said to Alison, "You don't need to make a reconnaissance to determine where to lay the mile of airstrip, because I wore a path for it, running to the release light and back last night. Just follow my tracks."

Wingate jungle parties were fanning out into the thicket. Patrols of fourteen to twenty men each went out in all directions for an average of five miles. They reported no Japs, no Burmese, no sign of life. The clearing was a natural jungle glade, a break in the forest, without human inhabitants anywhere near.

By ten o'clock in the morning they had the radio working. Bonham and his wireless crew had it fully repaired now, having dug the radio glider out of the rut into which it had crashed and set it up among the trees as a radio station. Wireless telephone communications were established with headquarters, and John talked to Phil. There has been many a dramatic telephone call in this phone-calling world, but never one quite so rich in tension and relief as this one, John telling Phil, "We think we'll be ready for the troop-carrying planes tonight. The boys are working on the airstrip." That and some quick, matter-of-fact phrases to explain what had happened.

"When I found they were not all killed," says Cochran, "I was so relieved I was bawling, I was that upset. I had been physically knocked out by discouragement. Wingate was equally happy, but he didn't show it."

The Man, his throaty voice unperturbed, conferred on the radio telephone with Brigadier Calvert, gave operational instructions, setting into motion his radio-controlled tactics of jungle war.

They discovered the reason for the puzzling factor that had almost reduced everything to calamity, the strange be-

MORNING AFTER: Clearing the field, Broadway, for incoming troops to land.

havior of the gliders, their sluggish climb, reluctant response to the controls, tendency to dive when cut loose and excessive speed in landing. Bill Taylor checked his own glider He found stuff that should not have been in it, an unscheduled excess of equipment and supplies. This had been loaded secretly and taken along by Wingate soldiers.

Weights had been calculated to the ounce, the maximum burden, the largest overload the gliders could carry and be handled safely. The British soldiers had been instructed to take along no extra weight. But in the Wingate jungle campaign of the previous year they had been in trouble because of shortages of ammunition. This time they were going to safeguard against shortages, and at the last minute had sneaked aboard extra cases of cartridges and grenades, rations, too, never dreaming how pounds of extra weight would affect the behavior of already overloaded gliders. In Taylor's glider, in places that had unbalanced it, they had hidden two extra crates of rations and three of ammunition.

In the afternoon, light planes landed on a hastily improvised small strip, and evacuated casualties. Three had been killed in the crashes on the field, a dozen injured badly enough for hospitalization. One of those killed was glider pilot William Ritzinger. Just before the take-off, he had thrust a note into a pocket of glider leader Bill Taylor, who now found it, a bit of verse that Ritzinger had adapted from Kipling:

> *We're the prophets of the utterly absurd*
> *Of the patently impossible and vain,*
> *But when the thing that couldn't has occurred*
> *Give us time to catch our breaths*
>   **AND GO AGAIN.**

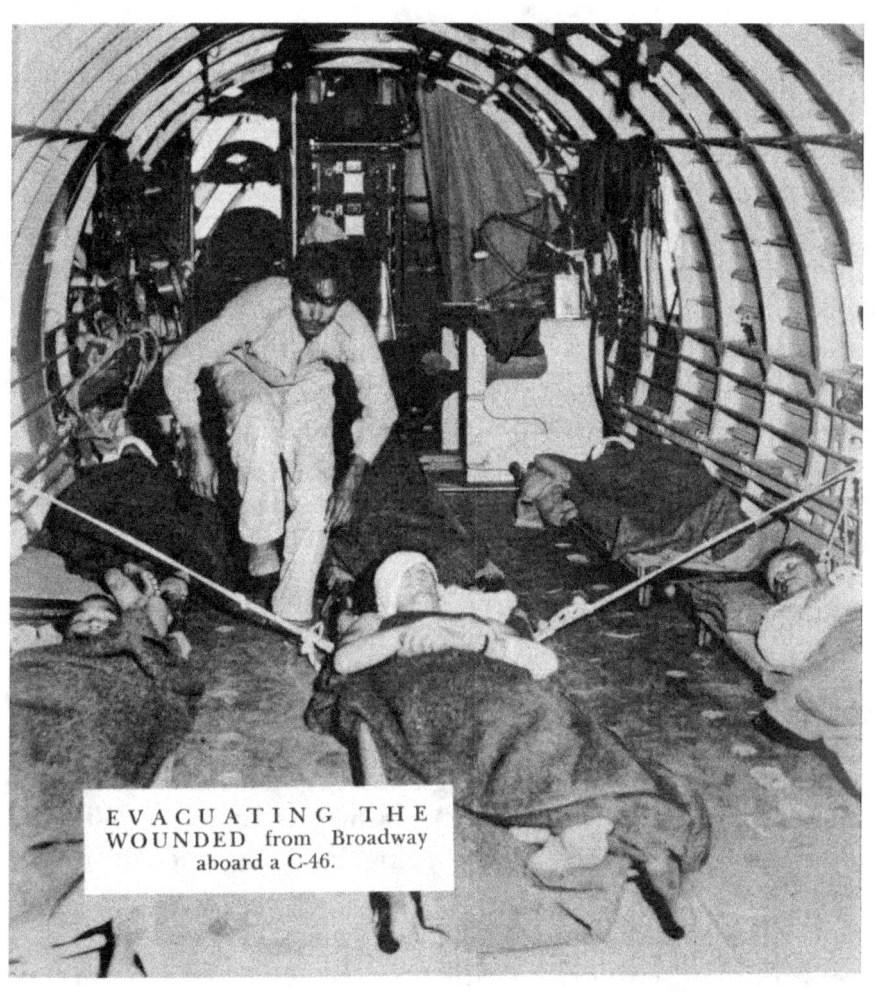

EVACUATING THE WOUNDED from Broadway aboard a C-46.

By nightfall they had a long airstrip laid down for the transports, a forty-eight-hundred-foot strip, nearly a mile runway on the rutted and furrowed clearing. They had a portable electric light system working for night landings, a decently lighted airport.

That night a large force of Chindits and tons of armament, munitions and supplies were flown in by big cargo planes of the Air Transport Command, which did a job thus set forth by Cochran: "Here were these fellows, troop-carrier pilots who had done odd things, and now they were asked to load up with British troops and heavy cargoes and take off from a field they didn't know and go into the center of Burma and land on a strip that had been built in one day. They didn't know where it was. They were to go homing to it by radio. They knew they were landing 165 miles behind the enemy lines."

The first transport in, landing after dark, was piloted by General Old. Twelve in all came in that night, and disgorged soldiers to hold Broadway against any force the Japs could bring up quickly. Night after night the transports flew in, operating on a regular schedule, flying a Wingate division to Broadway, and pouring in armament and munitions.

"We sent ammunition, barbed wire. Our plan was to push in materials for building a stronghold, like land mines, large-caliber machine guns and antiaircraft guns. We flew heavy cannon to Broadway."

Jungle Broadway was a busy airport. The Americans said it was like LaGuardia Field. The British said it was like Croyden.

TAPS: A Burmese chaplain reads the burial service for fifteen British soldiers.

17. "The Wildest Tales Are True"

O<small>N THE NIGHT OF</small> Burma D-Day, seventeen gliders, in all, broke loose. Of these, eight landed in friendly territory. Nine went down beyond the Chindwin in country held by the Japs. Care had been taken to route the glider trains over jungle areas where enemy forces were not likely to be found, but it had been necessary at one point to cross Japanese divisions massed for the enemy drive into India. Several gliders, upon breaking loose, were forced down in the vicinity of the Japanese 31st Divisional Headquarters. Some had the worst of luck. Chindits and Air Commandos were killed in crashes or by Japs, or were captured, some subsequently murdered by the enemy. Most often, fortune was good, and returning glider men told thrillers of escape.

One glider landed on a river sandbank. British and Americans burned their aircraft in the face of the surprised Japs, and made off through the jungle. Starving, days later, they dynamited a stream with a hand grenade, got seventy-nine fish, and finally walked into Broadway, to which they were to have flown. The way in was led by Peter Fleming, the British author.

One glider, flown by Pilot Robert Wagner, landed on an enemy airfield at Katha. The Japs were so astonished that the crew was able to climb out in bright moonlight, march across the flying field, and disappear in the jungle. This party reached the Irrawaddy, swam the river and came in safely.

The two-glider tow that was to have been second in at Broadway broke loose beyond the Chindwin. One of the gliders was Oley Olson's. Named to command at Broadway, Oley found himself and his companions in a very different situation. They were able to cast loose the tow line cleanly and quickly, and turn around for a long glide back toward the Chindwin and friendly territory. They landed not far from the river, for a walk through jungles.

The other glider had bad luck. The tow line, when it broke, whipped back over one wing. Before the line could be released and the wing got clear of it, the glider lost altitude and they had to make a quick landing. The ranking Air Commando aboard was Dick Boebel, a thwarted airman. Boebel had wanted to be a pilot, but he was twenty-nine, older than regulations had allowed. Yet he had contrived to get into army flying school. He had had eighty hours of flying, then had failed to make the grade, missing out on the last test for wings. Put in a desk job, he had jumped at the chance to take an administrative post with Project Nine, in charge of housing and similar details. Now he was having adventure, more than he had ever bargained for. As Dick Boebel tells the story:

"We were coming down over black jungle. Our glider pilot wanted to make a landing in the trees. He had been

COLONEL ARVID OLSON with the crutches he made for walking with a foot injury after his glider broke loose beyond the Chindwin River.

told in the States that you could crash-land in trees with little damage to the aircraft. But he had learned that bit of wisdom in orchards, not in the thick jungle where trees are of different heights, one very tall, with a smaller one alongside. In the moonlight I could see open fields below, and said to the pilot that we had better land in a rice paddy. It was hard to convince him. He was sure Japs would be right there ready to jump all over us. But I figured the chances of that would be slim. Anyhow, things looked quiet, so I pulled my rank on him, and we crash-landed in the paddy field.

"There was a crunching sound when we hit. We all piled out and gathered under the wings of the glider, seventeen of us. There were four Americans, five Burmese riflemen, including one Burmese captain, and eight Britishers. Suddenly shots rang out. We flopped to the ground, flattening ourselves. In the darkness we could see nothing. The Burmese captain whispered to me that it could only be a few Japs because it was just rifle shooting. Then we heard a machine gun, a stream of bullets cutting across the rice paddy.

"We decided we had better not try to attack them, we were so loaded down with guns and ammunition. I had a tommy gun, a carbine, a regular army forty-five and a small pistol, a lot of artillery for one man to be carrying around. We figured we'd better get out of there. We ran across the fields, away from the sound of the shooting, and toward a mountain that hid the moon. We were running in shadow. All the time the rifle and machine-gun fire was clipping through the paddy field. We didn't know it, but we had landed near a Jap military headquarters. So the glider pilot's hunch had been right. The Japs, hearing us crash, were shooting in the direction of the sound. None of us was touched.

"The Burmese captain led us. He took us up the mountain. We crossed a path. He made us walk backwards along the path for some distance. If the Japs spotted our tracks, they would assume we were going in the other direction. The Burmese captain knew all the tricks. He was small and apparently delicate, but really rugged. He had great big eyes. He had been educated in a university in England, and after it was all over, he gave me a Japanese bill on which he wrote, 'In memory of a lovely journey,' and signed it *Valentine Barr*.

"When we thought we were safe from Jap pursuit we crouched into a thicket to rest. We were worn out. I was lying exhausted when in the darkness a noise started cracking. I saw the shadow of a snake coming down the side of the gulley to my right. There was enough light to see that the thing was about five inches in diameter, a huge python. I didn't know what to do. Should I holler for help, pull out my weapons, or cut his head off with a knife? Luckily, I remained still. He came down. It all took about ten seconds. It seemed eternity. The python crossed over my right foot, straight across over my left, and up the other side of the gulley. He never hesitated a second, never slowed down. He must have been twelve feet long. I wondered later how I ever kept quiet. It must have been fright. I told the guys about it afterwards, and they were scared stiff too, just hearing about the monster snake.

"We were twenty-five miles inside enemy territory, and solid jungle lay between us and friendly country on the other side of the Chindwin. We traveled by night, hiding away in the thicket during the day and sleeping. The moon lasted for ten days. A dim light filtered down among the trees at night, enough light to enable us to pick our way. The jungle was so thick we had to cut through it. Burmese soldiers out in front hacked the thicket with their big knives. When we heard dogs barking we knew there was a village nearby. We stayed away from villages, the Japs having natives in their pay.

"One evening we were breaking camp, ready for a night of travel, when a fellow next to me said suddenly, 'Look, there is somebody up on the hill.' I looked—there were two Japs.

"We were at a place where the jungle thinned out, and the ground ran up steeply to a ridge without trees. There two Japanese soldiers were standing with their rifles at their side. They seemed to be looking down at us, as we moved among the trees.

"What should we do? Should we ask them down to have tea with us, or take a shot at them? I called over to the Burmese captain, and said, 'See what we've got up on the hill!' He took a look. Was he startled!

"At that moment the two Japs turned and ran, disappeared. There was no further sign of them. We never knew what it was all about, whether they took us for natives, or what. They were the only Japs we saw on the whole trip.

"After several days a couple of Chindits, British, came to me with confidential information. They told me quite coolly that they intended to kill their commanding officer. They were virtually asking my permission. I wasn't altogether surprised. Their commanding officer was a British lieutenant colonel, one of the worst individuals I have ever known. His men hated him.

"When he gave them an order it was with a tone of nasty browbeating. On the march through the jungle, he insisted on having a Chindit for his batman, to play valet to him. He took more than his share of our skimpy rations, and demanded that everything be arranged for his comfort. He was, by virtue of rank, in command of the whole party, yet his leadership was not only useless but a menace. His orders were ridiculous. We had to depend completely on the Burmese soldiers with us, they knowing the jungle. He treated them like scum.

"I knew what was coming, knew that his men wouldn't put up with him much longer. They'd kill him. But I acted surprised. The Chindits who informed me about it said it would be a simple matter. They'd get the lieutenant colonel out alone, on the black night-march through the jungle, and it would seem as if an unfortunate accident had happened to him. But I couldn't very well give permission for a murder. I told them to do nothing so drastic. I'd take care of things.

"I went to the candidate for the unfortunate accident, and told him plainly how things stood. He had better turn his command over to me and make himself inconspicuous, if he wanted to go on living. He understood, and said, 'Very well, very well.' I took command, and thereafter we had no more trouble with him, except that he still couldn't help making himself disagreeable from time to time.

"When we got back, I told Phil and John about it. They went to Brigadier Tullock, Wingate's chief of staff, who talked it over with me. The offensive lieutenant colonel was dismissed from the Wingate forces, the only officer that Wingate ever fired. The British learned that previously, in Africa, this same lieutenant colonel had been fired by Montgomery.

"On the fourth night we reached the Chindwin and had to make a river crossing. The Chindwin was wide, and had a strong current, and we had to get across at night. Of our seventeen men, eight couldn't swim a stroke. They had to be helped across. The British had a good trick. They took off their trousers, tied knots, and blew the trousers up like balloons. That helped in floating us across, swimmers towing nonswimmers in the darkness.

"The nonswimmers were told that, if they happened to get loose from the swimmer towing them, they were not to cry out. Some of our Burmese soldiers had gone on a scouting trip and found that a Japanese patrol had been in the vicinity recently. We were afraid that Japs might be near, and would be attracted by any loud sound.

"One of those who couldn't swim was a young glider mechanic, Corporal Nienaber. He was one of the few in the Air Commandos about whom we had been doubtful. He was small and thin, and wore thick glasses, and a tough campaign had seemed no place for him. We hadn't wanted to take him along, but tears had welled in his eyes and it had been just too much to tell him he couldn't go.

"He was the only one to be carried away from a swimmer. The current yanked him away. He was swept downstream, and could not be spotted in the darkness. A call from him might have saved him, but the little fellow, about whom we had been doubtful, grimly obeyed the rule of silence. He could have let out a yell, but there was not a sound from him. He was lost.

"The British were greatly impressed by the self-sacrificing courage of Corporal Nienaber. When we got back, newsmen attached to the Air Commandos featured the heroism of the little, bespectacled glider mechanic who had given his life so as not to endanger his comrades.

"In the swim across the Chindwin we had to abandon most of our clothes, and were nearly naked. We lost our shoes. Several British Mae Wests, inflated vests, had helped us in swimming. These we cut up, and tied sections to our feet. We decided we were near enough to friendly territory to march by day and sleep at night. At the end of the first day beyond the Chindwin, after darkness had fallen, we made camp on top of a hill.

"In the morning, when light came, we saw a large native village. At the foot of the hill were thatched huts and people moving about. Should we take a chance? We decided to approach the villagers, and ask if they knew where a British patrol might be.

"We started trooping down the hill and soon dogs were barking. When the villagers saw us they were frightened. Half naked and with bits of clothing tied to us, we looked like scarecrows. Our Burmese soldiers had a job on their hands before they could convince the villagers that we were friends.

"They brought out their head man, who derived his authority from his age. They told us he was 110 years old. Probably he was about seventy. We were informed that a British patrol had passed through a few hours before, marching along a trail pointed out to us.

"The villagers were about to celebrate a feast, a day which had something to do with the phases of the moon. They invited us to join. Probably we should have hurried after the patrol. We violated regulations, too, all the rules of being careful about eating native food, because of dirt and dysentery. After a starvation trip through the jungles, we were too hungry to bother. The feast consisted of curry of peacock. It was delicious, would have been a rare delicacy in an expensive New York restaurant. They served it in clay bowls. You reached in and took out a piece of peacock, and dipped it in the curry. We ate all we could, and the villagers seemed insulted because we couldn't eat any more.

"After the peacock and curry, we didn't feel like walking, but started out, one of our Burmese scouts going ahead to look for the patrol. Soon he brought back a British infantry

BURMA WARRIOR wearing native dress and armed in his own jungle style.

officer, a Captain Johnson, who took us to his outfit. They served us a collation, not peacock and curry, but the inevitable British tea.

"The captain told us that his patrol had located some Japs and expected to be in action soon. He didn't want to get us mixed into the fight. In our condition we would have been useless. We could get further help, he told us, by going along to an individual whom he merely referred to as 'this man.' He gave me directions for traveling along the trail to the place where we'd find 'this man.'

"We started out again, following directions, and a few miles along the trail saw a man sitting on the side of a hill, along the bottom of which ran a stream. He was sitting with his arms folded. He was smooth-shaven, and bigger than the Burmese. He had on ordinary civilian clothes, but the clothes were unimportant, he was that impressive. You could imagine that he was a king. Around him were villagers, cooking food and tea for him. As we came up the hill, as weird a band of castaways as has ever been seen, he looked at us, not at all surprised. He had a broad face and a fetching smile. He said, 'My name is Goldberg.'

"I was never so astonished by a name, Goldberg, this king of the jungle. When I started to tell him who we were, he remarked, 'Oh, I know all about you. You crashed a couple of days ago in a glider. There are about fifteen of you. You had a hell of a time getting out.' He spoke excellent English, although slowly, with some slight hesitancy in picking his words.

"He knew about us because Oley Olson and survivors of his glider had been through before us, and had been helped along by Goldberg. Oley had told the jungle king to be on the lookout for us, our glider too having broken loose."

Goldberg was half English Jew and half Burmese. He had

BURMA BEAUTY: Some were, by American standards, and some most definitely were not.

been educated in Rangoon, and gone into the British civil service. In peacetime he had been very small potatoes, just another Eurasian clerk. But the war had brought him into his own. The Jewish-Burmese Eurasian had become an agent for the British in dealing with the tribes along the Chindwin. He was in competition with Japanese agents, both sides buying the allegiance of the villagers with kerosene and salt, the two great valuables of those parts. Goldberg outdid and outsmarted the Japs.

"They offered a large reward for him, and one time a Burmese betrayed him. Goldberg had a narrow escape. He found out who the Burmese was, then asked the British to bomb the traitor's village. British planes leveled the village. That struck the people of the region with terror, and thereafter Goldberg was something of a king among them, the man who could bring the bombers on your village if you didn't watch out.

"Goldberg was not anxious for the war to be over. The situation was exactly to his taste. During peacetime he had been an unwanted sort of person. The Burmese avoided him because he was working for the British. The British wouldn't admit him socially because he was a Eurasian. Now, in the war, the British gave him anything he wanted, and the Burmese bowed before him as the man who could summon the bombers.

"He gave a feast for us, roast peacock without curry. The natives cooked and served the banquet. Goldberg had plates, forks, and spoons, and coffee served in cups. About tea, favorite of both British and Burmese, he said, 'I can't stand the stuff.' Goldberg was different. We didn't see the food cooked. It just appeared, natives carrying huge trays of it, while we sat talking with Goldberg.

"He put us up for the night, providing us with beds

slung on bamboo poles, comfortable beds four or five feet off the ground. For a day and a night we lived like kings, with King Goldberg.

"When we left I promised him that I'd send him some salt as soon as I got back to base, and some kerosene if I could find any, to replenish his supplies for paying off the natives. When I got back, I found that Oley Olson had already made arrangements to fly salt and kerosene to Goldberg.

"One of our Burmese soldiers was stricken with malaria. When we got back to base the doctor said the Burma boy was asking for me. I liked and respected the Burmese soldiers, whose knowledge of the jungle had saved our lives, and the one who was ill had been brave and competent. I recalled how all during the trip he had admired my carbine, the latest model in the American Army. I decided I'd give him the carbine. I knew no Burmese and he knew no English, so I took an interpreter along. Then in the hospital, a dugout, I handed the carbine to him, forgetting the interpreter.

"The Burma boy, faint with malaria, took the gun and said something. The interpreter translated it, 'He says he needs cleaning material. He understands you want him to clean your gun.' I had the interpreter tell him I was giving him the gun, and he nearly burst out crying with gratitude."

Dick Boebel's story is typical of the variety of adventure brought about by gliders breaking loose on the night of Burma D-Day. More important was the strategic consequence. The Japs were confused by gliders landing here, there and the next place. Suspecting landings of guerrilla patrols, they were thrown into turmoil over what they believed to be a widespread and complex pattern of guerrilla attacks. They wasted time and energy by sending forces out to hunt for what they thought to be raiding parties. They put special guards to protect their communication and supply dumps.

The accidental breaking loose of the gliders had the effect of a diversion, as good as if it had been planned. It delayed the Japs in finding out about the seizure of the jungle clearing for the Broadway base, and hindered their moves for assailing it. Wingate said to glider leader Taylor, "Bill, did you play a trick on me and have those gliders land to throw the Japanese off the scent?"

18. "How Long Will the Lull Endure?"

ONE HUNDRED AND SIXTY-FIVE MILES behind enemy lines, their jungle Broadway remained unmolested for eight days. During this time the R.A.F. moved in a force of six Spitfires, and kept them based there. This they did without the permission or the foreknowledge of Cochran and Alison. The flying-field fortress was not ready to accommodate fighter planes. It was designed to be a fighter-plane base, but it was not yet suitably equipped. Dispersal points had not been completed for the safety of planes, in case the Japs should attack by air. Nor was the radar adequate to detect, in time, the approach of hostile planes. Jungle Broadway was still operating by night, with a dim minimum of lights for landings and take-offs. Transports carrying troops and supplies came in under cover of darkness, and were gone by day. During the hours of light there were no planes on the field for Jap air observation to spot. There were ground troops but no planes.

Cochran explains: "The Japs figure funny. You could

have a ground base and fight their troops, and you'd never be bothered by Jap planes. But if you brought aircraft into a place where they thought they could get at them, they'd fight. We didn't believe the Jap air people and ground people spoke to each other. As long as the ground action was going on, the Jap air people would say, 'That is your business.' But when they saw planes on the ground, that was air stuff. I don't think the Japs would ever have seen anything to attack if they hadn't spotted the six Spitfires flying in and out and sitting on the field during the day."

Before the R.A.F. moved in to take advantage of the jungle base the Air Commandos had built, Wingate gave them permission. Cochran and Alison considered it a maneuver of his to get on better terms with the R.A.F. and procure some favor in return. The move angered Cochran because it invited air attacks for which they were not ready.

The Japs came over, there was air fighting, and the Spitfires did well. The lack of dispersal points and the insufficiency of radar, however, were fatal. The enemy air force jumped Broadway in strength. The Air Commandos had planes on the field—they might as well have, since the British were there. Expecting an attack, they got their planes out in time, all but one. The pilot delayed, and an incendiary bomb set his plane on fire as he was taking off. The Spitfires were caught taking off. They were burned on the ground or were shot down. Two of the six got into the air, and put up a brilliant fight against the overpowering odds of twenty attacking Japs. The British group leader, one of the bravest and most skillful of air fighters, alone engaged the entire attacking force. He shot down two Japs in flames, then was overwhelmed by numbers and fell flaming on the flying field.

Cochran and Alison protested bitterly to Wingate. "At

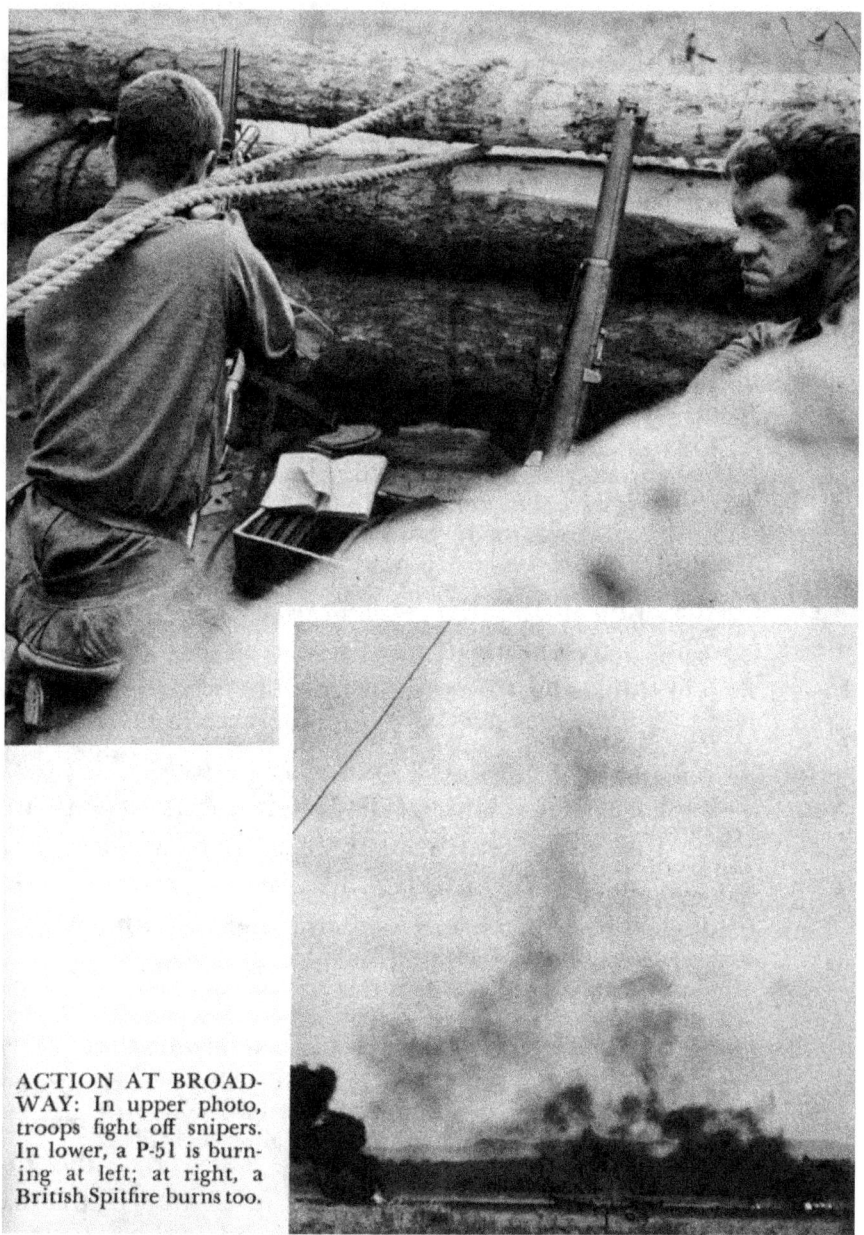

ACTION AT BROADWAY: In upper photo, troops fight off snipers. In lower, a P-51 is burning at left; at right, a British Spitfire burns too.

first he pretended he didn't know what we were talking about, and then said, 'I did do that, didn't I?' We told The Man that up to that time we had been loyal, but when it came to double-dealing we could be nasty little fellows, and that from then on we'd trust nobody. To make up for it, he wrote letters to Prime Minister Churchill, President Roosevelt, Lord Louis Mountbatten, and General Arnold, stating that the entire air invasion had been our party. He tried to rectify in some small way the trick he had pulled on us."

When the jungle base was completed, fighter planes kept enemy aircraft away, and Broadway went into full operation as a supply center for Wingate's Chindits. Led by Mad Mike Calvert, parties were moving through the equatorial forest. Their goal was the parallel railroad and highway through the Indaw-Katha bottleneck. Twenty-seven miles west of Broadway, in the sector of Mawlu and Henu, stood a strategic hill overlooking the railroad and highway. Held by a force of Japs, the hill was stormed in what was virtually a two-man assault by Mad Mike Calvert and his right-hand man, Squadron Leader Tommy Thompson. The two went up the slope with hand grenades, and blasted Japs in such fashion that little help from their soldiers was needed. The Chindits dug in, turning the hill into a fortress. From this roadblock they had the railroad and highway under fire, thereby cutting the life line of the Japanese to the north.

Troops, supplies, equipment and fortification, armament and mules, flown to Broadway, streamed from that base through the jungle to the Mawlu-Henu roadblock, reinforcing it. Twenty-five hundred Chindits were concentrated there. It was days before the Japs could rally any kind of force against them. By that time, with pits and trenches, entanglements of barbed wire and fields of land mines, the hill had been transformed into a powerful stronghold. A supply line by air was established, transport planes dropping provisions and munitions by parachute. Chindit patrols pushed out and seized forty miles of railroad and highway. Fighting developed against increasing Japanese opposition, and the Mawlu-Henu roadblock, keeping a stranglehold on the Japanese life line, became a major focus of the campaign.

Broadway functioned as a radio center in constant touch with the home bases. In Wingate's radio-controlled pattern of long-range penetration, wireless, its ways and problems, had a dominant part.

The British were addicted to ciphers. They never sent anything in the clear. The Americans argued with them: "You're ciphering yourself out of operation. You're so damned secret you're slowing everything. By the time you get a thing coded and decoded, it is too late."

The Americans tried to communicate in a way clear to themselves, but not to the Japs. They used American colloquialisms which no Japanese could understand, even if he had gone to an American university. Some Japs might know a bit of American slang. The Yanks twisted slang around so that only they could know what it meant.

It got to be a game. They tried to outdo each other, tried to get up trick phrases, outcipher each other. Cochran would think up a message and say, "Send this to John at Broadway and see if he understands it, I'll bet he won't." Then back would come a reply showing that Alison had understood.

"On one occasion, I told the radio boys to instruct Andy Rebori, who had the light planes at Broadway, that he must not fly in the daytime, because there were snipers in the hills, but that he could fly all he wanted in the moonlight. This is the message they sent: 'Andy from Phil'—Don't act like sunflower except in emergency. Act as vampire all you want.'

"When I saw that, I said, 'It doesn't make sense, Rebori will never get it. You're going too far with this thing.' Then Andy called me on the radio and announced, 'I get what you sent, Phil, I'll do it.'

"I finally caught John on one, sent him a message he couldn't figure out. I wanted to tell him that the radar warning device was coming in to him at Broadway that day, and that a pilot by the name of Hilderbrandt, whom he knew, was flying it. We never mentioned radar on the air, so I wrote up the following message: 'Air sniffer arriving soon. Meet man name of gal swooner with her guard down but her brand showing.' When John got that, he was puzzled. He knew I was trying to stick him, and it made him mad. He kept wondering what that fool Cochran was trying to say.

"Meanwhile, Hilderbrandt came flying into Broadway with the radar. When John saw him, he suddenly realized what the message meant. The key to it was the name of a New York night club singer whom we had often heard, Hildegarde."

A fighter pilot out on weather observation might report back by radio, "Elyse Knox." Or he might say, "Harmon." Elyse Knox was Harmon's girl friend. She was fair, and her name meant that the weather was fair. Harmon meant foul weather. Or the code report might be "California" or "Florida." If the pilot reporting was from the West Coast, "California" meant fine weather. If he was from some other part of the country, "California" meant rotten weather. It all depended, and the same sort of thing went for "Florida."

They called their light planes Maytags. Their P-51s were Fords. B-25s were Buicks. A cargo carrying transport was called a Two-Ton Tony.

They called their radio stations by odd names, all except one. Broadway was always Broadway, as if the Great White

THE RADAR TENT: Communications h. q. at Broadway, sandbagged for protection — but not on top.

Way in the Burma jungle was odd enough. The home base was "Red Dog," so named after the card game favored there. Tamu, when they had it, was "Easy Easy Lazy." The Imphal station was "Uncle Bud."

That went back to earlier events in Cochran's life. Uncle Bud, a gamecock from Groton, Connecticut, was the rooster mascot of the first fighter outfit that he had trained for war, the Sixty-Fifth Squadron. They used to take Uncle Bud back to Groton for fights. The Sixty-Fifth Fighter Squadron took Uncle Bud to Africa, all through the Tunisian campaign and up into Italy. Everywhere they had him fight, matching him against North African and against Italian gamecocks. They gave him a series of wives, Egyptian, Libyan, Italian.

Uncle Bud met his end when a jeep ran over him. His pals had him stuffed, and stood him up next to a picture of Phil Cochran, their first commander. "I suppose they figured that some day they'd stuff me and put me up there beside Uncle Bud."

In charge of the Air Commando radio was Ernie Bonham, who in civilian life had been a teacher of mechanical drawing in an Illinois high school. Bonham had gone to teachers' college for two years, not long enough for a degree, which hadn't mattered until Illinois law was changed, so that a high school teacher had to have a degree. That made Ernie mad, so he joined the Army. Having been a radio ham for years, he got into Army radio, and then served in China with the A.V.G., doing radio work with Chennault. Ernie was easy-going, chewed gum all the time, and seldom said anything. When he did, it meant something.

What he did say was usually about a fight he'd had with the British because of ciphers, their love for coding and decoding. One day Olson and Engelhardt flew over to Broad-

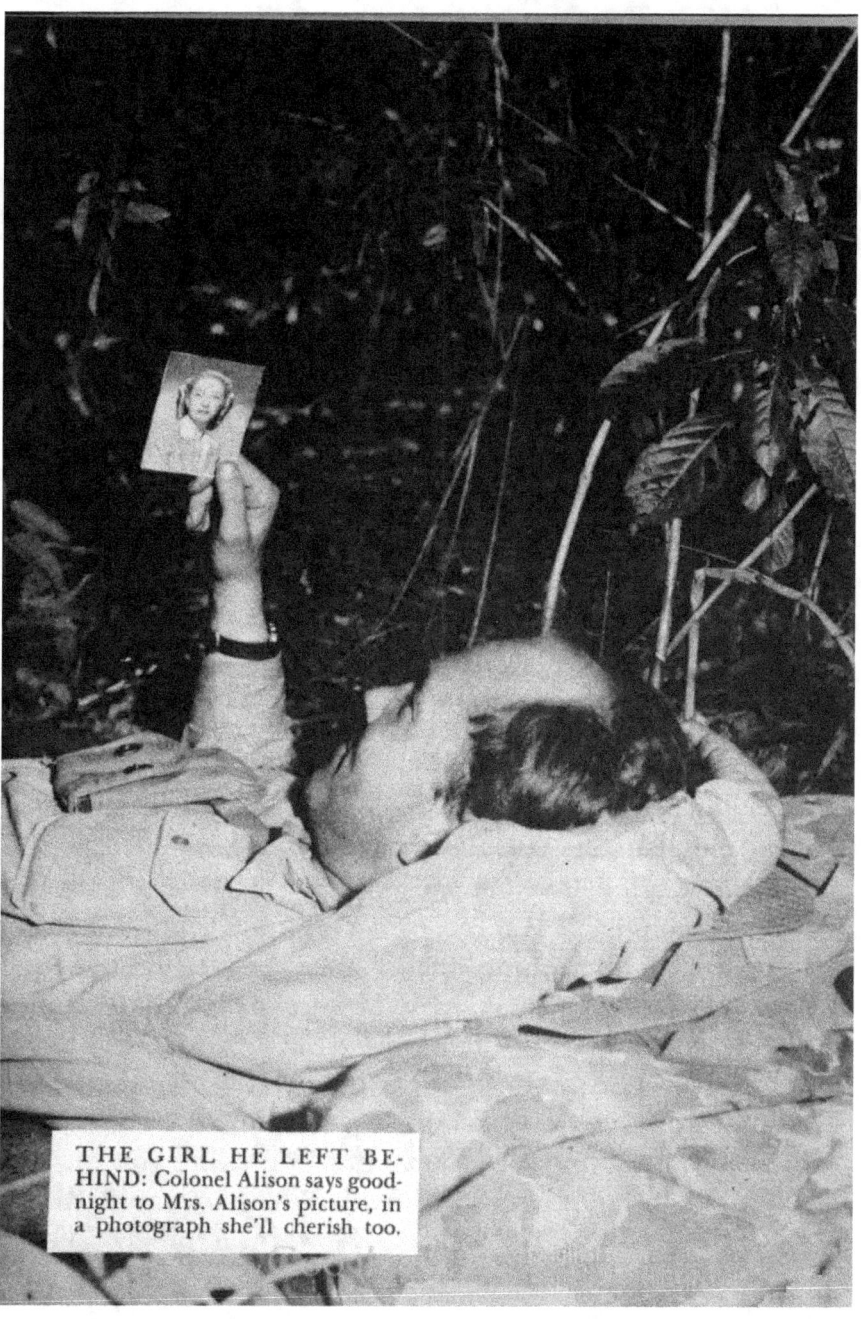

THE GIRL HE LEFT BEHIND: Colonel Alison says goodnight to Mrs. Alison's picture, in a photograph she'll cherish too.

way to see Cochran. They had a complaint to make about the British. They saw Bonham sitting, chewing gum and looking down at the ground.

"What's the matter, Ernie?"

"I'm mad, those damn British."

"Well, we're mad at them too."

Ernie smiled. "That's good."

They had their talk with Cochran, and when they came by again, Ernie was still sitting there. He looked up and said, "Stay mad."

Sergeant Orville P. Hawkins of the Air Commando radio was from Kentucky. An old-time Army sergeant, he had a Kentucky drawl, and his voice never changed. He had infinite patience. Anyone tuning in on the radio was likely to hear the slow Kentucky twang over and over again: "Red Dog to So-and-so. Red Dog to So-and-so. If you hear me, come in." When pilots got lost, he coaxed them in.

One pilot named Pitts got lost at night. Over black jungle, he reported by radio that he couldn't find his way in. They lit bonfires, opened drums of gasoline, and had flames rising high. They had a searchlight sweeping the sky, everything in the hope that in the darkness he'd see the light.

All the while Hawkins was talking to Pitts. "Keep on flying. Tell me what you see." Pitts didn't see anything. He announced, "I'm running out of gas, I'm going to jump." That was bad. If he survived in the jungle, the Japs would probably get him. Hawkins drawled into the radio, "Don't jump, I'll bring you in. Tell me what you see." Pitts saw nothing but darkness. Hawkins kept coaxing him, kept him flying a few miles more. "Don't jump, I'll bring you in. Just tell me what you see now." Finally Pitts exclaimed, "I see some light in the far distance." Hawkins replied, "That's it, head that way," and brought him in.

"HOW LONG WILL THE LULL ENDURE?"

The pilots used to make regular trips to visit Hawkins. They got to know his voice, and wanted to make his acquaintance. They'd drop in at his radio shack and thank him for the help he gave them. Hawkins, like a big, shy farm boy, was embarrassed.

Their radio communications were so good that it brought a crisis with the British. Says Cochran: "We did a lot of talking by radio. We'd call up a fellow at another base and ask him how he felt, or had he heard about the latest rumor. We cluttered up the air, so much so that at times we were blanking out the communications of the British Navy in the Indian Ocean. They asked us to stop. After that there was less radio chatting."

In the radio shack at Broadway worked Phil Cochran's brother, Joe. Back at Erie, Pennsylvania, Joe had worked in the trucking business of the oldest Cochran brother. He drove ponderous trucks on long-distance hauls, so in the Army they put him in transportation. Then he got a chance to go to flying school, but failed to make the grade as a pilot. Joe felt bad about that. He wanted to go to war. Cochran was against taking him. It might be a problem to have a corporal in an outfit of which the commanding officer was his own brother. While Cochran was in England, Alison and Engelhardt took Joe in. He did transportation work for the Air Commandos, then became the plotter for radar.

One night at Broadway Joe had word that an Air Commando plane, the code number of which was 34 Zero, was about to come in. He stepped out of the radio shack, and shouted, "Thirty-four Zero's over." Everybody thought he meant that thirty-four Japanese Zeros were over the field. The dives for foxholes were immense.

Then there was the time when Japs came over bombing and strafing. Americans dived into foxholes. British antiaircraft guns shot down five out of eight. Things quieted down, and then once again the roar of a motor, a plane coming in, a Zero. The Jap, going slow, moved over the field, and started a roll. The guns hit him. The plane disintegrated in the air. At the same moment the pilot bailed out. It was obvious that he had been shot up previously, and had come over the field to parachute down. He landed on the strip about a mile from Wild Bill Christian and a chap named Paladock (they called him Murphy). The two started on the run to get the Jap.

They passed a British major, an intelligence officer who wanted the Jap for questioning. He knew that if they got there first, they would probably knock the Jap cold in the process of grabbing everything he had for souvenirs. The major called to Wild Bill and Murphy, and ordered them to unload some mortar shells from a transport plane nearby. The Britisher then ran down to the Jap.

Wild Bill and Murphy unloaded the mortar shells according to orders, and still beat the major to the Jap. They did what the Britisher had been afraid they'd do. They slapped the Jap down, and came back with their pockets bulging, the loot including a cigarette lighter and a seal the Jap used to sign letters.

The British intelligence officer took the enemy pilot for questioning. No luck. He came back saying the Jap didn't know any English.

Wild Bill heard this and sounded off, "That buzzard understands English."

The major asked, "How do you know?"

"Well," answered Wild Bill, "when we got to him to take those things away from him, he gave us a little trouble. So I clubbed him on the jaw. A minute later I said to Murphy, 'Think I'll hit this no-good so-and-so another clout,

WOUNDED IN AIR ATTACK at Broadway, this man was flown to Hailikandi.

just for luck.' As I said it, the Jap put his hands up to his head."

The major took the Jap in hand again, and put him in the middle of a ring of Gurkha soldiers. They had fierce-looking knives in their hands and passed their thumbs over the edges. When the Jap was sufficiently frightened, the major said, "I know that you understand English."

The Jap broke down. The first thing he said was, "I never shot down American plane. I never shot down British plane. I never hurt American or British soldiers. I am a liability to the Japanese air force."

19. "They Come from the Ends of the Earth"

THE NIGHT AFTER BURMA D-DAY, while transport planes were flying troops to Jungle Broadway, the gliders struck out again and seized a second base behind the Japanese lines. The original plan had been for a two-base invasion, from which two Chindit brigades would raid enemy communications. Piccadilly had been eliminated, and now, flushed with the success at Broadway, The Man said, "We must press our luck." They reverted to the two-base plan.

The secondary base, in a clearing that Wingate selected fifty miles south of Broadway, they called Chowringhee, named after Calcutta's main street, in recognition of the Indian troops in Wingate's brigades. The pile-up of gliders at Broadway had shown the disadvantage of too many. So this time they struck out with a minimum force of twelve, carrying airfield building equipment and a small party of Wingate assault troops.

With Alison at Broadway and Olson and Boebel still

missing, Cochran had nobody to send to command the Chowringhee base but Clint Gaty. Clint was a good man, but in what kind of shape was he? His job had to do with armament, equipment, matériel. During the invasion of jungle Broadway, the previous night, he had been pressed into service for the task of directing the take-offs, sending the tow planes and gliders out, tense and exhausting labor. Gaty had not slept all night. His eyes were half shut. He looked ready to collapse.

Cochran said, "Clint, I know you're all in, but we've got to build Chowringhee, and you've got to do it. I'll get all the stuff ready and all the people. You won't have to do that. You'd better get a couple of hours sleep."

Gaty replied, "There's a war on, ain't there?"

He washed his face, shaved off several days' growth of beard to look decent enough for a commander of a base, and hurried to the task of assembling the glider force, which took off at nightfall.

The first glider in at Chowringhee was piloted by a tall, husky young fellow growing bald, who a few years before had been famous as a boy star of Hollywood, Jackie Coogan, in former times "The Kid" of motion pictures. Growing to manhood, he found Hollywood luck had deserted him. He had married and been divorced from blonde Betty Grable, who had gone on to become a fabulous star. Jackie Coogan had enlisted and gone into gliders. When the chance had come to join Project Nine, he had seized it and turned out to be a fine glider pilot. Now the first in at Chowringhee was Jackie Coogan, the Kid.

This brought a troublesome aftermath. Somehow an incorrect news story was sent, in which Jackie Coogan was represented as having been the first to land a glider in the air invasion, not in the second jungle clearing invasion, but in the first. It was made to appear that he had led the way, not into Chowringhee, but into Broadway. That transferred to the erstwhile Kid of the movies the distinction that belonged to Glider Leader Captain Bill Taylor. The story got a headline play in the United States, with elaborations of the romance of the onetime boy star of the films rising to such pioneer glory in the war of the air.

Word of this got back to the Air Commandos. The glider pilots resented it as an injustice to their leader, Bill Taylor. Jackie Coogan had had nothing to do with the false account, but incurred hostility nevertheless. He was advised to make a public and effective disclaimer of the false glory. This never came about, and the feeling of the other glider pilots was such that it was felt best, for the effect on morale, to transfer Jackie Coogan out of the Air Commandos, in which he had done a first-rate job.

The second seizure of a jungle air base went off smoothly. Landing conditions at Chowringhee were better than those at Broadway. There was one mishap: a glider flown by Lieutenant Robert Dowe overran the field and crashed into a buffalo hole. In it was a heavy tractor for airfield building. This broke loose, plunged forward and killed Lieutenant Dowe and the airborne engineer assigned to operate the tractor.

They found that the glider force had been too small, Clint Gaty reporting by radio that he needed more equipment for airstrip construction. Four more gliders, loaded with mechanism, were sent to him from Lalaghat. Another carried a bulldozer to Chowringhee from Broadway, sky transport from one newly seized base to another.

The airstrip was speedily constructed. Transport planes, the first one piloted by Captain Baker, poured in with forces of Wingate troops. Gliders and glider flyers were taken out in snatch pickups. The establishment of the Chowringhee base went so well that Wingate had a transport-plane load of tangerines and bananas flown in for his Chindits. It was a part of his mania for fresh fruit.

The commander of the Chindits at Chowringhee was Brigadier Joe Lentaigne, who always took out his false teeth when he went into battle. From the newly seized base, Joe led his long-range penetration column to the Irrawaddy. The river crossing was made in boats brought by glider. Four gliders, loaded with collapsible boats and outboard engines, landed on a sandbank of the river. It was the second boat-carrying job done by Air Commando gliders. Lentaigne's column crossed the Irrawaddy the same way Ferguson's brigade, pushing down from the north, had crossed the Chindwin.

Three of the four gliders were evacuated by a snatch pickup, one having cracked up. The glider pilots were taken out. So were four Japanese prisoners. For the first time in history, prisoners of war were transported in a glider pickup—bewildered Japs, who found themselves tied in a glider and snatched into the air.

Lentaigne's Chindits, having crossed the Irrawaddy, blew up the railroad line, ambushed parties of Japs, shot up trucks, and captured and destroyed enemy supplies. They harried the enemy supply line to the big northern Burma base at Bhamo.

Still another type of glider operation was staged. Five gliders loaded with a patrol of Chindits landed at night in the area north of Mandalay. The patrol, sent in to make guerrilla raids, was led by a young Scottish major who had risen from the ranks. He was a favorite of Wingate's and of the glider pilots. "He looked like a playboy, and stuttered," recalls Bill Taylor. "We knew him as an entertainer who played the piano and sang. His repertoire ranged from classic ballads to the troop songs famous in the British Army. In action he was one of toughest men I have ever known."

The gliders landed under fire. Japs nearby heard them, and blazed away in the darkness. The Chindits, led by their tough playboy commander, had a fight on their hands as they climbed out of gliders. These, commanded by Lieutenant Seese, had to be evacuated immediately, under fire. Lights were quickly laid out, transports came over in the darkness, and snatched the gliders, while Japs were shooting and being attacked by Chindits.

The jungle base at Chowringhee was held for only a brief time. They wanted it only as a landing field on which to set down Lentaigne's brigade for its jungle march, raiding the Japs. Then they evacuated it, just before the Japs shot up Chowringhee.

Wingate seemed to have an intuition. His guesses were often uncanny. Now The Man turned to Cochran and said throatily, "Phil, evacuate. You're through with it." They evacuated the base that night, and the next morning the Japs came over in force. Nothing was there except a couple of wrecked gliders. These fooled the enemy pilots. Mistaking the glider wrecks for planes on the ground, they strafed them with a tempest of machine-gun fire.

The Air Commando radio, monitoring Japanese broadcasts, heard enemy pilots flash back word of planes they were destroying on the ground, the base being wrecked, everybody killed. Jap troops moved into Chowringhee. Then Grant Mahoney's fighters and R. T. Smith's bombers cut them to bits with bullets and high explosive.

20. "The Blindfold Game of War"

THE THIRD JUNGLE BASE established by glider was Aberdeen, named after the Scottish home city of Wingate's wife. Aberdeen differed from Broadway and Chowringhee in that it was not an all-air invasion. The ground had already been occupied by Wingate troops. Ferguson's brigade, pushing southward on the right flank of General Stilwell's army, was in sore need of supplies, munitions and replacements. Transport planes had dropped food and ammunition on the march, but these had been insufficient, and it was decided to construct an air base at a forward point of the advance.

Ferguson sustained the only severe reverse of the Wingate campaign. A column of four hundred men was sent for a thrust through the jungle to seize the Jap airstrip at Indaw. A disastrous mishap occurred. In a skirmish an enemy shell set afire a flame-thrower on the back of a mule. The maddened animal, plunging with the flame-thrower hurling fire, stampeded the entire mule pack. Without mules, the Chindits could not transport their water supply. They marched fast for two days, hoping to procure water when they reached Indaw. They found the Japs in force. Having thirsted for two days, they had to fight for water to stay alive. They tried to get water under Japanese fire. Chindits reached the edge of the Indaw air base, but the entire force was cut off, surrounded. It looked as if the column of four hundred men was lost.

They were saved by air action. Among the trapped Chindits were officers who understood the way of the sky, and they were able to direct Air Commando planes in an assault that liberated them. The Japs were concentrating for an attack to wipe out the surrounded force. Air Commando planes smashed the enemy concentration with naval depth charges. This was a tactic already practiced by American Air Forces in the southwestern Pacific—giant explosions of depth charges used by ships against submarines. They blew a hole in the enemy line, and through this the Chindits streaked in a fast retreat. A British report stated later that the depth charges killed so many Japs the Chindits couldn't guess at the number. The whole plain was littered with enemy bodies blown apart.

The Americans guessed the Chindits had made a mistake. If, having lost their mules for the transport of water, they had called on Air Commando planes, these could have dropped water to them. Instead, they had fought a battle for water and been defeated. Tired and discouraged, they struggled back, but Wingate took the setback in characteristic fashion. "We will retrieve the defeat, and capture the airstrip at Indaw," said The Man.

Aberdeen was established with daylight glider landings. With Ferguson's troops holding the ground, there was no need for coming in at night. Six gliders, loaded with construction equipment and an airfield building crew, took off before dawn, flew most of the way under the cover of darkness, and landed at sunrise. The first one in, as at Broadway, was Bill Taylor, glider-force commander. Bill had a wild ride.

He had a co-pilot, Steve Oumanski, one of the rare characters of the Air Comandos. Steve said he was a descendant of Polish nobility. He had been in the Army for years, and, though now an officer, retained the toughness of the old-time sergeant. Everywhere he went he chiseled the local people as he had been doing in the Regular Army all over the world, in the Philippines, in Hawaii, in Panama.

Steve was an armament expert. He had built the steel tubing mounts for the antiaircraft machine guns of Project Nine, and had constructed a stock for shooting a .30 caliber machine gun from the shoulder. Not many men were strong enough to do it, but Steve put a .30 caliber to his shoulder and fired it like a rifle.

Steve was a demolition expert. He knew all about high explosives. He set booby traps and laid land mines in the fortification of jungle bases. He kept so much explosive material around him, his comrades were afraid to go near him. They never knew but what he might have the door of his *basha* booby-trapped, ready to blow up if opened.

Steve liked sardines. So did the jackals in the surrounding jungle. Every night they paid Steve's *basha* at Lalaghat a visit to lick the empty sardine cans. Steve booby-trapped the sardine cans. That night the Japanese air force paid a visit, and dropped some bombs at Lalaghat. The Air Commandos were in slit trenches when the bombs fell. The attack having ended, they were going back to their *bashas*, when the jackals arrived at Steve's sardine cans. A violent blast shook the night. Bombs, they thought, and went diving back into slit trenches.

"THE BLINDFOLD GAME OF WAR"

In the booby-trap explosion not a jackal was killed, but the blast blew out one side of Steve's *basha*.

Bill and Steve flew to Aberdeen in the first of six gliders. There was no moon, and it was pitch black in the darkness before dawn. "Down below," relates Taylor, "it was so dark that it was impossible to see any clearing in which we might land if compelled to cut loose. I thought of Johnny Alison's description of how he had landed his glider in the invasion of Broadway, 'by the close-your-eyes method.' We had in the glider a 4500-pound bulldozer and heavy crates of TNT, Steve's pride and joy. Perilous cargo for a crack-up landing in the black jungle.

"The air was turbulent, and in the moonless night I had a hard time holding my position behind the transport plane. We were building up a lot of slack in the tow line. Once the slackened rope whipped back over the glider and almost went around our landing gear. Steve thought it had fouled the landing gear, and that we would have to cut loose. He reached to release the tow line. I nearly took his arm off, knocking his hand from the release mechanism. Steve almost had us down for a crack-up with the bulldozer and the TNT."

Their landing at Aberdeen was one of the freaks of the Wingate campaign. "It was growing light when we arrived at the place for landing, an open space of ground, where Ferguson's Chindits were waiting for us. I released the tow line, and went into a slow glide, heading for a rice paddy below. I felt it was time to show my boys coming in behind me how to make a perfect glider landing. I misjudged a down draft. The glider began to stall. I had to try a pancake into the rice paddy. Ahead was a tall tree, which was just six inches too high. I couldn't get control of the glider, and one wing seemed sure to hit the treetop. That would mean a crash, with the bulldozer and Steve's cargo of high explosives.

The wing was just about to smack into the treetop, when the tree fell down. It was knocked over with a loud bang right in our faces. British soldiers on the ground were clearing out trees, and by luck had dynamited that one just as the glider was about to hit it.

"We sailed on over the fallen tree. The glider, out of control, crashed into a paddy bund, an embankment. The impact knocked off the landing gear and collapsed the glider wings so that they looked like a pair of hound dog's ears.

"As we climbed out of the wreck, I was embraced in a tremendous bear hug. It was Steve. The big bruiser was hugging and kissing me. I thought he had gone out of his head. Then he explained that, in the landing as the tree fell down, he had vowed that if he ever got to earth safely, he was going to kiss me. And he sure did.

"I never lived down that messy landing at Aberdeen. It was the only glider I'd ever wrecked. My glider pilots now had a chance to razz me, and they did. I'm not superstitious, but there was something I had overlooked. It had been my habit always, when starting on a glider trip, to write my wife's name, Kathy, on one side of the pilot seat. This had begun back in training days when I had taken my wife for glider rides. She was the first woman ever to fly in a big military glider. In the take-off for Aberdeen I had been in such a hurry that I had forgotten the ritual of writing Kathy's name."

The landings were made near a native village, and probably created a Burmese legend for the future. The villagers were astounded when out of the sky at dawn came big birds, out of whose bowels emerged jeeps, bulldozers and tractors. The whole village turned out and put on a parade, with a local priestess carried in state, a Burmese procession to hail what to the villagers was the utterly supernatural.

"THE BLINDFOLD GAME OF WAR"

The Chindits said there were Japs in an adjacent valley across a range of hills, and that the enemy would speedily be apprised of the air base activity at Aberdeen, as soon as a native or two slipped off to tell them. The Japs were paying large sums of money for information. The calculation was that it would be twenty-four hours before the enemy could get across the hills with a force strong enough to smash the airfield job. There was that space of time for the building of a strip and the landing of troops to hold the base. It was a race against time, a fast job of airfield construction directed by Lieutenant Di Sandro. The race was won by two hours. Wingate troops, fanning out through the jungle, made contact with an advancing enemy force two hours after they landed.

Japanese planes assailed Aberdeen. They made a strafing attack. One glider pilot was hit, Lieutenant Satron. A bullet drilled through his thigh. Two British soldiers came to his aid. They were leading him away, supporting him, with Satron's arms across their shoulders. They were halfway across the field when another Jap plane roared over, strafing. Despite his wound, Satron made a dash, outran the British soldiers who had been supporting him, and beat them to the nearest cover.

Chindit Commander Brigadier Ferguson was one of Wingate's best officers. He was a monocled Englishman with red handle-bar mustaches, who wore his eyeglass into battle. Dick Boebel knew him well. "I remember sitting in conferences with him time and again in an old native shack built on stilts twenty feet off the ground, with no light except a couple of candles. He was easy to get along with and interesting to talk to. He had written comic pieces for *Punch* in London, and was a poet. He always carried a copy of Byron with him. When we parted, he gave it to me, writing an inscription in the front of it."

"THE BLINDFOLD GAME OF WAR"

At Aberdeen, Ferguson refitted his brigade with airborne supplies and equipment, and eventually joined forces with Lentaigne's column, which had started out from Chowringhee. Together they raised havoc along the Jap supply lines.

21. "Jungle-Favor Go with Thee!"

THE ORIGINAL WINGATE IDEA had been a light-plane job for evacuating wounded, and that was not neglected. With the Chindits in the thick of their jungle campaign, the small-aircraft section of the Air Commandos assumed a major role. Taking out the wounded was one of the toughest of tasks.

In assembling light planes for Project Nine, it had been hard to find a leader. "We had trouble getting someone who lived and ate small airplanes. We knew that somewhere in the business there was one fellow who would give his eyeteeth to run the small-plane section of our show. But where was he? We made inquiries, but apparently there was nobody like that in the United States."

Then glider man Bill Taylor had said, "When I was in Panama, I knew a fellow down there who was doing just about everything that you could think up for small planes, even dropping bombs. His name was Andrew Rebori, and he may still be down there." They checked, and found that

"JUNGLE-FAVOR GO WITH THEE!"

Andrew Rebori was in Panama, still doing a light-plane job in the Canal Zone. Over jungle county too, in a region similar to Burma. Evidently here was their man. They made a long-distance call to Panama, although, as Bill Taylor put it, no telephone would be needed by Rebori. Said Taylor, "Just have him shout, and you'll hear him from Panama." Which was almost correct.

Rebori had a very deep, loud voice, which he didn't control. He talked with a noisy, discordant bellow. When they asked him on long distance about running a force of light planes in a risky and important show, he roared, "Okay, you fix it with my C. O. and I'll be there, pronto!"

Despite his name, Rebori was a redheaded Irishman, very thin. In Panama he had had malaria many times. He was a graduate engineer, and came from Chicago. He was opinionated and stubborn, argumentative and hot-tempered. He believed in directives. He wrote voluminous documents about everything, carried a typewriter every place he went, and pounded it every night, which Cochran didn't like. That fugitive from business administration scowled at the reams of documents Rebori ground out. But that was the Rebori way.

From Panama he brought pilots whom he had been training. His number-two man was Big Ed Smith. He took his gang to a Project Nine base at Raleigh, North Carolina, and trained them with a ferocious energy, teaching them to land in the smallest spaces—on roads, in cabbage patches, the most difficult places he could find. To Cochran and Alison he thundered, "Come on down to Raleigh and look us over. When you see a big pile of wrecked airplanes, you'll know we've been working hard." His pilots did wreck many planes, but not one of them was ever hurt.

Rebori, for all his light-plane enthusiasm and ability as a

H. Q. FOR TRANSPORT PILOTS: A tent at Broadway is their 'ome from 'ome.

leader, was not a skillful light-plane pilot. He knew what he wanted, but couldn't do it himself. Aware of this, he would stand in front of his men and rumble, "I can't do this thing but, by God, you're going to do it!"

An engineer, Rebori went to Wright Field and worked out a bomb rack that would drop either bombs, gasoline or supplies from the wings of his small planes. That was much in accord with the ideas of Cochran and Alison. "We were dreaming of doing things that small planes had never attempted before, dropping all sorts of things."

Immediately after their arrival in India, before even the maneuver in Gwalior, Rebori's light planes did a job. This was in South Burma. It had nothing to do with the Wingate campaign. A British division invading Arakan had got into trouble. It was cut off by the Japs. The British were sending big transports over, dropping food and munitions. But that wasn't enough. The surrounded division had numbers of wounded.

"Our light planes ran an ambulance service under the eyes of the Japs. For two weeks they evacuated wounded, taking out eight hundred. We put bomb racks on the wings, and the little planes, while on the ambulance job, hit the Japs with three-hundred-pound bombs. The troops in the trap, instead of being wiped out, were able to keep on fighting, because of the help from the sky. They gave the Japs a beating, killed three thousand of them."

This light-plane operation was a policy job. They did it to create good will, what they called "baksheesh to the British."

The Wingate ground campaign, the war of the Chindits in the jungle, brought to the light planes their test and challenge, the evacuation of thousands of wounded under the worst conditions of jungle difficulty and peril. The small planes had no possible protection against Jap fighters. Their

LT. COLONEL CLINT GATY ready to bring in planes with signal lamp at Broadway. Wingate can be seen in the rear.

only safety was in evasion, weaving in and out of treetop level—jungle hedge-hopping. The British called them "grasshoppers."

They conducted a shuttle service. Big cargo planes, flying at night, would land supplies at Broadway or Aberdeen. From there the light planes would fly the supplies, in daylight hedge-hopping, to small, hastily improvised airstrips laid down by advance parties of Chindits. There they'd pick up wounded and fly them back to hospital bases. In an L-1 or an L-5 they could evacuate one injured soldier or two per trip. Stretcher cases were difficult. They took out more than two thousand wounded. They evacuated Chindits who were tired out and replaced these with fresh soldiers, operating a system of replacements by air.

The attitude of the Wingate wounded was one of touching gratitude. They magnified in their own minds the job the light planes were doing in taking them out, so that they wouldn't have to be abandoned to the jungle and the Japs. The British voiced their gratitude in glowing terms. The West Africans, Indians and Burmese, who couldn't speak English, expressed their appreciation with glances and gesticulations. Wingate said the evacuation of the wounded meant everything for morale.

It had been so different the year before when they had had to leave the wounded behind. Ferguson told of one boy who had broken his leg in a fall. Attacked by Japs, his detachment had to get out. The boy wanted to be killed, rather than left behind. They gave him some food, and left him, but as they started off, they looked back and pictured themselves in the same plight. They never heard of him again. This discouraged them terribly.

The light planes picked up three survivors of the previous Wingate campaign. Abandoned, they had gone through hell.

"JUNGLE-FAVOR GO WITH THEE!"

They had been found by the natives and adjusted themselves to jungle village life.

Eighteen evacuations were made by helicopter. In one case a transport plane with three wounded men aboard had engine trouble, and was forced to make a landing on a road held by Japs. The pilot helped the wounded into the jungle, hid them, and radioed their location. It would have taken a hundred soldiers four days to get to them through the jungle. Light planes could not have got at the injured men. The order was given: "Send the egg beater." The helicopter took them out.

But, on the whole, they had bad luck with helicopters. They brought four from the United States. These came in halves. They got the nose of the first one, but the fuselage section never showed up. It had been shipped by air, but the plane carrying it crashed at Cairo. The two parts of the second helicopter arrived in India, but got lost there. The third they put together, and flew it around. It hit some telephone lines, crashed and was destroyed, killing one of two men aboard. The fourth helicopter was successful, and performed the egg-beater tasks of evacuating the wounded. Its pilot was a Lieutenant Harmon, a light-plane flyer who had been grounded by the doctors because he had asthma. He didn't let on about that, smuggled himself out, and became the first pilot ever to take a helicopter into combat.

The command of the light-plane section was shifted. Andy Rebori, who had done a tremendous job, moved on, and was succeeed by Clint Gaty and then Dick Boebel. After his jungle adventure, walking out, Boebel was made intelligence officer, and now light-plane commander. He was not a rated pilot. Having failed to make the grade in flying school back home, he had no wings. As light-plane leader, he felt he couldn't have the confidence of his pilots unless he flew with them. Without wings, he led rated pilots on missions, flying in combat.

"We had to let him do it," explains Cochran, "because we were short of leadership talent. There in the field, because of the necessity, we broke a standing rule for the Army Air Forces. Later, the British gave Boebel the status of a pilot. In fact, he won the American Air Medal and Distinguished Flying Cross for exploits that he performed without American wings. He was probably the only man in World War II to do so."

Boebel specialized in a method whereby light planes collaborated in bombing assaults. In jungle hedge-hopping, he'd spot a munitions dump or a camouflaged rice depot, to which he would afterward lead bombers and mark the target with a smoke bomb. Skimming low in a light plane, he could see clearly what was to be hit, could mark it accurately, and the planes above could bomb the smoke.

"One day," he recalls, "I went out in a light plane with Wild Bill Christian to a string of Jap supply dumps that I had located. We skimmed low and marked them one after another for the bombers following us. We put down smoke bombs in quick succession, and the targets were hit just as fast. Then, as we dropped the last smoke, we saw a bunch of Japs coming along the road in a truck. They spotted our light plane, and thought we were going to bomb them. They dived out of the truck, and ran to what they thought would be safety. They swarmed to the exact place where the smoke bomb had hit, and were there when the fragmentation projectiles from the bombers came down. They must all have been wiped out."

Smoke tactics were used extensively, with British ground troops as well as American light planes marking targets. Cochran tells the story: "We would inveigle the British to

"JUNGLE-FAVOR GO WITH THEE!"

send out a patrol of a hundred men or so, and find out where the Japs had their supplies. They would set up some smoke at a point where it would be a guiding beacon, and our planes would go over and slam the target. Or maybe the British would send word to us that one of their patrols last night saw fifty *bashas* loaded with so-and-so at such and such a place. But it got so that we wouldn't take any targets from the British unless they marked them with smoke or gave us exact locations. We didn't want to waste our time.

"We used our fighters as bombers, and often used our bombers as fighters. They didn't exactly do ground strafing, but our bombers had a cannon in the nose and shot up Jap targets on the ground."

Even a bomber on a photographic mission was always ready to attack with bombs or cannon shells. "I recall," says Cameraman Russhon, "how once, flying with R. T. Smith, I was filming a railroad line from six thousand feet, and saw a locomotive running along down there. I called this to the attention of R. T., and he peeled off for a kill. He came in broadside on the locomotive and put two 75 mm. shells into the boiler. You should have seen that locomotive blow up.

"R. T. was better with his 75 mm. cannon than a lot of fancy officers with their .45 automatics in target practice. I personally saw over forty locomotives destroyed by sharp-shooting with 75 mm. shells. It was great sport. Phil Cochran loved warehouse supplies and ammunition. Johnny Alison preferred aerial combat and close air support. Grant Mahoney enjoyed nothing like destroying Jap planes. R. T. Smith's delight was any and all rolling stock."

Russhon tells of a startling adventure with a bomb. "We had been on a bomber mission, and were coming in to land. I was in the rear compartment. Everything seemed calm and perfect, but the moment our wheels touched the ground I found myself up at the roof of the plane, hit by something heavy and violent. When we got out I told the pilot, R. T. Smith, that just as we had landed something had come up and kicked the hell out of me. He couldn't understand what I was talking about. Just then an ordnance officer informed us that a five-hundred-pound bomb had failed to leave the bomb bay. Over the target it had failed to drop. So when we landed, the bomb was hanging there. As the wheels touched ground, it fell through the bomb-bay doors, hit the runway, and bounced back up into the rear compartment, hitting me and knocking me against the top of the plane."

Notable among the Air Commandos was Flight Surgeon Cortez Enloe, an officer more at home in the laboratories of science than in the hurly-burly of war. Dr. Enloe had studied in Germany, where he had been a close friend of General Wedemeyer, at that time American military attaché at Berlin. It was General Wedemeyer, afterward our top general in China, who had taken Cort Enloe to the India-Burma theater.

Later in the war Enloe was to figure in phases of science that attended the collapse of Nazi Germany, leading one of the scientific teams that the Office of Strategic Services sent hastily into captured German cities to take over scientific establishments, the equipment, the secrets, the research technologists. Meanwhile, he was enjoying a fling of adventure as an Air Commando.

He studied problems of air operation in an area of tropical diseases, and went on flights for the excitement of it. It was in the character of this scientific research worker to note experiences and sensations with subtle perception and to write them down with sensitive skill. He tells of a flight he made with Cameraman Russhon in a bomber piloted by Captain Radovich, who was leading a squadron. They did some uneventful photographing, and it was time to go home.

"JUNGLE-FAVOR GO WITH THEE!"

"Radovich, the irrepressible boy of Serbian extraction, whose feather-trigger temper had earned him the nickname 'The Mad Chetnick,' would never think of going home without a fight. He led us west toward the broad expanse of the vital Irrawaddy. As we approached the river at about a thousand feet, we spotted a line of rafts loaded with trucks and a double-decked steamer and a large barge unloading at Tagaung.

"During the next twenty minutes I lived a year. I expected to be terrified on my first treetop bombing attack. Instead, all my fear was in being afraid of the fear itself, for now that it is over I can't recall having experienced any sensation at all during the raid itself. It was something like the stage fright that vanishes once the acting commences. Perhaps, I should have been stirred by the sight of the houses flying into the air as we overshot the boats, but there was nothing personal about our savage onslaught as we loosed our shells and our bombs. I can't recall having given any thought to the fact that we'd kill a hundred people, and destroy their cattle and wreck their homes. At such times the attack is the thing. The only thoughts in one's mind are, 'Will we hit those rafts down there? Can we sink that steamer, burn that barge?' Everything else is dismissed from consciousness."

Cort Enloe tells how Radovich's bomber squadron, escorted by fighters, pressed the attack, making repeated passes. One of the bomber pilots was Murrell Dillard, a Florida lad, who went charging into the antiaircraft fire that now was blazing at them. Enloe describes what happened:

"Suddenly, Grant Mahoney, who was watching the show from above, screamed into the radio, 'Rad, look!' We looked back on the target in time to see a wing fly into the air and a flaming rocket of yellow flame shoot up from just above the trees. It was good old enthusiastic Dillard riding to death.

"JUNGLE-FAVOR GO WITH THEE!"

The bomber careened as her tail section struck the trees. It seemed to come apart and fly into the sky. The broken plane skimmed along like a huge torpedo gone berserk, spending the momentum of Dil's last attack. It plunged into the trees, searing a path through the jungle foliage of the town for two hundred yards. Suddenly it came to a stop and there was a violent explosion which sent a pillar of black smoke rolling up high above us. Then there was nothing but silent flame.

"As if everyone hadn't seen it, Radovich, who felt the responsibility for his men more than they will ever know, kept calling, 'That's our plane down there. That's no bomb burst, that's our plane down there!' We had made four passes at the target and there was no stomach for going on. Calmly, quietly, Rad called the others. He pressed the throat microphone against his neck as he said, 'Rad to all planes. Re-form, fellows. Re-form, we're going home, we're going home. Over and off.' He switched the radio off, turned and said only, 'Goddam!'"

Fighter Pilot Bob Pettit had a streak of stubbornness. There was a bridge below Bhamo that the British had bombed many times without success. It was of vital importance for the Jap supply line to Bhamo and on to Myitkyina. The bridge was put on the target list for the Air Commandos. They said they'd get it, went over, and missed. That made Bob Pettit so angry he couldn't get over it. Time and again they'd see two fighter planes with bombs go out by themselves, and they'd say, "There's Bob and some kid going after that damn bridge again."

He finally got it with two one-thousand-pound bombs. They took pictures of the wreck, and remarked casually to the British, "Oh, by the way, we got that bridge below Bhamo today," never telling how many times they had

BULLSEYE: Smoke shows a hit on the motor pool and supply depot, Wunto.

missed. One British report stated that the bridge they had demolished had been a camouflage span the Japs had put across for deception. That incited the most copious picture-making job of the Air Commando show, Russhon's photographic department turning out an amount of elaborate camera studies of the bombed span to prove to the most skeptical that it was the real bridge that had been bombed.

They ripped out Japanese telephone lines by using a trick that Cochran had worked in North Africa. A fighter plane would fly with a dangling weight at the end of a cable and whip it around wires and rip them out. The Japs hardly ever had their telephone communications intact. Stubborn Bob Pettit was out on a wire-cutting job near Bhamo one day, and was coming up to the telephone line, when he lost the cable and the weight dangling under his plane. His wire-ripping equipment gone, he was so angry that he flew through the wires. He plowed his P-51 through the telephone line in four or five places. It was a wild but an effective job of disrupting Jap wire communications.

When Pettit got back he had cuts in the propeller and wings of his plane. The ground crew chief was annoyed. Pettit said, "I'm sorry to make trouble for the ground crew, but I was so mad I couldn't help it."

The major task for the fighter planes was dive-bombing and strafing to support Wingate's jungle columns in battle with Japs. British ground troops, held up by an enemy force, would call on the Air Commandos to clear a way through the Japs with accurate bombing and aerial machine-gun fire. This ground support was a specialty with Cochran and Alison, who had developed ideas for the collaboration of ground and air.

It irked fighter-plane-leader Grant Mahoney, with his one-man war against the Japanese Air Force. To Mahoney and his gang ground support was dull work. They wanted to fight air battles and shoot down Jap planes. A fighter pilot could drop dive bombs all day, but unless he destroyed enemy planes, it meant nothing to his career.

As old fighter pilots, Cochran and Alison understood this. They held a few meetings in which they explained to Mahoney and his pilots that they were not in Burma for air combat against the Japs. No matter how dull it might be, the job was to support Wingate's troops. Mahoney and his pilots saw the sense of it, but were not satisfied. They wanted to go down to the south toward Mandalay, where the Japanese Air Force was. "You'd think," says Cochran, "that old song about going back to Mandalay had got everybody." So Cochran and Alison had to compromise. Every so often they'd let Mahoney and his fighter pilots go south and fight air battles just to keep them happy.

Grant Mahoney had his eye on some airfields down toward Mandalay. He hoped the Japs would bring in a force of planes down there. One morning a job of ground support was to be done for Wingate. P-51s were to strafe a Jap position that was holding up a British column. Mahoney was unenthusiastic. He wanted to take his fighter squadron down to the flying fields near Mandalay, and play his hunch. He was itching with the belief that Jap planes would appear there. Cochran and Alison gave him positive orders. "No, Grant. It is likely enough the Japs may bring in planes, but General Wingate has got an important job for us to do this morning." Then they added a compromise. "You can do both. You can do the ground support job in the morning. Then in the afternoon you can fly down and have a look at those fields."

Mahoney agreed to the compromise. In the morning he and his fighters shot up Japs on the ground. They disorganized the enemy force, and the Chindits broke through. Then, in the afternoon, Mahoney took a squadron of fighters south. Back at headquarters, where Cochran and Alison were following Mahoney's proceedings by radio, they failed to hear from him. Time went by. Something seemed amiss. They had misgivings about having let Mahoney go. The flying fields near Mandalay were really none of the business of the Air Commandos, out of their scope of action, too far south.

"Then suddenly we realized that Grant's bullheadedness and opposition had paid off. There was a terrific noise on the air. Over the radio came Mahoney's voice yelling, 'My God, they're all over the place!'" They could hear him direct his fighter planes, attacking Japs on the ground, battling them in the air. "We realized that Grant had hit the jackpot. The Jap planes that he had been expecting had shown up, and how!

"We immediately got together all the other fighters, and a force of bombers, and sent them down to join in the fun. They shot down Jap planes and burned them on the ground. One boy made seven strafing runs, when usually you make only one. The Japs lost a lot of planes that day, because Grant Mahoney had been so stubborn."

In the month of March the Air Commandos got one-fifth of the Japanese Air Force in Burma. Once, eighty enemy airplanes were moved up against them. These were concentrating on a flying field late in the afternoon for an attack the following morning. Grant Mahoney's fighters caught them as they arrived, and burned forty-nine. Early the next morning they finished what the Japs still had left.

22. "There Was a Man"

The campaign had been successful. beyond all expectations. With time limited to the several months of the dry season, the effort had been so swift and decisive that now, less than three weeks after Burma D-Day, the strategy of the operation had been fully established against the Japanese. Jungle Broadway was a busy airport far behind enemy lines, a base from which radiated aerial supply lines to the Chindits. Aberdeen, likewise busy, was the main base for the light planes, the flying ambulances, in the evacuation of the wounded. These worked in and out, shuttling the injured from jungle fighting grounds to hospital bases in India. At the roadblock Mad Mike Calvert maintained a strangling grip on the Japanese railroad and highway life line through the Indaw-Katha bottleneck. Ferguson's brigade and Lentaigne's column made destructive forays against the river line of the Irrawaddy.

The original Wingate long-range penetration idea had now been so far transformed that it had reverted to the past.

The Man still called it long-range penetration, but it was back to the old idea of fortresses, infantry based on strongholds. To Cochran and Alison it suggested the American blockhouse system of the Indian wars, when the frontiersmen used the strategy of fort, from which parties sallied forth to fight the Redskins.

The dry-season flow of supplies to the Japanese forces in northern Burma was being choked off, and the dry season was the only period during which supplies could be moved effectively in the Burma jungle. Virtually cut off and deprived of supplies, the Japs would be helpless against the advance of Stilwell's army.

Wingate expanded with enlarged ideas. To Cochran and Alison he propounded new plans and projects. They collaborated avidly in visions of great action, their own imagination stirred by farther horizons of all-air invasion. The seizure of ground by air, which they had demonstrated, opened unmeasured possibilities.

Plans now envisioned the holding of jungle bases during the monsoon. Broadway, it was reckoned, could be maintained during the rains, Aberdeen too. During the wet season Chindits and Air Commandos could be reorganized and increased for new and greater thrusts into enemy territory, thrusts beyond Burma, into China to the Pacific. They saw a vision of repeating the seizure of bases by air, as at Broadway, in a leapfrog series, one air invasion after another along a line from Burma to the China coast.

The Man was everywhere, flying by light plane, transport and bomber from one base to another, from his headquarters at Imphal to Broadway to Aberdeen.

On the afternoon of March 24, nineteen days after Burma D-Day, Wingate took off for another of his aerial tours of inspection and meetings with his brigade commanders. He

THE MAN GOES ABOARD: General Wingate, wearing his African sun helmet, takes off on an inspection trip.

flew to Broadway in a B-25, escorted by fighters. There he conferred with the Americans and his own Chindit officers. From Broadway, he took a light plane to Aberdeen, where he visited Bill Taylor and his glider pilots and got reports from British leaders. He returned by light plane to Broadway, and there he called Cochran back at headquarters in Imphal Valley and asked for the B-25 to come and get him.

"He was always considerate of using our airplanes. He would phone in from a jungle base and say, 'I've been talking to so-and-so, they are enthusiastic about the air support you've been giving them, Phil. Will you send a plane for me?' I told him I had already sent the B-25 to get him. It should be at Broadway in ten minutes. He said, 'Thank you, thank you.' His manner was always one of courtesy and appreciation."

The B-25, piloted by Lieutenant Hodges, arrived on schedule. Wingate flew back to his headquarters in Imphal Valley, and stopped there briefly. He decided to go on to Air Commando base at Lalaghat, and took off in Hodges' B-25, accompanied by several British officers, two British journalists and an American colonel. It was night now, and they flew in the darkness.

Cochran relates: "The first intimation that I had, came when our bomber leader, R. T. Smith, called me and said that one of his pilots had just reported seeing what he thought was a plane crash and explosion in the hills. The pilot, Lieutenant Richard Benjamin, was flying along when he saw a great flash of fire in the night. The position he reported was about where Wingate's plane would have been. We were startled. We thought it couldn't be Wingate. It couldn't be. But Wingate failed to appear."

Thus they had their first flash of the news they couldn't believe. Their minds couldn't encompass it. Everything had been Wingate. The campaign had seemed like an extension of his personality. They had nicknamed him The Man. Now the shock, their appalled refusal to accept the meaning of the explosion in the hills, made them realize how truly he had been The Man.

They checked and rechecked, trying to find some other explanation. They called all their flying fields, hoping the Wingate B-25 might have got off its course and been forced to land. They checked with Benjamin, the bomber pilot who had seen the flame in the hills. The more precisely he gave the place and time, the more evident it was that the Wingate plane would have been at that place at that time.

All night after the dismaying flash they rushed around in nerve-racked anxiety, busily active, trying to do something, learn something, trying to disprove what more and more seemed to be true. They hoped the explosion in the hills would turn out to be something else. Or perhaps, if Wingate had crashed, he might have survived, although Benjamin's description of the explosion in the night made that seem unlikely.

The next morning John Alison flew with Benjamin, who directed him to the place. They saw the wreck of a plane that had smashed to scattered pieces and burned. The fragments looked like a B-25.

It seemed impossible that anybody could have survived such a crash, but still they could not be certain about what had happened to Wingate, not until a ground party had gone to the wreck. They sent a ground party. The smashed plane was deep in the difficult hill country. It took the searchers two days to get to it.

When the party reached the wreck they found little recognizable. The plane, upon crashing, had burned fiercely, and only charred remnants were left. Bodies could not be identified, but they corresponded to the party that had taken off with Wingate. There was one eloquent sign, a helmet. It was a burned shell, but unmistakably Wingate's sun helmet, the tropical headgear he always wore. It had been one of his many idiosyncrasies to go campaigning in the old helmet he had worn in war adventures in Ethiopia. A few telltale papers were found, scraps that had been hurled from the wreck and scattered. These had belonged to Wingate, letters addressed to him.

Exactly what had hapened they couldn't guess. The evidence at the scene of the wreck indicated that the bomber had not flown into the hill. It had fallen and crashed. Something had happened to the plane to make it dive down into the ground.

The death of Wingate was kept a secret. The British were afraid that the news might impair the morale of the Chindits, Wingate's personal power among them having been that great. Cochran and Alison, to conceal the truth, started the rumor that The Man, as one of his peculiar tricks, had flown to Delhi. They let out intimation that, having started for Lalaghat, he had changed his mind, and wasn't that a damnfool thing to do?

The Chindit command was taken over by Brigadier Lentaigne, leader of the force that had pushed through the jungle from Chowringhee, but that was kept a secret. Wingate's adjutant, Brigadier Tulloch, gave Lentaigne's orders in the name of The Man. At Chindit headquarters Cochran and Alison gathered with the British officers. "We got together and said now that Wingate was gone we had to work harder. We pledged ourselves to Brigadier Lentaigne. He said he needed our help. He was a man of broad vision and generous mind."

Cochran and Alison flew to Delhi, and conferred with

Mountbatten. The meeting was in the same stately office in which Cochran had faced the High Command of southeastern Asia and with Wingate's letter had saved the Chindits and the Air Comandos. It was a familiar scene for him, but now Wingate was gone.

"Usually people ham those things up as a bit dramatic, but the feeling was there, as Louis the Lord talked to us. He said that in Wingate's death he, John and I had sustained a great personal loss, and that we must carry on. A fire had been kindled in the three of us, and we must continue that Wingate fire."

They talked about keeping Wingate's death still a secret. Cochran and Alison stated that, so far as they knew, nothing had leaked out from their bases.

There were many among the Air Commandos who knew or surmised the truth, but they kept silent. "It's one of the nicest things I ever saw a bunch of American kids do," says Cochran. "They realized we had an awful thing on our hands. The bomber crews knew that neither Hodges nor the B-25 in which he had flown with Wingate had come back. At our headquarters the boys knew how badly we had been worried that night, rushing around, showing all the signs of anxiety. In the office they all knew that Wingate was dead. They knew also that we didn't want the word to get out, and they kept everything to themselves."

The British, on their side, were ruthless in imposing secrecy. At a hotel bar in Delhi a British major was talking to an Air Commando who, keeping the secret, spoke of Wingate as if he were still alive. The Britisher exclaimed, "My God, haven't you heard? Wingate is dead!" A British intelligence officer nearby heard the remark. He immediately arrested the major.

Says Cochran: "For a long time afterward we caught ourselves speaking of Wingate as though he were still alive. We still called the Chindits 'Wingate people.' His personal force had been such that its absence left a terrific hangover. We would talk in meeting as if he were still alive. Somebody would say, 'Find out what Wingate thinks about this thing.' The Man had exerted such influence on us that it still hung over our minds. A month after he was dead his spirit still dominated everything that the Chindits and the Air Commandos did.

"Even General Stratemeyer, American commander in India, would say, 'Wingate wants this or that. What do you think of his idea?' John Alison and I talked it over and said, 'We'd better tell him that Wingate is dead. He is our commanding general, and he should know.' So we went back and said, 'General, there is something I suppose we had better tell you, Wingate is dead.'

"He said, 'Yes, I know. I've known about it since the second day, but I didn't think we ought to talk as if we knew it.'"

Finally, the secret had to come out. The British had a notion of making a kind of Lawrence of Arabia legend out of Wingate by letting word leak out that he was off on an ultrasecret war mission, the way Lawrence of Arabia was so often rumored to be on an undercover job in some distant place or other. That way, Wingate could be kept alive in gossip and superstition. However, it was realized that the thing could be overdone. Fooling the Chindits too long could have a boomerang effect. One intention was to have Prime Minister Churchill make a solemn announcement of Wingate's death to Parliament in London.

Actually, the news was first made public when Wingate's wife put an obituary notice in a London newspaper. The Wingates, a devoted couple, had been childless, but Wingate's son Jonathan was born a few weeks after his father's death. Jonathan and his mother, who shares her husband's love for Palestine, now divide their time between Scotland and a second home at Tel Aviv.

MRS. WINGATE IN NEW YORK: This photograph of Lorna Wingate was made when she spoke at a dinner given by Hadassah in aid of refugees escaping from Europe to Israel.
Wide World Photo

23. "For Their Work Continueth"

GENERAL ORDE WINGATE died at the climax of his life's achievement, just as the stranglehold had been fastened on the Japanese life line. The success he had directed needed only to be maintained. For Brigadier Lentaigne, his successor, few offensive operations were left. The task was now to hang on, and block supplies for the Japs in northern Burma during the remainder of the dry season. Chindits waged defensive battles, American planes gave them air support.

The Japs were reacting increasingly through the air and on the ground. They made passes at jungle Broadway, air raiding and thrusting with ground troops. Their planes bombed the air base fortress, and sky battles were fought. Chindit patrols clashed with enemy parties in the jungle. There was one major crisis at Broadway.

Japs came by night, infiltrating through the jungle, and got inside of the barbed wire enclosure protecting the base. At first they were mistaken for British troops. Andy Rebori

WINGATE AND LENTAIGNE: "The Man" with the general who succeeded him.

says that in the darkness 250 enemy soldiers marched down the middle of the field, shouting commands in English. They were inside the gate before the alarm was given. A Gurkha soldier was the first to realize that these newcomers were Japanese. Shooting started. Nobody knew who was shooting at what. Rebori reckons that on the first night the Chindits fired two hundred rounds of ammunition and killed two Japs in the wild, confused fighting in the darkness. The Japs made their way to planes on the field, assailed them with bayonets, ran holes through them. Instead of burning them or knocking out the engines by firing bullets into them, they thought that by ripping the fabric with bayonets they were destroying the planes.

The second night, with the British doing little more than holding their ground, the Japs would crawl up to their positions and shout, "Hey, Joe!" A Gurkha would blaze away at the sound, the Japs would see a spurt of fire, and throw hand grenades. Then the Gurkhas learned their lesson, and crawled toward the Jap position. When a Jap shouted, "Hey, Joe," a Gurkha would jump him with a swing of a kukri, a Gurkha knife. A Gurkha never puts his kukri back in the scabbard unless the knife has drawn blood. If he hasn't slashed anybody with it, he will slit his own arm and draw blood.

Both Japs and Chindits were in foxholes at one end of Broadway. They fought for a week, the air base tied up, unusable during that time. They were in a maze of foxholes, so close together, so mixed up, that the enemy couldn't be bombed by air for fear of blasting the British, until, after savage fighting, the Japs were pushed into a corner, herded there. Then Air Commando fighters, carrying thousand-pound bombs, blew the Jap force to bits, killing 250. One Jap colonel sat on the barbed wire for a long time,

"FOR THEIR WORK CONTINUETH"

onto which he had been blown. They didn't have time to remove him.

The Japs had planned to establish themselves at one corner of the field and maintain a stronghold there, keeping the base tied up. They failed to reckon with bombing to blast them out. If they had established themselves in the jungle at the edge of the flying field, they could not have been bombed effectively, and it would have been a desperate job to dig them out.

The major ground battle of the campaign was fought at the Indaw-Katha roadblock. In this stronghold on the hill Mad Mike Calvert's Chindits found themselves surrounded by a Japanese division. The Japs attacked the fortress in waves. They were mowed down. They surged forward day and night, almost hourly. The Chindits found the shooting so good that, when the Japs failed to assault on their own initiative, parties of Gurkhas stirred them to action, slipping into their lines and provoking still another charge.

Losing heavily in infantry assaults, the Japs brought up armor, with which the Chindits couldn't cope. Light tanks thrust against the fortifications of the roadblock hill, and were driving through. Mad Mike called for antitank guns. Two gliders loaded with artillery to smash armor landed at the base of the hill, reverting to the original Cochran-Alison idea of glider transport of heavy armament to jungle forces. After this, the light tanks were knocked out as fast as they came to the attack.

The Japs brought up big guns, 90 mm. cannon. At one time they had 150 mm. artillery. They blasted away with a ponderous mortar that threw what the Chindits called a "coal scuttle," a shell the size of the conventional bucket for coal. The Chindits timed the guns with stop watches, timed the interval between gun flash and shellburst. They watched for the flashes, and knew how many seconds they had to duck for safety, checking with infinite care on the coal scuttle. They had nothing with which to reply, nothing to match the power and range of the Jap artillery. They had to sit and take it.

Air Commando planes came to the rescue. They watched for the flashes of the guns, and bombed. Their most destructive blow against artillery was struck when the Japs lined up twelve heavy cannon in a ravine and were smashing the fortress on the hill with a devastating fire. One of Wingate's officers reported by radio: "I'm afraid we can't take this. It's getting too rough." The next day Air Commando planes, spotting the row of gun flashes in the ravine, hurled bombs. Thereafter the guns were silent.

The Japs became aware that the planes were being guided by gun flashes. They refrained from firing the guns while hostile bombers were around. The Air Commandos retorted with tricks to draw enemy fire and gun flashes. The Japs were using 90 mm. antiaircraft guns as ground artillery. These, pounding the roadblock, could be swung upward against planes. R. T. Smith's bombers would fly over temptingly to lure their fire. The Jap gunners, holding back the fire of their cannon as ground artillery, couldn't resist the aerial targets. Their gun flashes would mark them for planes high above the bombers, fighters that then would swoop, dive-bombing.

The Japs concentrated twelve hundred troops for a rush against the roadblock, massing them on the slopes of a wooded hill, where among dense trees they couldn't be spotted from the air. The enemy force was discovered by deduction as much as anything else. The Chindits were expecting such a maneuver. It was the logical thing. Small signs confirmed their belief. They sent word to the Air

Commandos, whose planes responded. They flew over and blew the Japanese concentration to bits with marine depth charges.

In the Battle of the Roadblock, the Air Commandos used every trick in the book and some that were not. They dropped burning gasoline on the Japs. They shot up enemy positions with cannon in B-25 bombers. They resorted to novel tactics of serial cannonading. Six bombers going around in a circle would pound a Jap pillbox for an hour. They called that a "daisy chain." It was unorthodox, but it was effective.

They constructed a roadblock airfield for bringing in supplies and evacuating the wounded. Glider second-in-command Vincent Rose took five gliders loaded with engineers and engineering equipment and landed at the foot of the embattled hill. There an airstrip called White City was quickly constructed. No sooner was it completed than the Japs captured it with a savage and powerful attack. The Chindits drove them out after days of fierce fighting. White City, close to enemy guns and always subject to immediate attack, was the most perilous of air bases. Yet light planes flew in with supplies, and evacuated wounded.

Cochran went to the roadblock from time to time. "I'd take a light plane that would get right down on the treetops and scoot across. We'd land, climb out, and get a reception to warm the heart. You could feel as you walked along that people were looking at you and smiling. You could feel the excitement of the officers as they grasped your hand and said, 'Thank God for those Air Commando boys of yours.'

"At roadblock headquarters, dug in the side of a hill, they would rush and get you tea. There was nothing too good for you. You would feel they didn't know how to express themselves, they were so grateful because of the way our planes were saving their necks. The roadblock commander was a Chindit officer named Rose, serving under Mad Mike Calvert. He and his staff treated us like kings.

"I felt the praise, and wanted some of our boys to fly in and get the same impression that we had got. We sent some of our pilots over. They came back with Jap swords, Jap flags, Jap postcards, souvenirs of all kinds, which the British Chindits had given them. The British were so appreciative that they gave keepsakes which they themselves cherished a great deal. Then I had a job on my hands—to keep all the boys from going over. They all wanted souvenirs."

The Chindits couldn't leave their stronghold to go out and bury their dead. The Japs didn't bother with theirs. Enemy soldiers blown apart by air bombs were left where they fell. A hideous stench hung over the battleground. Black swarms of flies were attracted by the unburied bodies. The vultures were the only saving grace. "In a situation like that," says Cochran, "the British soldier really proves himself." The besieging force consistently numbered some three thousand men in constant attacks. The Japs kept bringing up reinforcements, but these hardly more than made up for the losses. Some three thousand were killed.

The holding of the fortress in the Battle of the Roadblock kept the Japanese life line choked until the end of the dry season.

24. "Victory at Last"

THE RAINS WERE COMING. The wet season scheduled to mark the end of Air Commando operation for the year was closing in. All along the impelling urgency had been to drive the campaign through before the monsoon. "We had the rains always in mind. Out there you are forever impressed, consciously or unconsciously, by the inevitable coming of the rains. All life in India and Burma is adjusted to the wet monsoon. No matter who you are, you get that feeling about the rains. In our northern latitude we look for the coming of spring. That's our nature. Out there the seasons for the people are marked by the rains. For us they were the curtain that would close down on our air operation, the curtain of the rains. Now the monsoon was shoving us out."

The Wingate plan to hold jungle bases during the wet season was abandoned. Fresh troops, two brigades, had been assigned to relieve jungle soldiers worn out by weeks of incessant fighting, but that was canceled. The two brigades were taken away from the Chindits and sent to reinforce British units opposing the Japanese thrust from Burma into India. The Japs hit north of Imphal, and advanced along the Manipur road. It looked as if they might cut the Assam Railroad, and that would have been a disaster. The railroad was Stilwell's life line, and, moreover, the route for supplies flown to China over the Hump. The Japanese drive into Manipur plain alarmed the British and the American command in India, and the two brigades assigned to the Chindits were thrown into the defense.

Wingate would have resisted this. Says Cochran: "Wingate had foreseen the Japanese move. I heard him many times tell British Army people that the Japs would try exactly that strategy. Then he would add to me, 'I hope they do.' His argument was, 'Let them think they are smart by driving into India. I'll get behind them, I'll cut them off.' He figured that, with a Chindit Air Commando operation, he could cut in behind the Japs, and rip up their supplies and communications so badly that they would have to pull out. I think he would have done it, if he had lived.

"The Man would have gone around the command in India, would have gone to Churchill. I suppose, the moment he was killed, British commanders in India started to think of taking forces away from the Chindits. I believe that really, while Wingate was still alive, they were trying to get one of his brigades. He wouldn't have stood for it. He would have gone over the heads of everybody, to the Prime Minister in London, and I have no doubt that Churchill would have backed him up, saying, 'Here is one fellow with a fiery force. He has done a daring and unorthodox thing. Why not let him carry on?' Prime Minister Churchill might well have left it to Wingate to check the

Jap drive into India. Churchill might have said, 'Why not give him a chance to upset a whole lot of stodgy routine? He'll soon be running the whole thing.'

"But Wingate was gone, and Lentaigne, succeeding him, did not command the forceful influence. He was an excellent officer, an able commander in jungle warfare, but it would have taken a Wingate with all his willful power to have held onto the two brigades, in spite of the Japanese thrust into India."

The loss of the two brigades made it impossible to hold northern Burma jungle bases during the rains. The battle-worn and exhausted Chindits at the bases could not have carried on during the wet season in the jungle. They had to be taken out, some evacuated by air, some pushing through the jungle to Stilwell's army up north.

The Air Commandos were called upon to support the evacuation. This extended their task beyond the time set for it. They were to have discontinued at the end of April, but carried on through the middle of May, as long as they could while the curtain of the rains closed down. "There were two- and three-day periods when our flying fields were under water. The ground would dry out, and we could get in a couple of days of flying."

They were utterly tired by the end of April, the time set for the conclusion of a job that had been planned to be one of killing exertion. The evacuating Chindits kept calling on them for air support. They wore themselves out.

"We were showing signs of wear and tear," says Cochran. "My fighter pilots were getting sick with extreme fatigue. Some were losing their desire to fight and fly. It was the same with the bomber pilots. The transport and light-plane flyers were losing their fire, were growing ill. They had some of the heaviest of the evacuation jobs. We had harder work than ever in winding up the job, and wore ourselves out, wore ourselves ill."

Flight Surgeon Major Cortez Enloe rates the period of intense strain and the building up of fatigue as beginning with the move into bases in Imphal Valley. "It was a combination of bad living conditions and unremitting work. The food was bad. Living in the *basha* huts was trying. There was no letup in the backbreaking labor. We hadn't enough men for the necessary daily tasks, and could not get enough native labor to take care of the coolie jobs. We all were doing things we were not supposed to do, in addition to our regular tasks. Planes were flying on too many missions, more than the human element could endure. The result was an increasing fatigue, with its invariable symptoms, lethargy, heedlessness, nerves."

Nerves took the form of a plague of rumors. Everybody was going home, rumor would say. The Air Commandos were to be given magnificent jobs in new outfits training in the States. One report said that glider pilots were to be sent to flying school back home and get their wings as pilots on regular planes. Glider pilots came to headquarters insistently, to be sure that they were on the list for going to flying school.

Administration Officer Engelhardt was a prime victim of the rumor epidemic. "Every day the boys would come to me, asking, 'Is there any truth in this or that?' We got so fed up with it that we decided to start a rumor of our own. We mentioned, as a gossipy sort of reminder, that John Alison had been in Russia. We had a couple of the boys go over to the gliders, sit around and ask casually, 'Have you fellows ever been in a cold climate?' Soon boys came in to volunteer, saying, 'I hear we're going to hit

Japan out of Russia, and I'd like to get in on that.' That was an example of how rumors can start."

Wild Bill Christian, who had distinguished himself in the fighting at Broadway, was badly tired out. One night at Aberdeen, Dick Boebel was awakened suddenly by a noise of shouting. He threw open the flap of his tent and looked out. There was Wild Bill yelling, "Get away from here, you damned Japs. Get out and stay out." His nerves were beginning to get him.

Cochran fell ill of fatigue. The malady from which he had suffered previously came back on him severely. He went to a hospital at Delhi. "I didn't want my men to see I was sick." Yet they were able to establish two more jungle bases to aid the evacuating Chindits, Blackpool and Clydeside. The latter was the final task for the gliders. Chindits were moving north to join Stilwell's army. One group in the area of Pinbaw was badly in need of supplies and the evacuation of wounded. Four gliders loaded with engineering equipment were flown to Pinbaw, and there an airfield was constructed, Clydeside. The task was accomplished under enemy fire. One glider, after cutting loose from its tow plane, was shot down, its pilot and co-pilot killed. The next day another glider was sent to Clydeside with engineering equipment. Then two more, one carrying a British armored car, flew to the air base. That ended glider operations in the campaign.

The aerial ambulances continued the evacuation of wounded until the monsoon rains made further flying impossible. Dick Boebel took them out, the light planes transferring to the British base at Ledo. "We told the British we were sorry we couldn't do any more evacuation work; too much water.

"At the Ledo base," Boebel relates, "I was talking things

over with a couple of our fellows at the bar. Somebody spoke up and asked where Sergeant Smith was.

"'Sergeant Smith, who is he?' I asked.

"'He is at that polo field.'

"That polo field! I had forgotten it. Outside the town of Jorhat in the Brahmaputra Valley we had a strip on a polo field. Eight light planes had been stationed there, pulling out wounded. I had forgotten them; everybody had forgotten them.

"I flew down to Jorhat, and the boys were glad to see me, Sergeant Smith among them. I hated to let on that I had forgotten them. I said, 'How is the weather, getting pretty rough?'

"'Yeah, it's wet.' They said it was hard to fly in the rains, but they were doggedly carrying on. How long they would have stayed, except for that remark at the bar, I don't know.

"I told them we were getting out, so pack up and leave. To this day, I suppose, they don't know they had been forgotten."

Alison had been taken out early, a week after Wingate's death, called home to form new Air Commando units. Studying reports on the successes in Burma, General Arnold had decided to create new units for air-invasion tactics, Alison's job. He was to build three more, each twice as large as the original. Actually, he supervised the setting up of two. One of these was sent to India to join the First Air Commandos Unit in the new campaign the following year. This was needless. The Japs were collapsing.

The success of the Wingate operation had been greater than they had known at the time. The Japs in northern Burma died on the vine, because of the way their supplies had been cut off by the Chindit-Air Commando campaign. They had been so strangled and starved they couldn't resist the dogged push of Stilwell's army. North Burma fell. If Wingate had lived, and had carried through with his plan to hold jungle strongholds in northern Burma during the rainy season, he still would not have had a campaign the next year, because the Japs collapsed. All Burma fell.

Nevertheless, during the following year, some Air Commando work was done in Burma. Two members of the old force, the First Air Commando Unit, were the first Americans in Mandalay. One of the two was Phil Cochran's brother Joe. There wasn't much to it. The Japs had evacuated Mandalay. But getting to Mandalay had been a dream in the Wingate campaign and the two Air Commandos made it a reality.

Cochran and Alison were left with the larger ideas they and Wingate had formed, ideas for a series of air invasions to the China coast. "We thought of successive jumps of about five hundred miles all the way across China. Our idea was jungle-hopping, rather than island-hopping. The concept was to close in on Japan from the China side."

Cochran talked this over with General Stratemeyer. He and his staff were for it. They had the great air transport theater of the war. Southeast Asia, with the immense amount of cargo-carrying over the Hump, was the mass transport sector, just as Europe was the strategic bombing and tank area and the Pacific was the Navy's carrier district. But the plan for Air Commando jungle-hopping across China also turned out to be needless. Japan was wilting because of developments out in the Pacific, the Navy drive from island to island. This was proving to be decisive. Japan was being overthrown on the island side.

Alison, returning home to build new units, had gone by way of England, where he had stopped off. To officers in the European theater he explained Air Commando tactics employed in Burma. General Eisenhower had him give advice about gliders for the glider phase of the approaching D-Day invasion of France. Bill Taylor was sent to Eisenhower's invasion forces, and took part in the planning of the glider landings on D-Day. Lessons derived from the all-air invasions in Burma were applied to the blow that began the end of the European war.

Cochran was to have gone back to India for new air operations in Burma, but the Japs were disintegrating so rapidly that General Arnold ordered him to Europe. He joined the first Allied airborne army, "to peddle my wares there and see if any of my ideas could be used."

"I went to Europe and dreamed up the largest Air Commando thing that was ever thought of, an airborne army to land far behind the Germans. My idea was to seize airdromes inside of Germany, create a fortress area thirty-five miles in circumference, and then fan out." The plan was never used. It wasn't necessary. The Germans collapsed at the Rhine, and the end was in sight.

Alison wound up in the Pacific, attached to the air forces assailing the Japanese islands. Cochran was on his way to the Pacific when Japan surrendered. According to the Cochran-Alison way of thinking, Japan was a country ripe for airborne invasion.

"We reckoned with the fact that the Japs were good at a thing they had practiced, but went to pieces when something came that they didn't know anything about. We figured that airborne invasions would have thrown the home islands of Japan into complete confusion. But distances were difficult, and so were the problems of transporting Air Commando equipment, gliders. In any case, Japan surrendered before air invasion or any other kind of invasion could happen."

25. "Lest We Forget"

BY NOW, the jungle will have crept back over the airfields. Since Wingate died, the world has not ceased from jungle fighting, but Burma has had a respite. After a few months the sites of Broadway and Chowringhee and Aberdeen, and the whole country south to Mandalay returned to what it was in Kipling's day, when the mists were over the rice fields and the elephants were piling teak in the sludgy, squdgy creek.

What then of the whole adventure? What did it all add up to, in terms of men and war, for men of today to turn back to Mandalay in remembrance?

As Wingate was the planner, it may help to go back to Wingate's original plan, to the seventeen-year-old resolution to be a soldier because in the absence of an international police force, soldiers would still be needed. We are in the same position today, except that the war in Korea has been fought in the name of the United Nations by the national forces engaged.

"LEST WE FORGET"

During his last difficult days in the first Burma campaign, when Wingate and his men whiled away the time by discussion of everything under the sun, he said, "This time, a league of nations or some federation of nations must be made to work." Wingate's own forces were international, and his coordination with Cochran and Alison in Project Nine proved that the best men recruited from the services of different nations can work together, no matter how widely their backgrounds may differ and their temperaments clash.

That Wingate was one of Britain's best was clear from the praise that rose at his death, from Churchill's "Here was a man of genius, who might well have been also a man of destiny," to Michael Foot's "Without such men our Empire is an infamy." Wingate himself would probably have been best pleased by the comment of one of his officers, who said that "Wingate's conception of greatness lay in the nation's contribution to human progress and ideas." In evidence, Lorna Wingate quoted her husband's saying that "the British Empire can live only if it builds a tower of justice, with a Jewish Palestine as a stone."

That Palestine remained the cause nearest Wingate's heart was clear when, in the last letter sent from Burma before his death, he quoted in Hebrew the verse *If I forget thee, O Jerusalem, let my right hand forget her cunning.* He would have been touched that the flags in Jerusalem flew at half-staff when the news of his death reached there. He would have been pleased when they planted a memorial forest in his name on the slopes of Mount Gilboa, where his Night Squads once routed Arabs and captured Axis-supplied guns. He would have been glad that, in dedicating Wingate Forest, a speaker said, "It is good to remind ourselves that there was a military man who symbolized to oppressed peoples the best tradition of the British."

ELEPHANTS A-PILIN' TEAK as ever, in Burma, now that planes are gone.
Ewing Galloway Photo

"LEST WE FORGET"

In the life of a man whose convictions made him virtually a minority of one in the world, the years in Palestine were probably the happiest. So strong was his dissent from popular beliefs that Wingate was destined to loneliness, but in Palestine he found a union of duty and inclination. He could believe in the cause for which he fought, and like and respect the people with whom he worked. He had company. He liked the country, smelling a native orange with all the enthusiasm of its grower. He watched Jewish dances with delight, forgetting the doubt of such pleasures fostered by the Plymouth Brethren. He loved to be asked to Seders, occasionally borrowing a skullcap that he might show off his Hebrew by joining in the Shir Hamatot. He always asked for the verse from the Psalms about the return to Zion, *Then was our mouth filled with laughter.* On one gala occasion, with Night Squad rapid transport, he managed to attend two Seders in one night, one with Chaim Weizmann at Haifa, another with younger friends at Hanita.

In Palestine, the army experts realized, Wingate put into practice the effective guerrilla tactics which, though they didn't know it, he had based on the Bible. But in Palestine he himself found confirmation of his faith that mountains could be moved, giants slain, great armies defeated, by a combination of physical endurance, mechanical aptitude and conviction. Any army could be trained to endure, could be given effective mechanical equipment, but for conviction there must be understanding of the essential issues, faith in the rightness of a cause. That was why, in Palestine, even the Arabs who loved to fight and were supplied with Axis arms had to be continually high-pressured by the Italian radio into attacking their neighbors.

The Jews knew what they were fighting for. So, asked

whether he thought peaceful Jewish farm boys would go willingly to war, Wingate said, "What if their ideals stood in danger? If the work of their lives was attacked, if it would be a matter of self-respect, and of helping their persecuted brethren to find a home? You have got here the makings of one of the finest military forces in the world's history." To his first force assembled at Ein Harod, he said, "You men lack only the arms to be the most efficient and devoted soldiers in the world. In our squads you will be provided with arms so that together we shall be able to guard what is holy to you, and to defeat the dark forces of reaction."

Wingate did not, of course, stress conviction to the neglect of his other two requirements. He never missed an opportunity to improve equipment and apply new scientific advances in the profession of war. And he trained his men mercilessly. As one in Palestine put it, "He did not coddle anyone, but made the highest demands on himself and on everyone." Whether it was asking the last ounce of endurance in jungle penetration, or waking an officer at midnight to discover why the mules were braying, he demanded the utmost in human efficiency.

He did, however, stop short, and ask his men to stop short, of methods which dishonored the undertaking. In Palestine, the Night Squads were told that although irresponsible murder and terror might be the tactics of the enemy, they could not be theirs. They must wage full and fair warfare.

In Burma, similarly, Wingate spoke against the tough methods of "unarmed combat" taught in a revival of primitive warfare that brought eye-gouging and garroting back into favor. Illogical as these gentleman's restraints on war may seem, they show Wingate's feeling for police action rather than fighting for fighting's sake. Some of Wingate's talents as a general, his care for his men, concern for their food and morale, and proper treatment of the wounded, he shared with great soldiers from Napoleon to Eisenhower, but these are also the virtues of great civil administrators. His sympathy for the civilian population in disturbed areas, perhaps his most remarkable virtue as a military man, suggests that he was, in fact, best equipped to be an officer of the peace. He lived and died an officer in a United Nations police force not yet born.

As an international hero and a seasoned professional soldier, Wingate naturally dominated the Burma campaign, but in the Air Commandos the American people are entitled to feel that their side was at least as well represented. To the British, who asked only for equipment and got it in supercolossal quantity and quality, it must have been a surprise to watch the young flyers in action. Here was heroism of a daredevil, youthful sort, wholly different from Wingate's considered action, yet highly effective.

As a representative of hair-trigger American action, Colonel Philip Cochran, either as himself or in the Flip Corkin character, was outstanding. Colonel John Alison was no less splendidly representative of perhaps a larger number of Americans who stay quietly on the job while they think fast, and prove themselves more than adequate in time of emergency. But although Americans themselves may not realize it, the nature of the country's contribution to war—complex mechanisms whose effectiveness depends not only on the skill of the user, but on that of the inventor—means that a large part of America's war effort is invisible in action. The mule just grew, but the plane had to be made. Its designer and the skilled workers who made it have a direct responsibility for its performance, and are as much a part of the victory as the pilot who flew it.

Although the Air Commandos staged the first all-airborne

invasion in history, whether Project Nine came up to expectations in testing the new uses of air power is a secret buried somewhere in the Pentagon. Certainly there were opportunities for testing, and a good many of the ideas tried further in Korea and now taken for granted were really first proved there. The practical uses of gliders are admitted, and although there are still arguments about double tow, it is taken as axiomatic that, for troop movements and transport of heavy material, gliders have no competition in their field. Better crash a glider, the experts say, and save the lives that would be lost in the crash of a transport plane. Helicopters too have their sphere of usefulness defined, as do the rockets first carried by Project Nine planes.

With its wonder-working equipment produced by many minds and hands, it was appropriate that Project Nine should have had the divided leadership that it did have—two heads, two heroes, and a number of lesser stars. It may be appropriate too that the men who headed the Air Commandos lacked Wingate's gift for pungent self-expression and could never quite explain themselves. With all his gay talk and engaging manner, Phil Cochran consistently underplayed his own important talent, the talent for cooperation. He talked about competition. That was like saying he was going to Casablanca and heading, instead, where his planes were needed to fight. He talked a tough, hard-boiled war; actually he fought a fair one, considerate of men and fellow officers. This was clear not only from his generous praise of fellow officers but from his fury on at least one occasion when newspapers gave Flip Corkin the glory he felt belonged to "the kids, these American kids that are just automatically wonderful." He stood up for his gang and his generation—pilots, ground crews, aces, grease monkeys, young Americans at war in distant lands.

Cochran spoke for them, and if he spoke rather quickly at times for his silent co-worker, Alison, he spoke fairly or Alison would not have stayed on. Alison's continued loyalty was endorsement of the partnership. For he was obviously a steadfast and able soldier, intelligent, ingenious, competent, diplomatic, firm under his mild manner.

Subsequent careers of the Project Nine leaders proved their ability and their diversity of talent.

Oley Olson, Grant Mahoney, Bob Pettit and Clint Gaty all stayed in the Air Force, Olson in an executive job. Mahoney finally lost his one-man war with the Japs, shortly before his country's war was won. He was killed diving on a dummy Jap target in the Philippines. Pettit took jet fighters to Japan while Gaty, still in Burma, flew out on a fighter mission from which he never returned.

Bill Taylor went back to his civilian job but transferred from St. Louis to New York. His assistant, Vincent Rose, went through harrowing war adventures only to be killed in a civilian plane crash. Bill Cherry is an air-line pilot. Dick Boebel returned to advertising and marketing problems, and R. T. Smith is a writer for radio and television.

Alison, with his graver approach to flying, became Assistant Secretary of Commerce for civil aviation. Later he joined a research project concerned with transportation problems.

Those who heard Cochran tell a story of breath-taking action and end it "It was just like a movie!" failed to foresee that this laughing comment was prophetic. For where is Cochran now? In Hollywod, as technical adviser on jet planes to Howard Hughes, RKO executive and plane manufacturer.

A happy peacetime ending, "just like a movie!"

www.ingramcontent.com/pod-product-compliance
Lightning Source LLC
Chambersburg PA
CBHW071955110526
44592CB00012B/1099